COURTING HISTORY

JAMES F. SIMON

COURTING HISTORY

A SUPREME COURT HISTORIAN REFLECTS ON HIS LIFE AND CAREER

BRISCOE CENTER
FOR AMERICAN HISTORY
THE UNIVERSITY OF TEXAS AT AUSTIN

DISTRIBUTED BY TOWER BOOKS, AN IMPRINT
OF THE UNIVERSITY OF TEXAS PRESS

TO MY FAMILY—PAST, PRESENT, AND FUTURE

Printed in the United States of America
First edition, 2025
Distributed by arrangement with the
University of Texas Press

Requests for permission to reproduce
material from this work should be sent to:
Office of the Director
Dolph Briscoe Center for American History
University of Texas at Austin
2300 Red River Stop D1100
Austin, TX 78712-1426

∞ The paper used in this book meets the
minimum requirements of ANSI/NISO
z39.48-1992 (r1997) (Permanence of Paper).

Library of Congress Control Number:
2024952829

ISBN 978-1-953480-16-3 (hardcover)
ISBN 978-1-953480-17-0 (ePub e-book)
ISBN 978-1-953480-21-7 (PDF e-book)

CONTENTS

PREFACE

I first met Jim Simon—legal scholar, author, and dean emeritus at the New York Law School—in April 2022 when he asked me if the Briscoe Center would have any interest in preserving his papers for teaching and research. He had read a *New York Times* story about historian and bestselling author Doris Kearns Goodwin's decision to place her papers as well as those of her late husband, famed presidential speech writer Richard Goodwin, at the Briscoe Center. What Jim read in the *Times* about the center's program and its collections impressed him. He explained that he had reached a time in his life when he was eager to find a good home for the collection he had accumulated documenting his professional career, which included his work authoring nine highly regarded books on American history, politics, and constitutional law.

An initial exchange of emails was soon followed by discussions on the telephone, as well as in person at his home in West Nyack, New York, where I met his charming wife, Marcia. Those discussions happily led to Jim's agreement to donate his archive to the Briscoe Center. During my visit with Jim and Marcia, I reviewed the contents of Jim's papers, which he had stored in his home office. His scholarship revealed his deep understanding of the history of the tensions that have frequently existed between the Supreme Court and the executive branch of our federal government. His research and teaching at New York Law School explored the Supreme Court across three centuries in detail. I quickly determined that the collection would be a valuable addition to the center's holdings documenting American legal history. Those collections include famed trial lawyer Louis Nizer's case records documenting the *John Henry Faulk v. Aware, Inc.* lawsuit in the 1960s that helped to end blacklisting in the entertainment industry; the Pennzoil Company's extensive legal records documenting its lawsuit against Texaco in the 1980s challenging the legality of Texaco's acquisition of the Getty Oil Company; the massive trial records of Timothy McVeigh in the Oklahoma City bombing case in the 1990s; and the papers of human rights lawyer Ramsey Clark.

I was also pleased when I discovered that during Jim's early career he had worked as a journalist, first as a summer intern in the Washington bureau of *Newsweek*, where he was mentored by famed newspaper editor Ben Bradlee, later as a reporter for the *St. Louis Post-Dispatch*, and, from 1969 until 1974, as a legal correspondent and contributing editor of *Time* magazine. At one point he covered the trial of the anti-Vietnam War activists known as the Chicago Eight. That assignment was of particular significance to me, because the Briscoe Center's archive includes the papers of Abbie Hoffman, one of the activists on trial. That portion of Jim's papers also related well to one of the center's specialties: the history of American news media.

James Frank Simon was born in Fort Worth, Texas, in 1938. He graduated from Yale College in 1961 and Yale Law School in 1964. His met his wife, Marcia, at Yale, where she was a graduate student in art history. He joined the faculty of New York Law School in 1975, where he served as the Martin Professor of Law and Dean. Jim's papers were transferred to the Briscoe Center in 2023. Among the most significant portions of his archive are his research files, including recordings and transcripts of interviews and correspondence with Supreme Court Justices, including William J. Brennan Jr., William O. Douglas, Harry Blackmun, Sandra Day O'Connor, John Paul Stevens, and Ruth Bader Ginsburg.

The Simon collection also includes the research material and draft manuscripts for his books, which includes *Independent Journey: The Life of William O. Douglas* (1980); *The Antagonists: Hugo Black, Felix Frankfurter and Civil Liberties in Modern America* (1989); *What Kind of Nation: Thomas Jefferson, John Marshall, and the Epic Struggle to Create the United States* (2002); *Lincoln and Chief Justice Taney: Slavery, Secession and the President's War Powers* (2006); and *Eisenhower vs. Warren: the Battle for Civil Rights and Liberties* (2018). Jim's first book, *In His Own Image: The Supreme Court in Richard Nixon's America,* published in 1973, won the American Bar Association's prestigious Silver Gavel Award. *What Kind of Nation* was a 2002 *New York Times* "Notable Book." Now other scholars can learn not just from his published works, but from the extensive research materials in his papers.

I'm pleased that Jim accepted my invitation to write his fascinating memoir *Courting History: A Supreme Court Historian Reflects on his Life and Career*, which the Briscoe Center is now proud to publish. I want to acknowledge the skilled and dedicated work of Dr. Holly Taylor, the head of the center's publication program, who served as Jim Simon's editor. Freelance book designer Derek George has done a masterful job, as he has done with many of the Briscoe Center's previous books. I also want to thank Robert Devens, director of the University of Texas Press, and his talented staff for their invaluable support as the distributor of *Courting History.*

And finally, and most importantly, I want to thank Jim Simon for his generous gift of his papers, for writing this very personal memoir, and for his friendship.

DON CARLETON
Executive Director
Briscoe Center for American History

INTRODUCTION

"The justice will see you," Justice William O. Douglas's secretary told me when I called his chambers. For two years, I had made the same request for an interview in telephone calls to the justice's chambers. Each time, before this call in the spring of 1978, I had been turned down.

I was stunned and slightly unnerved by the unexpected invitation to interview Douglas, the iconic judicial liberal who had championed the expansion of civil rights and liberties for more than three decades. But I had the presence of mind to ask what time would be convenient for him. "He will see you at two o'clock," she said. It was after one o'clock when I hung up the phone. I had not eaten lunch or prepared questions for the interview.

During my career as a journalist and author, I had interviewed other justices of the US Supreme Court, but never without careful preparation or on an empty stomach. For my biography of Justice Douglas, I had already spoken with four of his judicial colleagues: Justices William J. Brennan Jr., Abe Fortas, Lewis Powell Jr., and Potter Stewart. For my other books on the Court and its justices, I would ultimately meet with justices appointed by Presidents Harry Truman, Dwight D. Eisenhower, Lyndon B. Johnson, Richard Nixon, Ronald Reagan, and George H.W. Bush.

I had made my call to Douglas's chambers from the Securities and Exchange Commission, where I had spent the morning researching his tenure as chairman of the SEC during the New Deal. After hanging up the phone, I grabbed a sandwich at a nearby café, hastily scribbled a few basic questions to ask him, and took a taxi to the Supreme Court Building.

After I arrived at Justice Douglas's chambers, his secretary ushered me into his office. The justice lay motionless, his frail body warmed by a wool blanket and supported by a reclining leather chair. His thick white hair was hanging shaggily over his ears. His blue eyes still penetrated, and his high cheekbones were more prominent than ever, owing to the weight loss that had followed his severe stroke in 1974. He was dressed in a brown tweed sport coat and a high-collared white shirt and tie. The formal dress and the weak body seemed incongruous, though in earlier, happier days, this attire would have seemed equally incongruous with his then robust body.

For the first five minutes of the interview, I tried desperately to make conversation with the justice in a way that would put him at ease. I told him of the members of his family and his friends that I had seen. And I recalled that Kay Kershaw, his Goose Prairie, Washington, neighbor, had sent me on a "special" trail up a towering mountain in the Cascades. The trail "went straight up," I said, smiling. "I guess it was Kay's initiation rite for all eastern slickers." He did not return the smile.

I asked what he considered to be his greatest achievements at the SEC.

"Cleaning up the Street," he replied. His direct, concise answer was encouraging and accurate. As chairman of the SEC, Douglas had forced the New York Stock Exchange to reform its trading practices during the Great Depression.

When I asked what he considered to be his greatest achievement on the Court, however, he simply shrugged, brushing the question aside. To my chagrin and embarrassment, he then closed his eyes. I assumed the interview was over.

I left the room, and, shaken, asked his secretary if I should leave.

"No," she replied calmly, and suggested that I wait in her office. She returned after a brief conversation with the justice. "The justice, unfortunately, has been very tired today," she said pleasantly. "Let him rest. Perhaps he'll see you a little later."

I then fell into an easy, informal conversation with the secretary and her husband, who was Douglas's law clerk. The topic was babies, specifically our own. Their two-and-a-half-month-old was propped up in an infant seat on the secretary's desk. They offered affectionate commentary on their baby, and I spoke with immodest pride about Sara, my eleven-month-old daughter.

The conversation eventually returned to the justice. I told his secretary of the excruciatingly awkward five minutes that I had spent with him.

She laughed sympathetically. "That's the justice," she said. "He controls every situation."

But a few minutes later, we heard the secretary's buzzer. She walked into Douglas's office. When she returned, she said, "The justice would like to see you."

When I sat down in a chair across from Douglas, he appeared more relaxed. And he was much more talkative, recalling his days at the SEC and on the Court. He sprinkled the conversation with stories about famous people he knew, including Franklin D. Roosevelt, Joe Kennedy, and Justices Hugo Black and Felix Frankfurter. I asked about widespread reports in 1944 that he had been on the short list to run as vice president on the Democratic ticket with FDR. He said he had not talked to FDR about it and denied that he ever had political ambitions. He recalled a conversation with Joe Kennedy, John F. Kennedy's father. "He told me that he thought his son Jack and I were the two most able men in Washington. 'And I don't agree with one damn thing that either of you stand for!' he said. That was Joe Kennedy." Douglas then offered brief, subtly cutting opinions of Justices Black and Frankfurter: "At heart Hugo was a Baptist preacher," he said. Frankfurter was "divisive, Machiavellian." On the resignation from the Court of his close friend Abe Fortas, he said, "I thought Nixon was behind it, and I was right."

We had talked for almost an hour when Douglas pressed the buzzer for his chauffeur, Datcher, to take him home. The interview was over. As I walked down the front steps of the Supreme Court Building, I knew I had conducted one of the most unforgettable, and difficult, interviews of my professional career.

* * * * *

How did I, a privileged white kid growing up in segregated Fort Worth, Texas, in the late 1940s and 1950s, interview Supreme Court justices over a period of four decades and write numerous books on the US Supreme Court, largely devoted to the Court's expansion of civil rights and liberties? My story begins in Fort Worth in November 1938.

CHAPTER 1

GROWING UP

On the night of November 9, 1938, Nazis destroyed more than 1,000 synagogues and 7,500 Jewish businesses throughout Germany. The attacks on that night would be known in history as Kristallnacht, translated from German as "Crystal Night," a tragically ironic reference to the shards of broken glass that littered Germany's city streets.

More than 30,000 Jewish men were arrested and taken to concentration camps that night. Many of them, and tens of thousands who followed them into the camps during World War II, were upper-middle-class professionals—attorneys, physicians, professors. They were patriots: many had fought for their country in World War I. And a large number were secular Jews, members of the growing Reform Jewish movement that had been founded in Germany in the early nineteenth century. They considered themselves to be German Jews, with the emphasis on their nationality more than their religion.

I was born less than three weeks after Kristallnacht in Harris Hospital, Fort Worth, Texas, the second son of Natalie and Richard U. Simon, American Jews who had comfortably assimilated into the city's southwestern culture and small but thriving Reform Jewish community. My grandfather

Uriah Meyer Simon had been born in Moore's Landing, Mississippi, in 1879, one of six children of parents who had emigrated from Lithuania. The family then moved to Tyler, Texas, where Meyer grew up before enrolling at the University of Denver Law School (where the weather helped with his chronic asthma). After graduation, he returned to Texas to practice law in Fort Worth; in 1905 he married Hattie Weltman, a tall, demure young woman who had grown up in the city.

They made a striking couple. My grandfather—or "Poppy," to me and his three other grandchildren—was 5'2", with a beak nose and penetrating blue eyes that could be both kind and fierce. My grandmother, or "Bamie," was 5'7", elegant, soft-spoken, and matronly.

My grandparents joined Temple Beth-El, a Reform synagogue founded in Fort Worth in 1902. Poppy was one of the first presidents of the temple, and he and Bamie were regular attendants at Friday night services. Poppy also took a leadership role in settling Eastern European Jews in Fort Worth and other southwestern communities.

My grandfather quickly became a respected and highly successful lawyer in Fort Worth, forming a lucrative partnership with William (Bill) Slay, a prominent gentile lawyer in the city. The thriving civil law practice of Slay & Simon allowed my grandfather to provide for his growing family in grand style in a three-story mansion on South Adams Street, a few miles from Poppy's law office in downtown Fort Worth. There was a tennis court on the property and Black servants to tend the grounds and to cook and serve meals on the family's fine china and crystal in a large, formal dining room. My grandfather bought beautiful Dutch genre paintings as well as Romantic nineteenth-century French works (for example, by Jean-Léon Gérôme) from a New York art dealer that were displayed throughout the house.

In addition to his law practice, Poppy purchased and sold, at considerable profit, vast tracts of real estate on the south side of the city. His wealth accumulated rapidly in the 1920s, allowing him to send his two sons to an exclusive private prep school in Dallas and to Yale, where my father graduated in 1928 and his brother three years later. Both attended the University of Texas Law School in Austin and, based on their high grades, were selected for membership on the law review. Their younger sister studied elocution at Emerson College in Boston.

The stock market crash of 1929 and the Great Depression that followed severely diminished my grandfather's handsome income, and the family had to scale back its opulent lifestyle. In 1938, Poppy was nonetheless able to give each of his three adult children valuable property that he owned in south Fort Worth. Because he owned not only those three properties but also all of the other tracts on the street, the city permitted him to name it, and it became Simondale Drive.

✦ ✦ ✦ ✦ ✦

My father met my mother, Natalie Levin, in 1928 at the University of Texas in Austin when he was a law student and she was a freshman. Her grandparents' families had immigrated to Mexico City from Germany in the mid-1850s. Married as teenagers in Mexico City, in the early 1870s they had crossed the border and entered McAllen, Texas, with their five children. They eventually settled in rural Arkansas, where my great-grandfather eked out a meager living as a dirt farmer.

Mother was born in Little Rock, Arkansas, in 1912, the eldest daughter of Helen and Frank Levin. Her father had been born in Baltimore but had moved to the Southwest as a young man to work as a traveling salesman for the Interwoven Sock Company. When Mother was a small child, the family had moved to Dallas, where she and her younger sister, Frances, grew up. My maternal grandfather, whom my brother and I called Grandaddy, became a regional salesman for Interwoven, spending the remainder of his career selling his company's socks to men's department stores throughout West Texas.

The Levin family lived in a small house that Grandaddy had purchased in a predominantly Jewish neighborhood in Dallas (Mother's childhood friends included Stanley Marcus, the future president of Neiman-Marcus stores). Mother was a petite (5'2") and vivacious beauty who was courted by an entourage of eager young suitors throughout her teenage years. Her high school yearbook contained photos and multiple references to "Nat" Levin, whose popularity and academic honors were duly and often archly noted.

Despite the economic stresses of the Depression, my grandfather, an exceedingly frugal man, was able to save enough money for his two daughters to receive college educations. Mother graduated from the University of Texas in 1931; my aunt Franny graduated from the University of Missouri and later earned a master's degree in social work at the same institution.

After her college graduation, Mother returned to Dallas, lived with her parents, and worked for the *Dallas Morning News*, writing a breezy weekly cooking column that she pieced together from a variety of published sources. Her greatest challenge was answering readers' letters asking her personal advice for their home cooking: Mother had rarely cooked a meal.

Meanwhile, my father had begun to practice law with Poppy in Fort Worth at Slay & Simon. He was 5'8", fair-skinned, with light brown hair and a firm, square jaw, much like Poppy's. Well-built and athletic, he had been a starting guard for his prep-school basketball team and had run track both at prep school and as a freshman at Yale. A sophisticated but reserved man with a dry sense of humor, he wrote to Mother regularly from Fort Worth, regaling her with the complexities of his law practice. But he always ended his letters with uncharacteristically impassioned expressions of his love for her. He drove to Dallas to see her every weekend but found the commute exhausting. Finally, he wrote to her that they would either have to break up or get married. On June 8, 1932, my mother, twenty years old, and father, twenty-five, were married in her parents' living room.

After their marriage, my parents drove to Mexico City for their honeymoon before moving into a small apartment in Fort Worth near Texas Christian University (TCU). Two years later, my brother, Richard Jr., was born. By 1938, my father's law practice provided sufficient income, so that he could ask his childhood friend Charlie McDonald, an architect, to design a house for his family. Later that year, shortly before I was born, they moved into a large white clapboard and brick two-story, three-bedroom house, set far back from the street at 2628 Simondale Drive.

Our living room was furnished with a plush three-cushion green sofa, a comfortable easy chair for my father, a handsome mahogany secretary, and several paintings from Poppy's collection. There was a front porch surrounded by prickly bushes, a screened-in back porch, a breakfast room with brightly painted yellow walls, and a large, formal dining room for evening meals with visiting relatives and friends. Our food was cooked and served by a Black servant, Clara, who lived in a small, one-bedroom dwelling behind our house. In addition to preparing and serving our meals, she cleaned our house and took care of me when I was a small child.

My uncle Henry; his wife, Sammy; and their son, Henry Jr., lived across the street in a comparably large two-story yellow brick house. Uncle Henry had joined Dad, Poppy, and his partner, Slay, in their law practice after his graduation from the University of Texas Law School.

* * * * *

After Japanese planes bombed Pearl Harbor on December 7, 1941, and the United States declared war on the Axis Powers, our family's life in Fort Worth appeared unaffected. But in 1943, our lives changed dramatically. My father was drafted into the army at the age of thirty-seven and shipped to England in the buildup for the Normandy invasion. Suddenly, our family's tranquil life was shattered. My mother was left with two small children while her adored husband, an American Jew (and, in 1943, the president of Temple Beth-El), was sent overseas to help win the war against Nazi Germany.

Mother tried mightily to shield my brother and me from the anxiety she endured worrying about our father. It helped that her sister, my aunt Franny, pregnant with a third child, temporarily moved to Fort Worth from her home in Kansas City, Missouri, with her two young daughters. They lived with us for a few months after Aunt Franny's husband, Lawrence, was drafted into the army infantry and sent to fight in Italy. Although Uncle Lawrence discovered a bullet hole in his helmet one day during combat duty in the trenches of southern Italy, he was unscathed.

The week before Dad was to be shipped overseas, in 1944, Mother took a train to New York City to see him. Their rendezvous was against military regulations. They dined at a popular restaurant, and, to Dad's consternation, he noticed that his commanding officer was seated at a nearby table. Dad was promptly demoted from sergeant to corporal. Although Mother often recounted the incident, I don't recall her expressing any regret that their rendezvous caused Dad's demotion. After Dad went overseas, we moved to Kansas City to live with Aunt Franny for the summer. My brother, Dick, was deeply unhappy there, spending his time in Aunt Franny's basement suffering from colitis and homesickness.

His spirits were briefly lifted by listening to radio reports from the Democratic National Convention in Chicago, where President Roosevelt was nominated to serve a fourth term. Dick returned alone to Fort Worth to stay with Aunt Sammy and Uncle Henry while Mother and I remained in Kansas City for a few more weeks. By that time, Uncle Henry had been turned down for military service because of a heart condition. In physical stature and temperament, my uncle was strikingly different from my father. He stood over six feet tall, weighed more than two hundred pounds, and was an exuberant extrovert. He revered my father. After Dad was drafted, Uncle Henry did not want to practice law without his older brother. He left the law firm temporarily to buy and operate the Sunbeam Cookie Company. Every week during the final years of the war, he brought home boxes and boxes of unsold, sugarless cookies, the very worst I ever tasted in my life.

At home, Mother was outwardly upbeat, but anxiety lay just below the surface. She complained that the men in the security service she had hired to patrol our street every night were unreliable. Were they incompetent, or irresponsible, or were they slacking off because we were Jewish? One day, the quiet, genial barber who had given me my first haircut at the TCU barbershop called my mother to tell her, in a tone of voice she apparently perceived as scolding, that I had not given him the money in my pocket for my haircut. Did he think we were trying to cheat or "Jew" him? Mother immediately rushed over to the barbershop with the change that had been in my pocket.

• • • • •

Thanks to my mother's protective shield, World War II, for me, was a time of bright sunshine and happy play, tinged by the romantic notion that my father was a war hero. My mother let me wear a soldier suit, complete with an officer's hat, to Mrs. Massey's Nursery School. After my father was drafted, I proudly displayed a flag with a star outside my second-story bedroom window to announce that Dad was serving his country in the war. My cousin Henry and I never tired of playing war games, wearing miniature gas masks and brandishing toy guns.

Mother eagerly read Dad's latest "V-mail" letters from Europe, but she knew they were heavily censored. All she would tell me was that Dad was safe, and that he loved and missed us very much. In fact, Dad never saw combat, although he was often perilously close to the front. As a member of a transportation unit, he helped to provide supplies to our soldiers on the front lines. After the Normandy invasion, the closest he came to the front was in northeastern Belgium, where his unit took supplies to the American armies before the final push into Germany.

After Germany's surrender in May 1945, my father shipped home a trove of war souvenirs, including a room-size Nazi flag, two Nazi helmets, a Luger pistol, and a toy German bomber, my prize possession. That summer, when Dad returned to the United States, he was sent to the United States Army's Judge Advocate General's (JAG) Corps at the University of Michigan in Ann Arbor to become a military lawyer.

So we packed our suitcases and headed for Ann Arbor. Mother and her friend Selma Brine, with Dick and me in the backseat, drove our black 1939 Ford for five days in the sweltering heat to reach our destination. I recall long delays to change flat tires, but despite the heat and the car troubles, we were deliriously happy. Our family was going to be whole again, united for the first time in two years.

Soon after we settled into our rooms in the University of Michigan's student union building, my brother and I were gleefully running up and down the university's football field. Later, we laughed at the slapstick antics of Abbott and Costello in a local movie theater. But, most of all, we savored every waking moment that we spent with Dad.

The Japanese surrendered on August 15, 1945. A few days later, Dad drove us to Detroit to celebrate. We heard the popular crooner Nat King Cole perform at a nightclub and had bleacher seats for a Detroit Tigers game at Tiger Stadium. Our seats were in right field, but we could still watch the Tigers' star pitcher, Hal Newhouser, from a distance. It was a dream come true for this baseball-crazy six-year-old.

But the best was yet to come. One late afternoon in the early fall of 1945, after we had returned to Fort Worth, I watched Uncle Henry's car pull slowly to our curb. My father, wearing a broad-brimmed fedora hat and business suit, stepped out of the car. I rushed toward him, shouting with joy.

Yes, he was really home for good, and I was the happiest boy in the world. With my father back at home, life settled into a comfortable routine.

Summer temperatures in Fort Worth, when I was growing up in the 1940s, frequently rose above 100 degrees. And there was no air conditioning. Yet, for me, those sizzling hot days were pure joy. I spent every sunny day in my bathing suit jumping over a lawn sprinkler or diving into a swimming pool or lake.

My fondest memory from those summers was our first family vacation after Dad had been discharged from the army. In 1946, Dad drove Mother, my brother Dick, and me to Galveston. We stayed at the Jack Tar Motor Courts, spare accommodations to be sure, but to this seven-year-old, a novel, exciting experience. Every day, Mother watched anxiously from the beach while I rode the waves for as many hours as she would allow. One night, we dined at the dark, mysterious Balinese Room on the Galveston pier, which was famed as a nightclub with an illegal gambling operation hidden in a backroom.

When I became a first-grader at Alice E. Carlson Elementary School, my parents trusted me to make the twenty-five-minute walk home alone. Weekday afternoons I always took the same route, walking past my best friend Bill Paddock's house and across an open field full of weeds, then jumping over a tiny creek before climbing the hill on Simondale. Once home, I was free to do as I pleased for the rest of the afternoon, so long as I was on time for dinner at six o'clock. I often played in my room with my Lincoln Logs or drew imagined scenes with crayons. On sunny, warm days, I headed for the dirt trail behind our house to explore what seemed to me a vast wilderness, actually a wooded area that was later transformed into the Tanglewood housing development.

On Saturday mornings I usually accompanied Mother on her errands, bribed with a Bugs Bunny or Captain Marvel comic book at the Park Hill Pharmacy. But weekends were primarily devoted to sports. My cousin Henry and I tossed a softball or football in our front yard or batted fly balls on the vacant lot across the street. I also passionately rooted for the Fort Worth Cats, our hometown professional baseball team, joining the Cats' "Knothole Gang" in exchange for the autograph of the team's right fielder, Moe Santomauro. In football season, I followed Texas Christian University's Horned Frogs and idolized their quarterback, Lindy Berry. Before long, I started taking a detour from my route home after school to watch my hero, Berry, and the rest of the team on TCU's practice field preparing for the Saturday games.

The price for my freedom was good grades. I regularly pleased Mother with straight-A report cards. But this did not mean that I was a model student. I have never forgotten the punishment meted out by my first-grade teacher, Mrs. Hinckley, after I exacted rough justice for what I considered an unforgivable sin by the girl who sat next to me. While I was away from my desk to participate in my reading group, I noticed that she was copying my homework. When I returned to my desk, I slugged her. Mrs. Hinckley, a stern taskmaster, then exacted her own version of rough justice, sending me to the corner for the remainder of the morning, keeping me after school, and calling my mother to complain about her uncivilized son. When Mother arrived to pick me up, I cried, feeling humiliated but still not convinced that the severe punishment fit my crime.

After we returned home in silence, Mother did not allow me to complete the first sentence of my defense. What I did to my classmate was wrong, she scolded, and must never be repeated. At Mother's insistence, I apologized to my assaulted classmate the next morning. She must have forgiven me, since we remained friends through high school graduation. As for Mrs. Hinckley, so long as I behaved myself, she treated me in the same strict manner that she did my classmates. My short, unhappy, pugilistic career was over.

• • • • •

For the first fifteen years of my life, we lived in the big house on Simondale Drive in Fort Worth. In 1954, shortly before my mother gave birth to my sister, Mary Elizabeth, Dad decided that we should build a modern one-story house to provide for our expanded family. He chose a lot and builder in the new Tanglewood development just behind our Simondale residence. It would have central air-conditioning and heating, a washing machine and dryer, and no steep stairs to climb to the second floor. It made perfect practical sense. But I knew Mother was reluctant to leave the spaciousness and memories of our house on Simondale, not to mention the cachet of living on a street named for the family. And so was I.

When we packed our belongings and made the move, we were not only leaving our longtime residence behind but ending a lifestyle reminiscent of the Old South. We had always had a full-time Black female servant who cooked and cleaned for us and a Black yard man who mowed our large lawn. I knew them only by their first names—Clara, Lulu, Joe. For all those years, I never asked whether they were happy working for us, or how they felt about the racial segregation that was imposed on them every day of their lives.

During my boyhood, I sometimes accompanied my mother on her weekly ride to an unpaved block of crumbling shanties on the west side of town. That was where our Black "washer woman," Mary, cheerfully greeted us. Mary then hauled the two large mounds of our family's laundry from the trunk of our car into her tiny, wooden house. I never asked my mother how much we paid Mary, why she had to live in such poverty, or the reason the city did not pave her street.

In the late 1940s, my father's law firm, Simon & Simon, bought box seats from which we watched the baseball games of the Fort Worth Cats, an AA farm club of the Brooklyn Dodgers, which were played at LaGrave Field. I was a fanatical baseball fan in those days and attended more than twenty games a season. I knew the batting averages and pitching statistics of every Fort Worth Cat player. I did not question why there were no Black players on the Cats or the other teams in the Texas League—even after rooting for the great Jackie Robinson when the Dodgers played the Yankees in the 1947 and 1949 World Series. Nor did I wonder why my family and friends could sit in the comfort of a box overlooking the visitor's dugout while every Black baseball fan was relegated to a single, segregated section of the bleachers in far right field.

At Monnig's and Stripling's, two of the city's downtown department stores, the water fountains on the ground floor were clearly marked "White" and "Colored." I always drank from the "White" fountain and was not troubled by that abhorrent form of racism. For the twelve years of my education in the Fort Worth public schools, I never attended a class with a Black student. In 1957, three years after the US Supreme Court declared, in *Brown v. Board of Education*, that public school segregation in this country was unconstitutional, I graduated from Paschal High School, which remained segregated.

As a professional historian and constitutional law professor whose career has been devoted primarily to teaching and writing books on the protection of civil rights and liberties, I have often pondered why I had been so oblivious to the pervasive racism of the society in which I grew up. My vocal opposition to discrimination, particularly toward racial minorities, only began during my high school years. The opposition accelerated later, when I was an undergraduate at Yale, culminating in a revelatory experience as a member of an interracial group of students who, as participants in a cross-cultural program, Operation Crossroads Africa, lived and worked together on the coast of Ghana in the summer of 1960. But more about that later.

* * * * *

My mother first subtly raised the issue of prejudice in her conversations with me about her childhood growing up in Dallas. Her father had made a calculated choice to buy a modest house in a predominantly Jewish neighborhood of Dallas. The security of a Jewish neighborhood, she suggested, offered protection for the Levin family against antisemitism. All of my mother's many high school boyfriends were Jewish. At the University of Texas she joined a Jewish sorority, and she married my father, a member of a respected Fort Worth Jewish family.

In her conversations about growing up in Dallas, Mother never spoke of incidents of antisemitism directed at her or members of her family. But after the United States entered the war against Nazi Germany and Dad was drafted, my mother's sense of vulnerability as an American Jew must have been acute, although I did not know it at the time. My awareness of her wartime anxiety only surfaced years later when I recalled her distrust of the security patrol in our neighborhood and her panicked reaction to the phone call from my barber.

As a boy, I loved and admired both of my parents, but my mother had the more profound influence on me. Whereas Dad was suave and undemonstrative, Mother was openly empathetic and did not hesitate to tell me when I was not. I vividly remember my temper tantrum in our living room after Mother told me I must invite Virginia, the most unpopular girl in my fourth-grade class, to my birthday party at a local roller skating rink.

"She is fat and ugly and nobody likes her," I wailed.

Mother was unmoved. "Jimmy, you cannot hurt that little girl's feelings by not inviting her," she said. "Either you invite *all* of your classmates," she said, "or none." Mother, of course, prevailed, and the invitations were mailed to every member of my fourth-grade class. That roller skating party was the best birthday celebration I can remember. No one had a better time than me, except Virginia, who never stopped grinning as she skated merrily around and around the rink.

Why was my mother, such a sensitive member of a religious minority, willing to accept and benefit from racial segregation in Fort Worth? Unfortunately, I never asked her directly, but I believe that her explanation would have been complicated. Mother, the daughter of a traveling salesman, loved her life in Fort Worth as the wife of a Yale-educated attorney whose family had deep roots in the community. She certainly enjoyed the material comforts of that life. Having a full-time Black servant made life easy, even luxurious, by the standards in which she had grown up in Dallas.

But I think the greatest factor in explaining my mother's acquiescence to segregation was her devotion to my dad, his parents, and his siblings. It would have been unthinkable for her to bring negative attention to the Simon family by loudly, or even quietly, protesting racial segregation in her adopted hometown.

I suspect that her failure to speak out against racism created a slow, uncomfortable internal burn. Finally, it erupted in a confrontation with me after I came home from elementary school one day. Testing my preadolescent swagger, I blurted out the N-word.

"Don't you ever let me hear you say that word again," she shouted.

I was shocked by the vehemence of her reaction. I don't recall that she offered a long explanation for her outburst. Using the N-word was disrespectful and wrong, she said.

I never uttered the N-word again.

It would not have occurred to me to question my parents or friends about racial segregation in those days, even if I were troubled by it, which, obviously, I was not. The reasons for my own passive acceptance of racial discrimination growing up in Fort Worth may not have been so different from my mother's. I was grateful to have a happy childhood in a family that I loved dearly. Lazy summer days were the best. But winters weren't bad either. I looked forward to sledding on the hills of nearby Worth Hills Golf Course on the one or two days a year that it snowed. I made straight-A report cards at Alice Carlson that were signed by my beaming mother. The only consistent blemishes on my elementary school report cards were checks next to "Talking" (during class), "Does Not Follow Instructions," and "Handwriting," shortcomings that have remained lifelong traits.

McLean Junior High School provided a much more rigorous education than Alice Carlson, in large part because of the leadership of the principal, Mr. E. E. Dyess, a gaunt, white-maned disciplinarian who demanded excellence from his teachers as well as his best students. He introduced a "97 Club" for the top students, awarding them a large capital M letter in an effort to show that academics, as much as athletics, deserved recognition. I was placed in an accelerated class in seventh grade composed of the best students from the four elementary schools that fed into McLean. By the end of the first week with my new classmates, I realized that my days of easy A's were over.

At the same time, I was introduced to the best teacher I was fortunate enough to have in my twelve years in Fort Worth public schools. She was Margaret Sullivan, my seventh-grade English teacher, a middle-aged Irish American with an icy stare that could rattle the bones of the cockiest student. When we diagrammed sentences at the blackboard, she became the no-nonsense drill sergeant who stood menacingly next to us. With the same sense of purpose, she taught us to appreciate great literature. Although strict, she was never cruel or demeaning.

I suspected that Margaret Sullivan was not so straitlaced and humorless as she appeared, and I acted on my hunch after she assigned the class to write a paper on a hobby. After English class that day, I sat at my desk in study hall trying to figure out an original topic for the assignment. I began observing other students doing just about everything but studying. One was busy gossiping, a second drawing cartoons, a third staring out the window at a baseball game on the school's athletic field. It suddenly hit me: my topic would be "People Watching in Study Hall." I attempted to write the paper with humor and flair. Apparently, Margaret Sullivan thought I succeeded. She called my mother at home to tell her how much she enjoyed reading my paper.

In contrast to Margaret Sullivan, Nancy Vick, my eighth-grade English teacher, conducted her classes in a low-key manner that never seemed threatening. But her quiet intelligence and droll sense of humor made her classes both challenging and satisfying. She continued to spark my interest in literature and introduced me to the great English Lake District poets Samuel Coleridge and William Wordsworth.

Despite stiff competition at McLean, I continued to bring home excellent report cards and received an invitation to become a member of Mr. Dyess's "97 Club." In other pursuits, however, I was not so successful. I quickly learned that my days of competing on my school's athletic teams had ended at Alice Carlson. These hard facts of life were explained to me by McLean's basketball coach when he called me into his office after practice one day. "Jimmy," he said quietly, "you are a good basketball player but, frankly, you really cannot compete with the players who will make McLean's varsity team." He gave the example of Dean Cozine, a fellow seventh-grader, who was bigger, stronger, and faster than me and made moves on the basketball court that I could only imagine. The coach did not have to spell out what we both knew to be true: there were other boys as talented as Dean Cozine on every varsity team at McLean.

Although discouraging, the realization that I could not compete on McLean's varsity teams did not dampen my enthusiasm for sports. On Saturday mornings, I joined my friends Larry Glazer, Vick Brown, and Joe Bob Wise for basketball in what was known as "the little gym" on the TCU campus. Officially, the gym was restricted to TCU students, but nobody at the university seemed to object when we joined two dozen or so other junior high school boys who converged on the building. The front door was opened earlier by one of our compatriots, who had climbed up to a second-story window, opened it, climbed down to the first floor, and unlocked the front door for the rest of us.

After a morning of basketball, we crossed the street, sat on stools at the Spudnut Shop, and hungrily devoured hamburgers and french fries, topped off by a scrumptious sugar-glazed doughnut. On Saturday nights a small group of friends, both boys and girls, usually congregated at one of our houses to listen and dance to records of The Clovers, Ruth Brown, and Chuck Berry, all popular Black rhythm-and-blues musicians. They sang sexually suggestive lyrics with an irrepressible, driving beat that enthralled us.

In the eighth grade, I decided to compete for the staff of the *McLean Mirror*, the school's newspaper. Nancy Vick, my English teacher, served as the faculty sponsor of the *Mirror*, which she supervised with a keen eye for excellence. As a result, the *Mirror* annually collected numerous journalism awards. Eighth-grade students who aspired to join the *Mirror* staff in their last year at McLean were required to take a standardized English test; the twenty students with the highest scores made up the staff. I made the cut and was then honored when the incoming staff voted that I serve as coeditor of the *Mirror* with my classmate and good friend Ann Baker.

As coeditors, Ann and I worked extremely hard to live up to the newspaper's lofty reputation. I named my editor's column "Simply Simon," which I thought was clever, but Ann's was better—"Ann-alyzing." Under Nancy Vick's expert tutelage, we published issues throughout the fall and winter. In the spring, the Columbia University School of Journalism announced that the *Mirror* had been awarded the highest rating in its national competition for junior high newspapers. Our principal, Mr. Dyess, celebrated our award as enthusiastically as he did the football team's championship, a remarkable display of pride in football crazy Texas.

CHAPTER 2

HIGH SCHOOL YEARS

The academic mission of Paschal High School often appeared to be of incidental interest to the school's longtime principal, overshadowed by his passion for the Paschal Panther football team. During football season, pep rallies for his heroes were choreographed with the solemnity of a High Mass. Each week the players were reverentially introduced on stage, presented as brave warriors in a noble cause. The climactic moment of each rally was the "Silent Yell," which required the student body to shout out six words—"Paschal, Panthers, Purple, White, Fight, Fight!" What distinguished this yell, and made it crucial to the team's success, were the silences between the shouted words. If any student was so careless or irreverent as to cough or belch during the silences, the ritual would have to be repeated until it was perfectly executed.

None of my English classes at Paschal compared to the outstanding instruction that I had received at McLean. My tenth-grade English teacher at Paschal was kind, soft-spoken, and very boring. She asked the class to read chapters aloud from George Eliot's *Silas Marner* in the same plodding manner that my second-grade teacher had instructed us to read aloud simple, grade-level books. I wondered if that was the reason *Silas Marner* seemed so dreary and interminable. With a large faculty to teach a student body of 1,500, Paschal also had its share of dedicated, competent teachers. One of my favorites was my math teacher, who shared her delight in solving complicated algebraic equations. I also appreciated my American history teacher, who tried mightily to make the subject come alive in her classroom. She was severely handicapped, however, by our thick textbook, which was full of dates and names but provided few insights into the causes of historical events. My chemistry teacher, who surely realized early in the term that I possessed no aptitude for her subject, was my most compassionate instructor, patiently repeating her explanations of the periodic table and other basic concepts until I grasped them.

• • • • •

My social life during my three years of high school was lively and fun. I attribute those happy times to three factors. First, Texas law permitted fourteen-year-olds to drive, which gave me the independence that all teenagers crave. I bought a used 1954 Ford Fairlane from one of Dad's clients with money I had earned during the summer. Mother and Dad were out of town when I made the purchase. Dad was not pleased with me or his client, but the car, with its powder blue body and cream-colored roof, became my pride and joy.

Second, my friends and I had no trouble buying beer at convenience stores or Jax's, our favorite nighttime haunt, where we listened to music and danced. And third, we formed "the Tanglewood Ten," an informal group of guys who drove to the wooded area of Tanglewood, the partially developed housing project behind Simondale Drive, to drink beer, joke, and tell tall tales. Our activities soon expanded to regular parties with our dates. The camaraderie that developed among the "Ten" in high school has lasted, in many cases, for a lifetime.

Two of my friends in the "Ten" deserve special mention for the unique roles they played in my life during those years. The first was Gene Dozier, whom I had known since our days together at Alice Carlson. Late one night I received a phone call from a classmate I knew only by name and sight, who ran with a tough crowd that always seemed to be looking for trouble.

Obviously drunk, he mumbled a series of antisemitic insults and challenged me to a fight. He told me to meet him the next day after school behind the main building. I told Gene about the phone call, and he immediately offered to accompany me to the showdown. Gene stood 6'2", possessed a tightly muscled body, and was a star end on the Paschal football team. After school the two of us walked together to meet my challenger. He did not show up. I never heard from him again.

Joe Bob Wise, the second "Ten" member of note, and I decided to write a short story for publication. Joe Bob lived in a room above his family's detached garage, which gave us privacy to create our literary masterpiece. We met in Joe Bob's room on weekends late at night, the time, we assumed, that all aspiring writers did their best work. We took periodic breaks, seeking additional creative energy by driving to the Toddle House, a twenty-four-hour diner, where we ordered coffee and the best pecan waffles in the city. In time, we wrote "Thank You, Harry," a story of intrigue and murder, in which the murderer kills his office rival with a poison he had discovered in the darkest jungles of Brazil. The murderer accomplishes the dirty deed by sending his victim a gift box of holiday cards and envelopes to thank him for being such a good colleague, carefully applying the liquid poison to the adhesive on the back flap of the envelopes. We were extremely pleased with our story. But the harsh world of commercial publishing quickly intruded. We received a brief, printed rejection slip from *Collier's*, the national magazine that we had counted on to launch our professional careers.

◆ ◆ ◆ ◆ ◆

My first awareness that racial discrimination was wrong almost certainly began with my mother's emphatic dictum not to say the N-word. But in summer jobs during my high school years, I witnessed discrimination against Black laborers that focused my attention on racism that went far beyond semantics.

I made $1.10 an hour the summer I worked at a grain elevator just east of downtown Fort Worth. My job was to climb on the giant, grain-filled trailers of the trucks from West Texas that lined up every weekday outside the elevator. With a slotted aluminum spear, I dug into the mounds of grain—wheat, oats, and corn—that were piled high. I twisted open the slots so that the grain seeped in at every level. Then I poured the grain onto a cotton cloth and took the sample to the elevator office, where Kenneth, my boss, evaluated the overall quality of the grain and determined the price to be paid for storage. The third member of our crew, Ray, directed the truck traffic and generally made sure the operation ran smoothly.

Willy, the fourth and final member of our crew, was a muscular young Black man who provided the hard physical labor for the operation, shoveling the mounds of grain out of the large truck trailers and, during slack hours, cleaning the platform where the trucks were weighed, as well as sweeping up the rotten grain that had seeped underneath.

Willy and I were buddies. He took me seriously, never suggesting that I, a rich white kid, was just passing through and would resume a comfortable life at the end of the summer. Whenever there was a break in the truck traffic, Willy and I joked around. He would sometimes challenge me to do a chin-up on the enormous muscle of his flexed left arm.

Our easy camaraderie ended abruptly in late August when I discovered one Monday morning that Willy was not at work. I asked my boss, "Where is Willy?"

"Willy doesn't work here anymore," he replied. I asked what had happened, but he ignored my question and walked away. The subject was closed. And my friend Willy disappeared from my life, just like that.

Willy may have quit for personal reasons unknown to me, but I thought it unlikely that he would have suddenly left a steady job, even if the pay was meager (I assumed that his hourly pay was not much more than mine). I was certain that he could not have been fired for cause. He had not missed a day of work while I was there. I would have known if he had been drinking on the job. And he was the hardest-working member of our crew. It occurred to me that he might have asked for a raise and was dismissed for his brazen request.

I never learned why Willy left. But I kept mentally switching the skin colors of our crew. It was inconceivable to me that the two white men, or even this tow-headed teenager hired for the summer, would have vanished from the grain elevator without a trace or explanation. And if the hardworking Willy had been white, would the boss have said, with such peremptory finality, "He doesn't work here anymore"?

The next summer, I was hired for a menial, boring job at a meatpacking plant on the city's north side. For me, the highlight of every day was watching two huge Black men seize great slabs of beef hung from hooks and, wielding large knives, furiously and expertly cut the slabs into manageable chunks. The chunks were then thrown onto a conveyor belt and grabbed by white men and women seated on each side of it who, using small, precise knives, cut the beef into marketable size for sale.

That spectacle, which I so enjoyed observing, came to a halt one day. The two Black men had demanded that they be paid the higher wages earned by the white men and women. It seemed more than fair to me, because their skills were indispensable to the success of the operation. After a three-day standoff, the two Black men prevailed and were back at their jobs, presumably at higher wages.

I suppose it could be seen as a triumph of risky negotiations by two Black laborers who knew the value of their work. But again, as at the grain elevator, I imagined a switch of the skin colors of the participants and was outraged. What if the two Black men had been white and the men and women on either side of the conveyor belt Black? Was it conceivable, under my imagined scenario, that Black men and women taking chunks from the conveyor belt would have been paid more than two white men expertly slashing the slabs of beef? I had the further suspicion that the victory of the two Black men would be short-lived once management could find two more Black men to do their job for lower wages.

• • • • •

By the time I entered Paschal High School in the fall of 1954, I was more sensitive to political issues—not just racial discrimination, but also related issues, such as the collective bargaining rights of labor. Gradually, I became a vocal, underage liberal Democrat. That transformation was not inevitable in our family. My father was a moderate Republican whose vote was canceled out in every presidential election by my mother's vote for the Democratic standard-bearer, beginning with Franklin D. Roosevelt.

My political education began in 1952, watching the first live, gavel-to-gavel television coverage of the Republican National Convention. It was high drama, with conservative forces aligned behind US Senator Robert Taft of Ohio against those of General Dwight D. Eisenhower. My dad was an enthusiastic backer of Ike and, therefore, so was I. I was thrilled when the convention delegates nominated Eisenhower and, with Dad, celebrated Ike's landslide victory over the Democratic candidate, Governor Adlai Stevenson of Illinois. That election year Mother was pleased to note that in our affluent precinct she had cast one of only two votes tallied for Stevenson. Her good friend Norma Mack cast the other.

I had by then begun to devour *Time* magazine, which was delivered every week to our house. *Time* endorsed Ike, no doubt influenced by the preference of Henry Luce, the magazine's founder and publisher, who was a moderate Republican. After Eisenhower's victory, *Time* featured the president-elect's portrait on its cover.

But for me, *Time*'s most memorable cover of the 1950s was not the one picturing Ike in 1952, but, three years later, the one bearing the triumphant face of Thurgood Marshall, the lead counsel for the NAACP Legal Defense Fund, after he won the historic victory in *Brown v. Board of Education*.

• • • • •

By the mid-1950s I had begun to challenge the racist assumptions of some of my close high school friends, many of whom I had known since kindergarten. I was kidded mercilessly by my buddies, but I returned their ridicule with a steady smile and straightforward argument. I was convinced that facts and the law were on my side. Surprisingly, neither friendships nor feelings were hurt by these exchanges.

My next political challenge—engaging my father in discussions on the subject of race—turned out to be neither good-humored nor satisfying for either of us. Dad was a prominent lawyer and civic leader in Fort Worth. His clients included the mayor as well as some of the city's most successful businessmen. As an expert on zoning law, he often appeared before the Fort Worth City Council. He was elected president of the downtown Rotary Club and had become cochairman of the local chapter of the National Conference of Christians and Jews. We were one of the few Jewish families invited to be members of Colonial Country Club, where Dad played eighteen holes of golf every Saturday afternoon and early Sunday morning.

Dad was a voice of reason and moderation in both his professional and private lives. But, as I discovered in our tense discussions on race, he was also a proud Texan who was prepared to defend the laws and culture in which he had been raised. Like President Eisenhower, who also grew up in a segregated society, Dad favored gradual desegregation, always sensitive to the mores and history of the segregated South.

When I insisted that gradualism just wasn't good enough in eliminating racial discrimination, he reacted coldly, confronting me as he would a courtroom adversary who needed to be put in his place. It was not a fair fight, but I would not back down. Our discussions became verbal jousts of combat with neither side giving an inch. Those charged and often painful discussions continued for many years, much to the extreme discomfort of my mother and, later, my wife, Marcia.

✦ ✦ ✦ ✦ ✦

During my senior year at Paschal I was preoccupied with college applications. Yale was my first choice, which pleased my mother, the daughter of a traveling sock salesman. My father, a Yale alumnus, frequently sang the "Whiffenpoof Song" (named for Yale's leading singing group), but otherwise showed no allegiance to his alma mater. He neither encouraged nor discouraged my decision to apply.

Mother warned me that Yale, like other Ivy League schools, was reputed to impose a Jewish quota, an accusation that Yale and the other Ivy League schools denied at the time but was later documented to be true. Even if I was handicapped by a Jewish quota, other factors counted in my favor. I was a Yale legacy student and would graduate from a public high school in Texas, important to an Ivy League admissions committee in search of geographical diversity. My application would also highlight that I was coeditor of the award-winning *McLean Mirror*, had been selected for the editorial staff of Paschal's yearbook, had been initiated into the National Honor Society, and would graduate magna cum laude.

In preparation for my college essay, I studied a paperback called *Thirty Days to a Better Vocabulary*, and I was determined to use every one of my newly acquired words. The result was an essay that was not just ostentatious but also clunky, akin to gargling with a mouthful of rocks. Mother read it and said, "Jimmy, this essay doesn't sound like you." At first, I was indignant. But after rereading the essay, I agreed with her and rewrote it.

The greatest reward for serving as an editor of Paschal's yearbook was not the work, which was rarely absorbing, but the opportunity to become close friends with another member of the staff, Sherwin Goldman. I had known Sherwin for years, since both of us had attended Alice Carlson and Sunday school at Temple Beth-El. He was a year younger than me and a class behind, but had skipped his junior year at Paschal to graduate with my class. He was acknowledged by all who knew him to be "a brain," and he always stood at the top of his class. He also exhibited a sophistication well beyond his years. While I was drinking beer with my friends in Tanglewood, Sherwin was attending performances of the Fort Worth Symphony Orchestra as well as city ballet and opera events.

Sherwin and I devoted most of our conversations during the afternoon period set aside for work on the yearbook to discussions of our shared commitment to liberal politics. He was my only classmate, and that included my friends in the "Ten," who spoke openly about civil rights, especially discrimination against racial minorities. He had read more widely on the subject than I had and took the lead in our discussions. On the second subject of mutual interest, admission to Yale, he eagerly listened to me. Whereas his father, a Polish immigrant, had dropped out of high school, both my father and my uncle were Yale graduates. Moreover, my cousin Henry was then a Yale sophomore who spoke expansively at every opportunity of the fascinating world awaiting us in New Haven.

During the first week of April, Sherwin and I each received a letter of acceptance to Yale. I was ecstatic but wondered, with a mixture of satisfaction and regret, if the two of us, plus cousin Henry, had filled Yale's Jewish quota for Fort Worth for years to come.

• • • • •

Shortly before graduation from Paschal, I signed up with several friends, including Larry Glazer, for summer school at the Universidad de Monterrey in Monterrey, Mexico. My cousin Henry, after taking Spanish classes at McLean and Paschal, had spent the summer at the university before entering Yale and could speak the language fluently. I, too, had taken Spanish classes at McLean and Paschal, but I was not remotely close to speaking the language. Since I was scheduled to take Spanish at Yale to fulfill my foreign language requirement, my parents agreed with me that taking a prep course at the Mexican university was a sensible decision. It occurred to me that spending a summer in a foreign country with friends could also offer many pleasures.

Once I recovered from a severe case of diarrhea in my first week in Monterrey, the summer was, as expected, enjoyable. The university campus, on the outskirts of the city, was large and framed by beds of bright summer flowers. Our group from Fort Worth quickly became friendly with college students from several southern states. And though it was uncommonly hot, even by Texas standards, we soon looked forward to the traditional three-hour afternoon siesta. After our siestas, my friends and I would sometimes take a taxi into the city of Monterrey, where we had drinks at our favorite hotel bar and dinner at a nearby restaurant. We would then walk to the city square, hoping to look irresistibly attractive to the small groups of Monterrey girls strolling there. Though we failed in that endeavor, we never tired of trying. We also attended a couple of bullfights, but neither the matadors nor the bulls fit the romantic images portrayed in Ernest Hemingway's fiction.

After the first week of classes conducted in Spanish, I wished that I had had the good sense of my friend Larry Glazer, who had enrolled in an English class, for which he would receive credit in his freshman year at the University of Texas. I was relieved that I was not taking my Spanish classes for credit. By the end of the summer, I was no closer to speaking Spanish fluently than when I had arrived, an unsettling thought as I contemplated five Spanish classes a week in my first semester at Yale.

CHAPTER 3

YALE

One morning in late August 1957, Sherwin Goldman and I boarded an American Airlines flight for New York's LaGuardia Airport. We arrived nine hours later, after our plane had made stops in every Gulf Coast state, beginning with Louisiana, then moving on to Mississippi, Alabama, and so on up the Atlantic coast. After finally landing at LaGuardia, taking a bus into New York City, and making the two-hour train ride from Grand Central Station to New Haven, we were beyond exhausted when we dropped into beds at the Taft Hotel, located less than a block from the Yale campus.

When Yale had informed me of my freshman roommates by mail during the summer, I had been particularly intrigued by the name and education of Walter Bell Lockwood III, a graduate of Choate, the venerated Connecticut prep school. I envisioned late-night discussions with Lockwood on great Russian novels while a Beethoven symphony played on a phonograph.

"Hi, I'm Walt," he said, when I entered our room on the third floor of Wright Hall on Yale's freshman campus. He was solidly built and blond, the very picture, I thought, of a typical "Yalie." But Walter Bell Lockwood III was playing Elvis Presley's latest hit on his phonograph, not a Beethoven symphony. And while listening to Elvis, he was sipping a can of beer and smoking a cigarette. So much for my expectations. As it turned out, Walt Lockwood was exactly as he appeared that first day, easygoing and unpretentious, the perfect roommate. We would room together for all four years at Yale.

Later that week, we met with our counselor, a graduate student who lived on the first floor of our dormitory. He was friendly but slightly formal, and his advice scared the hell out of me. As freshmen, he told us, we would be assigned more reading in our courses than we could possibly digest in the six hours of study a night available before going to sleep. I had rarely devoted even two hours a night to my studies at Paschal, and I was a slow reader! He advised us not to let a single idle moment go to waste, beginning at our early morning breakfast in the freshman dining room. While standing in line for breakfast, he suggested we have a book in hand to continue our studies from the previous night.

It did not help my morale to start every weekday morning at eight o'clock with Spanish, taught by a young instructor who spoke only Spanish, grilled us daily on grammar, and expected us to read and discuss the poems of García Lorca. My troubles multiplied when I later attended classes in biology, no more fathomable to me than high school chemistry had been, and philosophy, in which I was introduced to the works of Plato and Aristotle.

My spirits improved slightly in my English class, with assignments to read Greek myths, Shakespeare plays, the short novels of Henry James and Herman Melville, and William Faulkner's *Light in August*. But I hesitated to speak in class, intimidated by my classmates, who seemed to understand the assignments at a deeper level than I did and could discuss the works with enviable sophistication.

My favorite class was European History, taught by a captivating young professor named Charles Garside. He presented his subject cinematically, full of human drama and consequence. When he discussed the reign of Charlemagne, emperor of most of central and western Europe in the Middle Ages, I felt as if I'd been transported to the ninth century. In preparation for breakout discussions of Garside's lectures, we were assigned a workbook that presented each major historical event from five different perspectives.

My high school history textbooks, weighed down by dates and names, seemed hopelessly obsolete.

I wrote Mother and Dad every week, bravely telling them how interesting my classes and classmates were. In our Sunday evening phone calls, I continued my exercise in positive thinking. But I was miserable, and Mother sensed it. She began to send me care packages filled with brownies, which made me more homesick.

Sherwin Goldman almost single-handedly lifted my spirits that first semester at Yale. He insisted on introducing me to his world of classical music, signing us up for two concert series performed in Yale's Woolsey Hall, the first by the world-renowned Boston Symphony Orchestra and the second by the New Haven Symphony. During the intermissions, Sherwin took my comments on the music seriously and then subtly expanded my understanding of what we had just heard. I was helped through a particularly complex symphony with the comforting thought of finishing the evening at Spot Pizza, feasting on the thick-crusted specialty of the house.

After a week of classes and long hours in the library, Sherwin and I, often joined by one of his roommates, sometimes splurged for a Friday night dinner at Casey's, New Haven's best restaurant, ordering lobster and talking for hours about the shortcomings of the Eisenhower administration.

Thanks to Sherwin, the Thanksgiving holiday took on a new, glorious meaning having nothing to do with turkey and cranberry sauce. We took the train into New York City for a long weekend in which Sherwin introduced me to my first ballet, a performance by George Balanchine's New York City Ballet at City Center. I was awed by the extraordinary grace and strength of two of the company's principal male dancers, Jacques d'Amboise and Arthur Mitchell. We purchased standing-room tickets to see my first opera at The Met. We also heard jazz at the Village Vanguard in Greenwich Village and watched Jason Robards star as Hickey in an off-Broadway production of Eugene O'Neill's *The Iceman Cometh*. We topped off our weekend on Sunday with a sumptuous lunch at Lum Fong's Chinese Restaurant.

In early October, I made my plane reservations to spend the Christmas holidays in Texas and then counted the days until my departure. The first week of my vacation in Fort Worth was all I could have asked for—tender loving care at home and rollicking good times with my "Ten" buddies.

But I spent most of the remainder of the vacation writing papers and dreading the three-hour final examinations awaiting me.

After returning to New Haven, I began to feel an intense pain in the big toe of my right foot. A physician at the Yale health center diagnosed it as "traumatic arthritis" and gave me a cortisone shot. It did not help. A week before my first exam, I was admitted to the university infirmary, where pain medication slowly began to work. I was released shortly before my first exam, fantasizing that I would overcome adversity, like heroes in Hollywood melodramas, by making spectacularly high grades on my exams. Only in Hollywood movies, I discovered. In fact, I did dismally on all five exams, receiving no grade above C.

Years later, after I had taken the Texas bar exam with a similar pain in the big toe of my right foot, I consulted a doctor in Austin. After reviewing my blood tests, he told me the pain I had experienced during the bar exam was similar to what I had felt before my freshman exams. Both painful episodes, he concluded, were the result of gout attacks, almost certainly caused by stress. I failed the bar exam. A year later, after returning from a fellowship in India, I again took the Texas bar exam and passed.

* * * * *

Between semesters, I took refuge in the beautifully appointed apartment of my aunt Ruth and uncle Zeke Rosen in Brookline, Massachusetts, a suburb of Boston. Aunt Ruth was my father's sister. Their corner apartment was located on a lower floor of one of two modern high-rise apartment buildings that Uncle Zeke had recently built. It was his most ambitious project, and he was justifiably proud. My aunt and uncle welcomed me as if I were their son, and I eagerly soaked up their affection. I slept late, read cheap paperback novels, and engaged in relaxing conversations about family at our meals together. Aunt Ruth and I spent afternoons at Boston's major art museums, the Gardner and the Museum of Fine Arts. At night, Uncle Zeke and I watched the Boston Celtics in the Boston Garden, marveling at the incredible athleticism of Bob Cousy and Bill Russell, who led the team to a string of National Basketball Association titles. Great art and great basketball, all in one brief vacation—sublime!

I returned to Yale with new resolve. My first decision was to try out for the college radio station, WYBC. The competition was called "heeling" and required freshmen to spend several hours a day for six weeks at the station performing menial tasks and learning about the twenty-four-hour broadcasting cycle. There was a sense of community among the "heelers," even as we cleaned the offices. And the substantive assignments (e.g., writing news copy and apprenticing with a member hosting a program of popular or classical music) were interesting. At the end of the trial period, I was voted to be a member of WYBC, which immediately created a new group of friends who had fun together while doing interesting work.

An unexpected bonus to becoming a member of WYBC was that the substantial amount of time I spent at the radio station forced me to organize my study time more efficiently. As a result, my grades on papers and quizzes began to improve. I even found the second semester of my philosophy course, so daunting in the fall, to be one of my favorites. It was taught by an elderly professor, Brand Blanchard, who lectured with remarkable lucidity. Just as important, we were assigned a book that made philosophy both challenging and accessible, presenting problems—such as the proof of the existence of God—based on the writings of five distinguished philosophers.

Having fulfilled Yale's distribution requirements for a foreign language and a science in my freshman year, my schedule sophomore year was a relative breeze. I enjoyed my class in English poetry, which included studying the works of Geoffrey Chaucer, John Milton, and Alexander Pope, though my instructor confessed with bemusement that he had never heard Chaucer recited in Middle English with a Texas accent. My psychology class was primarily devoted to the study of laboratory experiments on mice, which I found tedious. But when we read Sigmund Freud's *The Interpretation of Dreams*, I was fascinated. I also took a studio art course at the Yale School of Art and discovered anew that I had peaked as an artist in Mr. Caraway's fourth-grade class.

The first A's I earned at Yale were in two subjects that would remain lifelong interests. One was in a survey course in art history, taught by the cream of the Art History Department's faculty. The most popular lecturer was Professor Vincent Scully, an esteemed scholar of early Greek art and architecture, who became so engrossed in his subject that he frequently came dangerously close to falling off the stage with excitement. We were assigned papers on works at the Yale Art Gallery, including an abstract steel sculpture by David Smith and an awkward, stylized painting entitled *Mother and Child: First Steps* by Pablo Picasso. In writing papers for the course, I trusted my observations and aesthetic judgments, and that confidence carried over to the final exam. I received one of the highest grades in the class of over one hundred undergraduates.

I earned my second A in the most important course I took at Yale: twentieth-century American political history. It was taught by Professor John Morton Blum, who paced briskly across the stage, delivering his lectures with erudition and humor. What made Blum's course so valuable to me was not just his superb lectures, but also his reading list. Instead of the hated textbooks of my high school days, Blum assigned two dozen books, mostly paperbacks. They were written by the nation's most respected scholars, including Eric Goldman, William Leuchtenburg, and Blum himself, who made history read like riveting fiction. Years later, in the books I would write on American history, politics, and constitutional law, I attempted to emulate Blum and the other historians I had been introduced to as a Yale sophomore. After taking Blum's course, my choice of a major was easy: history.

During the year, a group of undergraduates organized a major colloquium on campus entitled "America's Role in a Revolutionary World," featuring addresses by prominent leaders of independence movements in Africa, Asia, and South America, as well as US Senator Hubert Humphrey of Minnesota, then a potential presidential candidate for the Democratic Party. One of my colleagues at WYBC, Ron Etra, and I persuaded the governing board of the radio station to provide gavel-to-gavel coverage of the three-day event. Etra and I served as on-air analysts. To say that we took ourselves seriously would be an understatement. But we also had the time of our lives, analyzing every major address in the hushed tones of CBS-TV's anchor, Walter Cronkite.

• • • • •

In the late spring of 1959, shortly before the end of the second semester of sophomore year, Sherwin asked if I would like to join him and two other classmates, Mike Samuels and Charles Schwartz, for a summer tour of Europe. I enthusiastically accepted his invitation, paying my expenses with money I had saved from summer jobs when I was in high school. Our trip began in grand fashion when we were met at the Glasgow Airport by Stewart Lang, a dapper Scotsman who drove a sleek late-model Jaguar. Lang was the owner of a major Scotch whisky distillery and an important business associate of Sherwin's father, Mickey Goldman, who owned and operated a hugely successful wholesale liquor business in Fort Worth. Lang served as our tour guide for two days of sightseeing in Scotland.

Our next stop was London, and then, for the next two months, we crisscrossed Europe in a rented Citroën, from Paris to Madrid to Berlin and from the Greek coast to Copenhagen. We were among hundreds of American college students who had invaded the continent, a phenomenon later described in an article in *Life* magazine. A *Life* photographer took my picture for the story with my passport sticking out of the back pocket of my jeans. He then advised me to place my passport in a more secure pocket. My photo did not appear in the magazine, but I was grateful for the photographer's advice.

We visited major museums in London, Paris, and Rome, but my favorite was the Prado in Madrid; I spent a full hour in front of Francisco Goya's powerful, disturbing painting *The Third of May*, commemorating Spanish resistance to Napoleon's armies. After Madrid, we drove to Pamplona, where I planned to "run with the bulls," inspired by Hemingway's description of the spectacle in *The Sun Also Rises*. At the last minute, my better judgment prevailed, and I sensibly watched from a safe distance.

An eye-opening lesson in Cold War politics occurred when we drove to the divided city of Berlin two years before the Communist government in East Berlin built the Berlin Wall to prevent East Germans from escaping to the West. We spent a day in the eastern sector and were startled by the contrast between its bleak, austere neighborhoods and those in bustling West Berlin.

Our most anticipated destination, and one that promised a second Cold War experience, was the Communist Youth Festival in Vienna, held for the first time outside of the Iron Curtain that had been imposed by the Soviet Union on the Communist countries of Eastern Europe. When I told Dad of our plan to attend, he insisted that I write to the State Department to declare that I was not and had never been a member of the Communist Party.

The festival was both fascinating and scary. Every program was replete with Communist propaganda. And each day we were there, we were confronted by American Communists who obviously had been trained to debate naive American college students from the decadent West.

* * * * *

My grades continued to improve my junior year, placing me in the top 10 percent of my class and entitling me to the designation of "Ranking Scholar." The dramatic rise from my dismal grades as a freshman to those I received two years later elicited a questionnaire from the university's psychology department seeking an explanation. I do not recall the questions or my answers to the questionnaire. In retrospect, I think my improved grades were the result of better study habits and a keen interest in my classes (two history seminars, a class in the history of modern art, an English course in tragedy, and a fascinating seminar on the psychology of religion taught by a gentle, wise professor).

Even as I exulted in my grades, my thoughts during the second semester of my junior year turned to my plans for the summer. I had been accepted into the Operation Crossroads Africa program, which promised adventure and an opportunity to test my commitment to racial equality.

CHAPTER 4

GHANA AND ISRAEL

In September 1957, during the first week of my freshman year at Yale, I met Ted Ledbetter, a bright, funny Black classmate who lived across the hall from me. Ted was the son of a well-known minister in New Haven and one of only a handful of Blacks admitted to my class. We became friends, and I was pleased when he invited me to his home for a meal and to meet his family. Ted dropped out of Yale at the end of freshman year and, sadly, I never saw or heard from him again.

My next interaction with African Americans, actually several sixth-graders, occurred during my sophomore year when I volunteered to tutor elementary school students in reading in a poor, inner-city school not far from the Yale campus. I don't have clear memories of the students, possibly because I did not think I was a particularly effective tutor. But I was proud of myself for making the effort.

My personal education in race relations began in earnest during my junior year, when I was drawn to the tough-talking young Yale chaplain, the Reverend William Sloane Coffin Jr. Coffin practiced a muscular Christianity that welcomed Americans of all faiths to confront the problem of racial discrimination head-on.[1] While continuing to speak out against racial discrimination in the South, he announced in the winter of 1960 that he would lead a small student group to Guinea, West Africa, the following summer as a participant in Operation Crossroads Africa, a cross-cultural experiment in race relations. To encourage Yale undergraduates to apply for the program, he invited the program's founder, the Reverend James Robinson, a Black minister in Harlem, to speak from the pulpit at Yale's Battell Chapel one Sunday in February.

I liked to sleep late on Sunday mornings and was not enthusiastic about attending my first sermon at the chapel. But I dragged myself out of bed that cold February morning to hear the Reverend Robinson and was not disappointed. In a rich baritone, Robinson told the story of the first group of Crossroaders, who had worked with African students in the villages of several West African countries. They had built schools and health centers and laid sewer pipes. Robinson said that the tangible results, while important, were not the greatest benefit of the program. Building bridges of understanding between young Americans and Africans would reap benefits of incalculable value for future generations.

I could not wait to fill out an application for Crossroads and was delighted to be accepted into the program. Given my raw conversations on race with my father, I did not think it was a good idea for me to ask for his financial assistance to support my summer in Africa. Fortunately, I had received a small inheritance after Grandaddy's recent death, which was the result of the sale of his valuable stamp collection. I used the money to support my summer adventure. I do not recall a long conversation with my parents about Crossroads beyond telling them of the program's ambitious purpose, and that I was incredibly excited to be a participant.

After completing my exams in May, I went directly to New York to meet the other Crossroaders. There were approximately seventy of us, all

1 In 1961, Coffin boarded a Greyhound bus in Atlanta with seven other "Freedom Riders," including the Reverend Ralph Abernathy, a Black minister and adviser to Dr. Martin Luther King Jr., headed to Jackson, Mississippi, to protest racial discrimination. When Coffin and the other passengers arrived in Jackson, local white men and women hurled taunts and threats at them. Undeterred, they sat down at the bus station lunch counter, where they were denied service and arrested.

from different colleges, divided into small groups. Like the previous groups, we would be working in various countries in West Africa. Although white college students made up a substantial majority of the groups, the number of Black students was by far the most that I had ever met. I immediately sensed the excitement and camaraderie among everyone who had signed up. We attended an exuberant performance by dancers from Guinea and a fine production of Lorraine Hansberry's *A Raisin in the Sun* on Broadway. But as enjoyable as those performances were, we were impatient to board our Pan Am plane and fly to West Africa.

I was a member of a group of eleven American students who were headed to Ghana. Two members of our group were Black: Ida Smith, an undergraduate at City College of New York, and Richard English, a doctoral student at the University of Michigan. In addition to Ida, the four other women in our group were students at universities and colleges in the South. The other men were either undergraduate or graduate students at universities in the East and South: MIT, Williams, and the Universities of North Carolina and Mississippi.

In late June, we flew to Lagos, Nigeria, then boarded a bus that took us to Accra, the capital of the Republic of Ghana. Formerly the British colony of the Gold Coast, Ghana had won its independence in 1957. We stayed overnight at the University College in Accra and were invited the next day to a student meeting at the college, where we met the new nation's first president, Kwame Nkrumah. Quite an introduction to Ghana!

My euphoria evaporated that evening when I attended a student party at the university. To my shock and chagrin, I was so emotionally upset to be one of only a handful of white-skinned guests, surrounded by a sea of Black Africans, that I quickly retreated to my dormitory room. Had I made a mistake in coming to Africa? Was I really as open-minded about race relations as I had thought? After spending a restless night trying to answer those questions, I woke up with new resolve to make the most of the experience.

A fellow Crossroader from the University of Mississippi, who had attended the same party, must have had a similar experience and wrestled with the same questions that I did. But he came to a different conclusion, leaving Accra the next day to return to the United States.

Our group boarded a small van the next morning headed to Pram Pram, a fishing village on the coast of the Gulf of Guinea about a two-hour drive south of Accra. After we arrived, we met a small group of Ghanaian students, who would be working with us to build a schoolhouse. We quickly put our gear in a vacant one-story concrete building a short distance from Pram Pram that would serve as our dormitory. Mattresses were strewn on the floor for us. Otherwise, we had to create a makeshift student village for ourselves. There was a long wooden picnic table with a canvas cover that served as our dining room. Meals were cooked over an open fire—usually fufu, which was boiled plantain, cassava, or rice pounded and shaped into a round ball. We built a small shower stall out of wood, where we soaped up and poured cold water over ourselves after work.

Soon after we had settled in, we walked to Pram Pram, a collection of small wooden huts with thatched roofs. We were introduced to our hosts, who did not speak English, but were nonetheless happy to welcome us. Later, we were invited to join them for a wonderful night of dancing. To the steady beat of large drums, we danced with villagers and each other for hours.

Before we started work on the schoolhouse, we strolled to the nearby coast, a beautiful beach overlooking the sparkling aquamarine water of the Gulf of Guinea. The beach later became a nightly destination for me where I marveled at the clear, dark sky filled with stunningly bright stars that appeared closer to earth than I ever remembered at home.

We used simple tools—hammers and saws—to construct the schoolhouse out of wood on vacant land near the village. We worked hard but so enjoyed each other's company that the hours went by quickly. And there were delightful daily breaks when local boys climbed the nearby palm trees to cut down large coconuts. We then gathered below the trees to drink the sweet milk from the sliced coconuts and scoop out the meat of the coconut from the shell. Delicious.

I set out on an adventure of my own one weekend after some of the local fishermen agreed to take me along on one of their daily voyages. Shortly before daybreak one morning, I met my companions from the village, who helped me onto their crude *Kon-tiki*-style wooden raft. The early morning sun was spectacular as we sailed out to sea. But, unfortunately, I spent most of the day with my head bent over the edge of the raft, heaving violently, relieving myself of any food I may have ingested over the previous twenty-four hours. After we returned in the late afternoon, the fishermen patted me on the back as if I had brought back a large bounty from the sea. My adventure had been spoiled by seasickness, but my companions were proud of me, nonetheless, for my eagerness to share a workday with them.

The most meaningful experience of that unforgettable summer was, as the Reverend Robinson had predicted, the friendships and understanding nurtured when working side-by-side with Ghanaian students. They were smart, fun-loving, and sophisticated. They knew a great deal more about our country than we did about theirs. They were eager, for example, to discuss the prospects of a young senator from Massachusetts, John F. Kennedy, who had just been nominated by the Democratic Party to become the next president of the United States.

I also formed close bonds with the extraordinary young men in my group, friendships that extended far beyond the summer. They included Ben Chertok, a graduate student at MIT who later worked as a physicist for Bell Labs; Dick English, the doctoral candidate from the University of Michigan who later pursued an academic career; Don Campbell, then a student at Williams, who later was trained as an analyst by Anna Freud in England and remained in that country as a psychologist; and Jim Alrutz, who, after graduating from the University of North Carolina, spent his career in Africa overseeing various large-scale development projects.

• • • • •

An obligation of all Crossroaders, insisted upon by the Reverend Robinson, was that we tell the story of our African experience when we returned to the United States. I eagerly fulfilled that obligation upon my return to Fort Worth, speaking to church groups and members of Temple Beth-El, to the Junior Chamber of Commerce, and to a reporter for WBAP-TV, the local NBC affiliate. I was particularly pleased to see my entire television interview aired on a newscast that included a segment on the Democratic presidential candidate, John F. Kennedy, who had been campaigning in Fort Worth earlier that day.

The one speaking venue that I sought above all others was the downtown

Rotary Club. My insistence on speaking at my father's Rotary Club was perhaps my slightly mischievous attempt to score points in our ongoing debate on race. Dad was not enthusiastic about the idea but reluctantly agreed to arrange for me to give a luncheon talk to his Rotary colleagues.

On the appointed day of my talk in a large dining room at the Texas Hotel, I was confident that my father was more nervous than I was. Would I embarrass him by lecturing his fellow Rotarians on the need to eliminate racial discrimination in Fort Worth, where the public schools were still segregated? Would I entertain the Rotarians with happy tales of my intermingling with Black Africans in Ghana?

I had thought carefully about my talk that day. I had no intention of embarrassing my father, either with a lecture on race relations in Fort Worth or by raising hackles with incendiary examples of interracial friendships made during my summer in Ghana. Despite our political differences, I loved him too much to subject him to public discomfort or humiliation before his friends.

I chose, instead, to tell the Rotarians about the vibrant young African nation that I had just visited. I recalled the intelligent, sophisticated young Ghanaians I had met and worked with and the mutual respect and understanding that resulted from those relationships. And I predicted a bright future for Ghana and suggested that the United States had a great opportunity to form meaningful partnerships with Ghana and other newly emerging independent African nations based on mutually beneficial political and economic ties.

I received enthusiastic applause following my speech. I was sure that the response was, in part, a show of respect for my father. But I was also confident that I had delivered a solid speech on international cooperation that was appreciated on its merits. Later, Dad received complimentary letters from several Rotarians in the audience, reinforcing my impression.

The greatest reward I received, however, came after I sat down next to my father. I could tell from his facial expression that he was pleased with my speech. And then I felt his gentle pat on my thigh. I had made him proud that day.

• • • • •

When my grandfather Poppy was alive, he conducted the Passover service for our family at Uncle Henry and Aunt Sammy's with straightforward seriousness. After he died in 1954, our family continued to read the service, but in a perfunctory manner, with the objective, it seemed to me, to eat dinner as soon as possible. We attended High Holy Day services at Temple Beth-El as an obligation rather than as a demonstration of repentance for our misdeeds of the previous year. Both Dad and Uncle Henry had served as president of the temple and my mother had served as president of the temple sisterhood, not as a reflection of their religious commitment to Reform Judaism, but to carry on our family's tradition of leadership in the Jewish community, which Poppy had begun shortly after the turn of the century.

I attended Sunday school and was confirmed at Temple Beth-El, but the six years of Jewish education and Hebrew instruction did not make much of an impression on me. I remember singing the Jewish hymn "Ein Keloheinu" with gusto, knowing that the benediction would follow and I could go home. And while I respected Rabbi Milton Rosenbaum, who taught our confirmation class, I did not retain much from his instruction. My most vivid and bemused memory of that confirmation year was the celebration arranged by our class's parents for a dinner at the Big Apple, a barbeque restaurant that specialized in pork ribs.

My serious Jewish education began when I was at Yale, primarily as the result of my discussions with Rabbi Robert Schur, who succeeded Rabbi Rosenbaum at Temple Beth-El. Sherwin Goldman had introduced me to Rabbi Schur after we returned to Fort Worth following our freshman year. Sherwin had been the first boy to be bar mitzvahed at Temple Beth-El, the year after I was confirmed, and had befriended Rabbi Schur shortly after he arrived as the temple's new rabbi. Sherwin had spoken often of Rabbi Schur and was eager for me to meet him. Schur was an outspoken advocate for civil rights and liberties and had joined other clergy in Fort Worth to protest segregation in the city and beyond. As Sherwin predicted, Schur became a close friend of mine as well as my mentor on Reform Judaism.

When I returned to Fort Worth during my undergraduate years, I often had long discussions with Rabbi Schur about Reform Judaism in which I would raise the question of whether I could be a good Jew when I had serious doubts about the existence of God. The rabbi spoke at length and with erudition about the Reform Jewish tradition and the Reform Jew's ethical responsibility to serve the larger community. He was, it seemed to me, an exemplar of Reform Judaism, providing spiritual guidance to his congregants at Temple Beth-El while serving as a civil rights leader in Fort Worth. He assured me that I, too, could be a good Jew in the Reform tradition by continuing to question my religious beliefs while engaging in the great issues of the day such as civil rights and liberties.

In addition to my discussions with Rabbi Schur, two courses at Yale stimulated my thinking on the question of my belief in God and, more broadly, my commitment to organized religion. The first was the philosophy class taught by Professor Brand Blanchard, who presented major philosophical issues, including the theological question of the existence of God, from the perspective of great thinkers through the ages. Later, I enrolled in a seminar on the psychology of religion taught by Professor Erwin Goodenough, a scholar of the history of religion. Like Professor Blanchard's class, Professor Goodenough's seminar questioned traditional religious beliefs. We read a wide range of books, from Harvard philosopher and psychologist William James's *The Varieties of Religious Experience* to Erich Fromm's *Escape from Freedom*, in which the author applied psychoanalytic methods to explain how individuals escape from isolation and alienation by making themselves dependent on others.

• • • • •

In the summer of 1962, following my first year at Yale Law School, I explored another aspect of my Jewish identity—my relationship as an American Jew with the state of Israel. I signed up with a national Jewish organization that sponsored trips to Israel for young American Jews to work on a kibbutz. I was assigned to Kibbutz Kfar Hanassi, located in the Upper Galilee on the Lebanese border.

A substantial portion of my expenses had been paid by Professor Harold Isaacs, a political scientist at the Massachusetts Institute of Technology, who had offered me an honorarium to keep a journal on my thoughts and experiences in Israel. Isaacs, whose field of research focused on group identity and ethnicity, had interviewed me several times in 1960 in connection with my summer experience as a Crossroader in Ghana. The result of his interviews, of both me and other Crossroaders, was the publication of his book *Emergent Americans*, an analysis of the Crossroaders' attitudes and experiences in Africa. His interest in my summer in Israel was in my identity as a Jew.

The boundary between Kibbutz Kfar Hanassi and the Lebanese border was patrolled by armed guards who were members of the kibbutz. Despite the presence of the guards serving as a reminder of danger, daily life on the kibbutz seemed as routine as if members lived in a suburban community outside of New York City or Chicago. The kibbutz had been founded by British Jews after the creation of the state of Israel in 1948, but it was a far cry from the pioneering kibbutzim of the early twentieth century. Kibbutz members picked fruit from lush, ripening apple, peach, and pear trees, ran a thriving toy factory, and could relax in a large, modern swimming pool during their free time.

My job, however, was not to pick fruit or work in the toy factory. Eight hours a day, six days a week, I moved heavy irrigation pipes from one row of fruit trees to the next. The strenuous work developed muscles in my arms and legs that I never knew existed. Our lorry picked me and the other men up at 5:30 every morning and took us to the fields for a full workday, which was interrupted at 8:30 for a splendid breakfast of eggs, hunks of cheese, fresh loaves of bread, huge tomatoes, and coffee. We finished work at 2:00 p.m., and after lunch in the kibbutz dining room were free to sleep, read, swim, or mingle with members of the kibbutz and the other young Americans who were there to live and work for the summer.

I roomed with Danny, a pleasant, quiet young Zionist from New Jersey who, like me, was spending the summer working in the fields. For my roommate, the summer's experience was part of his family's lifelong commitment to the state of Israel.

I also developed friendships with members of the kibbutz, including Gil, a strapping blond with a full beard. A proud sabra (a Jew born in Israel or Palestine before 1948) and committed atheist, he shared his fine collection of classical music records with me. Another friend of mine was Colin, a tall, bespectacled trained accountant who had immigrated to Israel from England anticipating a healthy outdoor life working in the fields of the kibbutz. But he was soon brought inside to keep the kibbutz's books. He didn't complain, noting that he had much more leisure time with his wife and two small children on the kibbutz than he had had in England. Every afternoon he spent two uninterrupted hours with his family followed by dinner together before the children were returned to the children's house, where they lived under the care of female members of the kibbutz.

During the summer, Adolph Eichmann, the Nazi SS leader who was a major organizer of the Holocaust, was hanged in Jerusalem after he had been found guilty of war crimes in an Israeli courtroom. Eichmann had been hunted down by the Mossad, Israel's national intelligence agency, in Argentina. Both his trial and punishment were the subject of animated daily conversations on the kibbutz and a grim reminder of the horrors of the Holocaust as well as Israel's essential role in providing a homeland for Jews around the world.

Living on the kibbutz that summer reinforced my support for the state of Israel. At the same time, I did not feel the deep, personal allegiance to Israel that my roommate had known since he was a boy. And though I liked my kibbutzim friends and respected their full-fledged commitment to the state of Israel, I did not want to join them permanently as a citizen in the new nation. My support for Israel, I concluded, was grounded in my identity as an American Jew whose first allegiance was to the government of the United States.

CHAPTER 5

LAW SCHOOL

My first glimpse of Senator John F. Kennedy occurred when he waved from the backseat of a limousine convertible that passed my residential college at Yale on an autumn afternoon in early November 1960. Huge crowds lined both sides of Elm Street, but I still was able to see Kennedy's uncommonly handsome, smiling face as he passed by. Long before his appearance in New Haven, I had made up my mind to cast my first presidential ballot for him.

His youthful energy and inspiring message, especially on the subject of civil rights, resonated with me. During the campaign, he had said that the president "must exert the great moral and educational force of his office to bring equal access to public facilities—from churches to lunch counters—and support the right of every American to stand up for his rights—even if it means sitting down for them." "Lunch counters" was a reference to sit-in protests by Black students at lunch counters that began on February 1, 1960, when four freshmen from North Carolina A&T College in Greensboro sat down at a segregated Woolworth's lunch counter, a protest that spread within weeks to sit-ins in nine southern states.

Kennedy also said during the campaign, "If the president does not himself wage the struggle for equal rights—if he stands above the battle—then the battle will inevitably be lost." No one could mistake his meaning: he promised a proactive, vigorous fight for civil rights, in contrast to President Eisenhower's perceived detachment.

On November 8, the day of the presidential election, I was in Washington completing research for my senior undergraduate history thesis on Arthur Bliss Lane, the former US ambassador to Poland, who had served in that diplomatic post immediately after World War II. My thesis adviser, Professor Howard Gotlieb, the chief archivist at Yale's Sterling Library, had suggested Lane as my thesis topic primarily because his papers were at Yale. I had arranged to interview Lane's widow, who lived in the nation's capital. By the time I interviewed her, I had lost all enthusiasm for the project since, as Lane's papers revealed, he had become a fanatical anti-Communist as well as an outspoken critic of President Truman's post–World War II foreign policy, which, he suggested, was not just soft on Communism but dangerously close to treasonous. Lane's attacks were similar to Senator Joseph McCarthy's reckless anti-Communist rants, though they predated McCarthy's by several years.

On election night I met Alice Huberman, my blind date arranged by a Yale classmate, in downtown Washington. Alice, a lively, attractive brunette, was then the national president of B'nai B'rith Girls (BBG), a Jewish girls youth organization, and had taken a leave from the University of California at Berkeley to serve as BBG's leader. She was as excited about Kennedy's candidacy as I was. After dinner, we spent an exhilarating evening in the lobby of the Mayflower Hotel watching election returns on a giant television monitor. By the time I said goodbye to Alice after midnight, Kennedy held what appeared to be an insurmountable lead. By the next morning, however, his Republican opponent, Vice President Richard Nixon, had almost closed the gap. I was relieved when final returns gave Kennedy a narrow victory.

JFK's inaugural address eloquently set the tone for his presidency: he was prepared to carry the torch for a new generation, sobered by combat in World War II but eager to set idealistic goals for the nation's future. "Ask not what your country can do for you," he intoned, "but what you can do for your country."

At my 1961 Yale graduation the following spring, our class orator, Bill Redpath, took up JFK's call to action, telling classmates and proud parents that we were prepared to follow our new president's lead. Many of us planned to defer graduate school to teach in a developing country in Africa, Asia, or South America, combining adventure, cross-cultural education, and meaningful work. I took quiet satisfaction in Redpath's words, since I had already worked in Ghana the previous summer and planned to spend the next two years teaching in Nigeria.

Shortly before graduation, I had been accepted in a program sponsored by the African-American Institute to teach English in Nigeria. At my father's urging, I had also applied and been accepted at Yale Law School. After I had received the offer from the African-American Institute, the law school agreed to hold my place for two years while I taught in Nigeria. Unfortunately, the teaching job in Nigeria fell through in early summer, so I made plans to start my first year of law school in the fall.

• • • • •

After I returned to Fort Worth early that summer, I studied the classified ads in the *Star-Telegram*, intent on finding a summer job that would be different from my past employment or any job that I was likely to have in the future. Two possibilities stood out: driving a cab or training as a dance instructor at the Arthur Murray Studio on Camp Bowie Boulevard. I decided to interview at Arthur Murray's. To my surprise, the studio's manager appeared eager for me to become a trainee with the promise that, after an intensive three-week course, I would begin instructing the studio's customers. It seemed highly improbable that I would excel at ballroom dance instruction since, as early as my first lessons in James Leito's ballroom dancing classes when I was in elementary school, I had demonstrated neither grace nor talent on the dance floor.

The agreement between the studio manager and me seemed to be risk-free for both of us. I would not be paid during the training sessions and very modestly if I became an instructor. Later, I learned that the manager shamelessly cheated every member of his staff. But I was living at home, so I did not need a salary and was unaffected by his chicanery. And the prospect of learning ballroom dancing taught by Arthur Murray instructors, and then being paid to teach dancing, appeared to be an irresistible opportunity.

I arrived at the Arthur Murray studio at ten o'clock the following Monday morning and met my seven fellow trainees: four young women and three young men. It was clear to me after a few conversations with them that I was the only one with a college degree. Some of the other trainees, I suspected, had not graduated from high school. But we immediately developed an easy, informal camaraderie, and we shared a common goal: to succeed as Arthur Murray dance instructors.

Six days a week, ten hours a day, we were taught ballroom dancing by our instructors, a young married couple. They were demanding but encouraging, so the hours went by quickly, and all of us became more confident and agile on the dance floor. We were so committed to our new craft that, after ten hours of instruction at the studio, we went to a nearby nightclub that had a small dance floor and tried out our latest steps. It was so much fun!

Before we graduated to become full-fledged instructors, we were drilled on sales techniques for prospective customers. We were taught to begin our sales pitch with an inspiring narrative of how much the dance lessons would bring enjoyment and enviable skill on the dance floor. Only later in the conversation should we discuss the high cost of the lessons.

The technique was surprisingly effective. When we did not have a customer, we were on the phone soliciting business. We received a small bonus for each potential customer we brought in. I remember calling my friend Larry Glazer's older brother, inviting him to come to the studio for a free lesson. I could then collect my bonus, but warned him against falling for the well-rehearsed spiel. He was assigned one of the most attractive and accomplished female dancers on the staff, and he was smitten. I felt a moral obligation to advise him to refuse to sign up for months of expensive lessons, advice he heeded reluctantly.

The summer I spent at the Arthur Murray studio was both entertaining and educational. I enjoyed ballroom dancing and, for a brief time (before I forgot the steps I had been taught), I was actually pretty good at it. And I delighted in the company of my instructor friends, who were plainspoken, fun, and wise in ways unknown to a recent Yale graduate. My experience as a dance instructor was as exotic, in many ways, as any other time in my life that I can recall, including as a Crossroader in Ghana.

* * * * *

My father's practical argument that I should go to law school was irrefutable: regardless of my ultimate career, a law degree was the best possible insurance that I could always make a good living. No doubt, he also hoped that I would return to Fort Worth to practice law with him, Uncle Henry, my brother Dick, and our cousin Henry. Even before I took my first class at Yale Law School, however, I thought it unlikely that I would practice in Fort Worth. Although I had no idea what my eventual career path would be, I was determined to strike out on my own.

In the fall of 1961, during my first semester of law school, I found the exercise in critical analysis in all of my courses to be challenging, but the only subject that really interested me was constitutional law. It was taught by Professor Alexander M. Bickel, a brilliant member of the young guard at the law school. Bickel had clerked for Justice Felix Frankfurter and made history, although it was not publicly known in 1961, by drafting five questions for the justices to ask attorneys in *Brown v. Board of Education* at the reargument during the Court's 1953 term.

The questions Bickel drafted at Frankfurter's request focused on the intent of the framers of the Fourteenth Amendment—that is, whether they had intended to outlaw public school segregation, and, if not, could the Court in the mid-twentieth century nonetheless rule that separate public school facilities for Blacks and whites was unconstitutional. Frankfurter's strategy, carried out by Bickel, was to present a rationale for the Court to schedule reargument in *Brown*, as the justices had been hopelessly divided after they had heard the first argument during the Court's 1952 term.

By the time the Court convened for the reargument in December 1953, California's former governor, Earl Warren, had replaced Fred Vinson as chief justice. And though Frankfurter could not have predicted the change in the Court's leadership, Warren's appointment justified Frankfurter's strategy for postponing the Court's decision in *Brown*. Under Warren's leadership, the justices voted unanimously to strike down public-school segregation.

None of this inside information was known to me or my classmates in Bickel's constitutional law class in the fall of 1961. The professor, always nattily dressed in a three-piece suit, was a Toscanini in his classroom, conducting a Socratic dialogue with mesmerizing precision. He spent six weeks on a single case, *Marbury v. Madison*, the seminal opinion written by Chief Justice John Marshall in 1803 that established the Supreme Court's authority to review the constitutionality of an act of Congress.

I was fascinated by Bickel's masterly analysis. But what distinguished constitutional law from the other classes I took that semester—contracts, torts, and property (all casebook studies of private law)—was that public law and policy were inextricably bound. Bickel's approach to constitutional law closely followed that of his mentor, Justice Frankfurter, who was the Court's leading proponent of the philosophy of judicial restraint. Bickel, like Frankfurter, believed that the Court should defer to the popularly elected branches of the federal government whenever possible. And the Court should, at all times, move cautiously and incrementally. Both Frankfurter and Bickel carved out an exception in *Brown v. Board of Education*.

Bickel's philosophy of judicial restraint was balanced by that of two other constitutional law professors who taught me at Yale. Professor Charles Black, a transplanted Texan who retained his drawl, supervised my independent study, in which I wrote a paper on the Court's civil rights and liberties decisions. Black had been one of the constitutional law experts brought to New York by Thurgood Marshall as he prepared for his reargument in *Brown* before the Warren Court.

Fred Rodell, my third constitutional law professor at Yale, taught a seminar on the modern Supreme Court. Rodell presented a jarring contrast to Bickel in philosophy and demeanor. Fred's politics, as well as his judicial philosophy, were decidedly left-wing, earning him a place on FBI director J. Edgar Hoover's suspected subversive list as well as the sobriquet "Fred the Red" among law students. He wore rumpled khakis and plaid shirts to class and insisted that students call him Fred. He was close friends with Justice William O. Douglas, Justice Frankfurter's chief nemesis on the Court, and, like Douglas, advocated a robust judicial activism to expand civil rights and liberties.

• • • • •

During the spring of 1962 when I was attending Fred Rodell's seminar, I spotted Marcia Solomon in the Yale Law School dining room. She was a petite brunette with large hazel eyes and a beautiful peaches-and-cream complexion. I managed to sit at her table for lunch one day and, fortuitously, Pauli Murray, whom I had engaged in an earlier luncheon conversation about her year and a half of teaching in Ghana, was also at our table. I did not know at the time that Murray, who was African American, had been a civil rights pioneer in her native South Carolina. At fifty-one years old, and already a highly accomplished civil rights attorney, she was now studying for her doctorate at Yale. Yale recognized her illustrious career in 2017 when it named one of its new residential colleges in her honor. As Murray and I discussed our experiences in Ghana, Marcia, in a high-pitched voice, said that she, too, had spent time in Africa.

"Oh, really!" I exclaimed with unbridled enthusiasm.

Marcia then recalled her time in South Africa during her junior year in high school when her father, a research chemist with the M. W. Kellogg Company, was working for the South African government to convert coal into petrol. I listened patiently until I had the opportunity to ask for her phone number.

When I called Marcia that night, I asked what she was doing.

"I'm painting," she replied.

"What are you painting?"

"Purple."

I had never met a girl who painted purple. I could understand painting a landscape or a bouquet of flowers, but never just purple. I was intrigued.

On our first date for coffee at George and Harry's, a favorite hangout for Yale students, I learned that Marcia had exhibited her artwork publicly at the Montclair Art Museum in New Jersey, and that she had chosen to attend Pembroke, the sister school of Brown, primarily so that she could take classes at the Rhode Island School of Design. At Pembroke, her academic interests had shifted to English literature, after she had studied with the novelist John Hawkes, as well as to art history. She had graduated Phi

Beta Kappa and received a full scholarship to the Yale Graduate School to study art history.

We later joked that each of us posed a language problem for the other. Marcia found my Texas drawl maddeningly slow and suggested that she could excuse herself to powder her nose in the ladies' restroom and return before I had finished my sentence. I countered that I had originally had such trouble understanding her accent that I had thought she was from Czechoslovakia. Imagine my surprise when I learned that she had grown up in northern New Jersey.

We had a few dates in the spring of 1962, but our relationship became serious after I returned from Israel for my second year of law school. That fall of 1962 we were practically inseparable, usually commuting between her apartment on Howell Street and my dormitory room in the law school quad. Our favorite date was buying ham salad sandwiches at a luncheonette near the Yale Art Gallery and eating in the museum's courtyard near a Henry Moore sculpture.

We were so in love that we were eager to share our happiness with others. I was tempted, for example, to invite the famous playwright Tennessee Williams to join us for a movie one night. He was standing glumly on a street corner, undoubtedly nervous while awaiting the first pre-Broadway reviews of his latest play, which was being performed at New Haven's Shubert Theatre. I restrained myself and did not issue the invitation, but wondered afterward if we could have boosted his spirits by taking him to the movie with us.

Marcia and I became engaged in February 1963 and planned a June wedding at a country club in Glen Ridge, New Jersey. But Marcia worried that her mother, who had complained of a heart condition for years, would not be able to manage the pressure of the wedding. In late March we flew to Fort Worth so that Marcia could meet my family. During the visit, Marcia expressed her anxiety about her mother's health around the time of the wedding. My mother suggested that we avoid the problem by having the wedding in our living room while we were in Texas. She had married Dad in her parents' living room thirty-one years earlier and both the wedding and the marriage had worked out well. We agreed to Mother's plan, and

Marcia's parents and younger sister, Judy, flew down for the ceremony in my family's living room.

Both Marcia and I later regretted our hasty decision. For Marcia, it meant that she was deprived of a traditional wedding with her friends as bridesmaids and guests. At the time, I thought it was a good idea. Mother and Aunt Franny, who had flown in from Florida, decorated the living room with large vases of beautiful spring flowers. In addition to my family, three of my closest friends from high school, including Sherwin Goldman, were there. Rabbi Schur presided, which was especially meaningful to me. But once we returned to New Haven, I realized that we should have stuck with the original plan to be married in New Jersey in June. Writing term papers and sitting for final exams was no way to start a marriage.

* * * * *

In the spring of 1963, the same semester that Marcia and I were married, I took a second seminar with Fred that had nothing to do with constitutional law but became the class with the greatest influence on my future career as a journalist and author. "Writing about the Law for Laymen" was one of the most popular electives at the school. Every year, as many as one hundred law students tried to enroll in it, but the seminar was limited to fifteen. Fred required each prospective student to write a brief essay on why he or she wanted to take the course.

The essay was quite a challenge for me. My only journalism experience had been as coeditor of the *McLean Mirror* when I was in ninth grade, hardly a compelling credential for Rodell's seminar. I expected that the seminar would draw applications from former editors of Ivy League newspapers as well as law review students.

So, how could I impress Professor Rodell? I decided to write a one-act play for two characters, one in the role of Rodell, the second as me. I turned the exercise into a slightly irreverent dialogue in which I tried to figure out what would impress the professor so that he would admit me to his seminar. It was risky, but it worked. And, yes, I was joined in Fred's seminar by former editors of elite college dailies as well as law review students.

But Fred's insistence on clear, unpretentious, creative writing struck a chord with me. And I became Fred's star pupil, whether writing a profile of a law professor, summarizing a Supreme Court decision, or analyzing a complex legal doctrine.

Encouraged by my success in Fred's seminar, I determined to land a summer job at one of the nation's top newspapers or newsmagazines. I wrote to every major newspaper and magazine in the country to apply, providing my résumé and expressing my strong desire to begin my training as a professional journalist. Most did not bother to reply. Those that did wrote brief letters of rejection. I received only one positive reply—from the *New York Daily News*, informing me that the newspaper might, just might, have an opening as a copy boy for the summer. I was devastated. How could these newspaper and magazine editors ignore my sterling Ivy League education and ambition to join their ranks? Easily, it turned out.

In desperation, I went to Fred to ask for his advice.

"Have you written to *Newsweek*?" he asked.

I replied that I had written to the magazine's New York office and received the all-too-familiar rejection letter.

"Write another letter to *Newsweek*'s Washington bureau and address it to Benjamin Bradlee, Washington bureau chief, but let me see it before you seal the envelope," he instructed.

I did as he said and brought the letter, essentially the same as the ones I had written to dozens of newspapers as well as to *Newsweek*'s New York office.

Rodell wrote in the margin, "Ben, take this guy. He's good," and scrawled "Fred." He then wrote on the envelope addressed to Bradlee "Personal."

Bradlee agreed to see me in Washington during a visit that Fred had arranged for the students in our Supreme Court seminar to hear oral arguments at the Court and meet with Chief Justice Warren. The day at the Court was fascinating. But I anticipated that the highlight of my Washington visit would occur the next morning when I was scheduled to meet Bradlee for breakfast at a Georgetown restaurant. At the appointed time, I entered the restaurant and waited for Bradlee. Thirty minutes went by and still no sign of *Newsweek*'s Washington bureau chief. Reluctantly, and with trepidation, I called Bradlee at home. He answered the phone and, when I identified myself, immediately apologized. He had forgotten our appointment. A few minutes later he arrived at the restaurant. He told me that Fred was a longtime friend of his family. We talked about my background and my work in Fred's seminar.

The next week I received a letter from Bradlee offering me a summer internship in *Newsweek*'s Washington bureau.

* * * * *

Marcia and I spent our first summer as husband and wife in a garden apartment in Arlington, Virginia. Every morning I boarded a public bus for Washington, DC, and my exciting job as an intern in the Washington bureau of *Newsweek*. Marcia's summer was not so satisfying. She spent her days working on her master's thesis on a single painting by the American neoclassicist artist John Vanderlyn, often doing her research at the Library of Congress. By this time, she was disillusioned with the graduate study of art history at Yale, which she considered obsessively fact-driven. It squeezed out the pure aesthetic joy and meaning of the great paintings that she had loved studying at Pembroke.

That summer, I reported to Ben Bradlee in *Newsweek*'s offices on the twelfth floor of the National Press Building. By then, Bradlee was already a well-known journalist, though he had not yet become the legendary managing editor of the *Washington Post*, and he was one of President Kennedy's closest friends. As a lowly intern, I would not have been surprised if I had never had personal contact with Bradlee. But, in fact, he treated me as if I belonged in the office. He read my copy and took me to lunch several times, always ordering a red Dubonnet on the rocks with a twist of lemon that, to this day, is one of my favorites. Before Dr. Martin Luther King Jr. delivered his "I Have a Dream" speech at the Lincoln Memorial that summer, Bradlee invited me and the other *Newsweek* reporters not covering the speech into his office to watch it on his television set. Soon after King began his speech, Bradlee sensed that it was historic and noted King's superb cadence in delivering it.

Bradlee was my hero. He was tall and handsome, wore wide, bright red suspenders, and cursed like the sailor he was in World War II. I was not tall (5'7") or handsome, and could not possibly have been taken seriously wearing wide, bright red suspenders. But I could curse, and my cursing that summer reached wondrously creative heights.

Bradlee handed me some legitimately important stories, including the failure of Congress to fund the multimillion-dollar Bokaro steel mill project in India under the US government's foreign assistance program. I also reported on a rally for Senator Barry Goldwater, who was a leading contender for the Republican presidential nomination in 1964. My most memorable assignment was to cover a press conference held by President Kennedy on the South Lawn of the White House. I do not recall any exchange between a reporter and the president at the press conference, but only that Kennedy was dazzlingly good-looking and clever, and that I was close enough to observe that this famously sophisticated president had what looked like egg on his tie.

At the end of my internship, Bradlee, unprompted, wrote a "To Whom It May Concern" recommendation letter that informed a future employer that I had demonstrated outstanding journalism skills as an intern at *Newsweek*. With Bradlee's letter in hand, I eagerly anticipated a future career in journalism.

After we returned to New Haven in the fall of 1963, Marcia was hired as a docent at the Yale Art Gallery, guiding tours of the permanent collection and special exhibits. By my third year of law school, I had completed my favorite courses in constitutional law as well as excellent courses in family law taught by Professor Joe Goldstein and psychiatrist Jay Katz. I therefore reluctantly signed up for what were known as "black letter" law courses, considered essential for the bar exam and law practice. I hated all of them—from Corporations to Trusts and Estates—and did not have the discipline to attend many of the classes or give the materials in the casebooks more than a cursory reading.

The one bright spot in my schedule was a seminar taught by Sigmund Freud's daughter Anna, along with Yale professors Goldstein and Katz. The seminar, entitled "The Best Interests of the Child," was the first that Freud offered in the United States. I was one of fifteen students admitted to her seminar, which was attended by an equal number of psychiatrists and psychologists from New York. Freud, a trained child psychoanalyst, was by then almost as famous as her father. She had written extensively in her field and established a center outside of London that provided research and training in child psychoanalysis as well as a child and adolescent clinic. She conducted the seminar at Yale with insight, grace, and understated authority. It was an incredible opportunity and experience.

Marcia and I enjoyed our first year of marriage together, but the uncertainty of our future weighed heavily on us. A national tragedy would trigger the decision to spend our next year abroad.

CHAPTER 6

A YEAR IN INDIA

November 22, 1963, was the most traumatic day of my life. I heard the first report that President Kennedy had been shot while I was being interviewed for a job by an editor of *The New Republic* magazine in New York City. When the editor received a call reporting the shooting in Dallas, our interview ended instantly. Marcia, who was at the Metropolitan Museum, and I returned immediately to New Haven, where we sat numbly in front of our television set absorbing the tragic event in disbelief.

My plan to find my first job in journalism seemed hopelessly inadequate. What could I do to honor JFK's legacy? My thoughts, once again, turned to Africa. I searched the law school bulletin board and found a promising opportunity. The Africa-Asia Fellowship Program, administered by the Maxwell School of Public Administration at Syracuse University, offered a limited number of one-year stipends for recent graduates in law, economics, and public administration to assist the newly independent governments in Africa and Asia. I could think of no better way to recognize the promise of Kennedy's brief presidency than to assist a newly independent African nation in drafting a new constitution or rewriting antiquated colonial-era statutes.

During the winter, I received a letter from Professor Arthur Osteen, the administrator of the Africa-Asia program, informing me that I was a finalist for the fellowship. Marcia and I were invited to spend a weekend at an inn in Amherst, Massachusetts, where the finalists and their spouses would be interviewed by experts in law, history, economics, and public administration, who would select the recipients of the fellowships.

Marcia and I prepared for the weekend as we would have crammed for a final exam. She concentrated on African art, architecture, and art history, while I studied African law, history, and economics. During the weekend in the Amherst inn, we met for hours with prestigious experts, including Professor Stanley Kutler, a distinguished historian at the University of Wisconsin. At each interview, we emphasized our prior experience in Africa and our strong desire to return to the continent to help one of the newly independent nations.

In the early spring, I received a phone call from Professor Osteen. "Congratulations, Jim," he said. "You have been awarded an Africa-Asia Fellowship to spend a year in India." I was so pleased to have been awarded a fellowship that it took me a few moments to realize that the offer was to go to India, a nation that had been independent for almost two decades, not a newly independent African nation. When the offer to spend a year in India sank in, I told Professor Osteen that my expectation, if awarded a fellowship, was to work in one of the newly independent nations in Africa. Would it be possible to send us to one of the African nations instead of India?

"No," he said emphatically, discouraging further discussion.

Had I turned down the offer to go to India, I later wondered, would Osteen have juggled the fellowships so we could have spent the year in Africa? At the time, however, I did not press the issue.

* * * * *

In August 1964, Marcia and I sailed from New York to England on the SS *United States*, one of the world's fastest ocean liners. During the voyage, Marcia gave a lecture on Indian art and architecture, which was delivered with both style and substance and was greatly appreciated by the other fellows and their spouses. Fortuitously, her lecture was given during the first full day of the voyage. The remaining four days were the roughest transatlantic crossing in August in the ship's history. The dining room was virtually empty for most meals, including the captain's formal dinner. Marcia and I, like other passengers, spent most of our time in our bunks or bathrooms coping, as best we could, with the tumultuous weather.

After we docked at Southampton on the southern coast of England, we traveled by bus to Oxford for a brief orientation for the Africa-Asia Fellows before our departures by plane for our designated postings. After the orientation, Marcia and I made two stops before arriving at our ultimate destination, New Delhi. The first was Rome, where we viewed Michelangelo's incomparable ceiling frescoes in the Sistine Chapel. The second was Istanbul, where we toured the magnificent Hagia Sophia mosque. Originally built in the sixth century as the largest Christian church of the eastern Roman Empire, it had been converted to a mosque in the early twentieth century when Constantinople (renamed Istanbul) fell to the Ottoman Empire.

When our plane landed in the early morning at the New Delhi airport, the late August heat was already stifling. After a cab ride to our hotel in the city, we reunited with Joel Henning, the second Africa-Asia Fellow assigned to India, and his wife, Grace. We had met the Hennings, both recent graduates of Harvard Law School, at the Oxford orientation. The four of us were soon introduced to Mr. Singh, a retired senior civil servant who had been paid by the program to oversee our year in India.

Singh was polite, but distant, refined, and subtly arrogant. During our meeting, I realized I should have held out for a posting to Africa. He made it clear that India, after almost two decades of independence, did not need two more lawyers, especially young, inexperienced Americans like Joel and me. It was ludicrous to think that we were needed to draft a constitution, new statutes, or, so far as Singh was concerned, anything else. He suggested that we spend a leisurely postgraduate year at the University of Allahabad, one of his nation's fine universities.

Joel accepted Singh's invitation. I did not. I had no intention of spending a postgraduate year at the University of Allahabad, if I had a choice. I had accepted the fellowship to work in one of the newly emerging nations of Africa or Asia. Assigned to India, I wanted to work in the field, if not as a lawyer, then as a trained professional who might be able to help solve, or at least learn about, problems at the district or village level. Singh said there was only one possible posting if Marcia and I did not want to spend the year at the University of Allahabad. He could arrange for me to go to Azamgarh, which, he warned, was in a poor, rural area of eastern Uttar Pradesh state, and considered by the elite civil service as a "punishment" district. I accepted his offer.

✦ ✦ ✦ ✦ ✦

Singh's bleak description of Azamgarh was not an exaggeration. It was a dusty, desolate town of about twenty-five thousand located thirty miles north of the city of Varanasi, with no amenities remotely familiar to our American eyes. Water buffaloes, as well as a smattering of camels, elephants, and monkeys, roamed freely in the surrounding fields. There was a health clinic run by Christian missionaries in the town and a single movie theater showing Hindi-language films.

My host was the district magistrate, Mr. Modwel, a tall, well-built man in his late twenties who had the confident air of a member of the nation's elite civil service. Western in dress and manner, he told me that Mr. Singh had contacted him on my behalf. He looked forward to our time together, although it was obvious to me that he had no idea what I would be doing in Azamgarh. He had arranged for us to stay in two rooms of a large, two-story stucco house owned by a retired schoolteacher. We would have a staff of servants, including a cook, a *chokidar* (watchman), a *dhobi* (a servant to wash our clothes), a bicycle rickshaw *wallah* (driver), and a messenger.

Our first visitors were the Lees, a Christian missionary family from Australia who had lived in Azamgarh for several years. Brian Lee, his wife, Lorraine, and their four daughters greeted us warmly and would become our good friends. Brian, a blond, balding Methodist preacher in his late thirties, had a pleasant smile and genial demeanor that, I later learned, disguised his thoroughly disillusioned state of mind. He had, by then, accepted the fact that the Hindu and Muslim populations in Azamgarh were not interested in converting to Christianity.

Once we had settled into our rooms, I was taken to meet Mr. Tiwari, whom Modwel had assigned to be my professional guide. A local civil servant in his mid-thirties, he was a man of slight build and quiet intelligence. I told him of the purpose of the Africa-Asia program, and how I had been assigned to Azamgarh by Mr. Singh. I said that I wanted to be useful and expressed an interest in visiting villages to learn about the problems in the district. Tiwari and I became friends as well as colleagues. Over the next several months, he accommodated me in every way that he could.

Tiwari and his driver arrived by jeep every weekday morning to take me to various villages, where I met with the chiefs and many of the local farmers. With Tiwari translating, they told me one depressing story after another. The intense heat beat down relentlessly on their small, arid farms. The farmers, whose faces were parched by the sun, told me of the primitive wooden tools they used, passed down from their fathers and grandfathers, with limited success. Their crops of rice, wheat, and sugar cane were meager year after year. They appeared to accept their plight fatalistically.

I suggested to Tiwari that I might start a farmers' newsletter in which the more successful farmers could share their methods with others in the district. Tiwari agreed to translate from the farmers' Hindi to my English; I would then edit their messages, and Tiwari would translate the messages back to Hindi. It was a cumbersome process and, since I was not aware of any noticeably successful farmers in the district, not likely to make much difference. Still, I thought it was worth the effort.

The district bordered on the Tons River, and the intermittent rainfall also supported a few shallow lakes. I arranged for the local government to stock one of the lakes with rohu, a local fish. My idea was to increase the local food supply with a modest, healthy alternative to the diet of rice and other starches.

When Tiwari told me that 200 rupees had been set aside by the local government for Dalits (members of the lowest Indian caste, also known as untouchables), I suggested that the money be used by two Peace Corps volunteers who had arrived in the district shortly after Marcia and me. The two volunteers, Bob and Paul, had been sent to India as poultry experts to help introduce modern methods for raising chickens. The irony of their presumed expertise was not lost on Bob, a native of New York City, and Paul, a resident of Philadelphia. They had seen precious few chicken coops before their Peace Corps training in Colorado. They were nonetheless eager to use the available rupees to build a chicken house and purchase local chickens for a nearby village of Dalits.

While I was busy with my various projects, Marcia found no comparable activities to engage her. She would have liked to teach English at a local school but was told by officials that they preferred teachers with a British accent. She expressed an interest in helping with family planning in the district. The only active program offered transistor radios to men willing to have vasectomies, but there were no more transistor radios available. And there was no program for women, either offering incentives or educational instruction, to encourage the use of birth control methods.

Marcia's days were mostly long and lonely. Our bicycle rickshaw wallah, Jungli, was available to take her into town, but she was reluctant to go and be subjected to the hostile stares of the local male population. The only bright spot for her was a series of lessons in Kathak, the classical Indian dance, taught by a local instructor. After completing the lessons, she performed at a recital in traditional Indian dress, tiny bells wrapped around her ankles, softly tapping her bare feet to the beat of a tambourine and the tablas (a pair of Indian hand drums), played by her instructor. The recital, attended by District Magistrate Modwel as well as Azamgarh's fire chief and other local officials, was a triumph.

Even living in the remote district of Azamgarh, Marcia and I could count numerous other memorable events during our months there. In November, Marcia arranged a surprise birthday party for me with a planned camel ride. But the surprise was inadvertently spoiled by a local official, who interrupted a meeting I was attending to whisper conspiratorially in my ear, "Sahib, the camel has come." When I mounted the camel at our residence, it let out a few moans, either of protest or pain. In any case, it did not move.

Undaunted, Marcia and I were later hoisted onto seats atop a large elephant at our residence and successfully rode it to a meeting in town. And on Christmas Eve, I dressed up as Santa Claus for the Christian children of the staff at the health clinic; Marcia and I then joined clinic families for the Yuletide celebration.

We also made periodic trips by bus to Varanasi, the spiritual capital of India on the Ganges River, where we watched hundreds of Hindu pilgrims bathe in the sacred waters. On New Year's Eve, we joined Bob and Paul and other Peace Corps volunteers working in northern India for a gala celebration in one of the city's Western-style hotels. And on another special occasion, Marcia bought a stunningly beautiful selection of silk saris in Varanasi, which is the sari center of India.

* * * * *

We had a very small circle of friends in Azamgarh: the Lees; the Peace Corps volunteers, Bob and Paul; and Dr. Suvi, the physician in charge of the health clinic, who had been expelled from Burma by the ruling military junta. As Americans, we did not fit into the caste system, or, it seemed, anywhere in the Indian social hierarchy.

Modwel never invited Marcia and me to his residence for lunch or dinner. Always mindful of his status as the top official in the district, he nonetheless made an effort to be a gracious host. I was invited to a number of official dinners for visiting dignitaries, but all were men-only affairs. They were culinary feasts of succulent tandoori chicken and lamb, spicy curries, naan and other Indian breads, and delicious sweets. In addition to attending Marcia's recital, Modwel invited me to play tennis and to duck hunt with him and other government officials. But there was an invisible barrier between the district magistrate and his American visitors, which was most conspicuously apparent when we were invited to accompany Modwel and his wife on a "winter tour," a holdover tradition from the colonial days of British rule.

As we set off on the tour, which Modwel carried out as part of his administrative duties, Marcia and I traveled in the back of a pickup truck, while the Modwels and the driver sat up front in the cab, which only had room for three. Our destination was a rural area of the district, where a small army of servants had set up an elaborate tent city. For the next few days, Modwel sat behind a small table in a clearing near the tents listening to the pleas of local farmers asking for government assistance.

On our day of departure, a thunderstorm erupted, creating a potential protocol dilemma for the district magistrate. Apparently, it did not occur to Modwel to sit in the back of the pickup with me, so that Marcia could ride with Mrs. Modwel in the dry comfort of the front compartment. Instead, he and his wife took their seats next to the driver while Marcia again sat with me in the back of the pickup. We became thoroughly drenched during the two-hour drive back to Azamgarh, and Modwel never apologized for, or indeed expressed any concern or regret about, the stormy conditions we endured on the return trip.

* * * * *

Even before leaving Azamgarh, I was sadly aware that my projects, as well as Bob and Paul's attempt to introduce modern chicken farming to a Dalit village, had failed. My newsletter never, so far as I knew, attracted any notice from the area's farmers. My fisheries project became mired in bureaucratic paperwork.

Bob and Paul's poultry project was the most ludicrous failure of all. Once the two Peace Corps volunteers had supervised the building of a first-rate chicken coop, the chief of the Dalit village insisted that only chickens from Bombay (approximately one thousand miles away), not local varieties, were worthy of the new coop. When he was told that there was no budget to transport the Bombay chickens to Azamgarh, the chief moved into the chicken coop himself. Later, when a disillusioned Bob was asked how he liked India, he responded, sardonically, "I like everything about the country except chickens and Indians."

At the end of my tour in Azamgarh, I was invited to join a planning team, as an observer, that was commissioned to devise a five-year agricultural plan for the Azamgarh district. The team was made up of high-level civil servants from Lucknow, the capital of Uttar Pradesh, and led by a sophisticated young Brahman named Bhargava. He was charming, articulate, and very intelligent. But it soon became apparent to me that he was focused exclusively on setting ambitious goals for the district. Had he made a realistic assessment of the conditions and productivity of local farmers, he would have been forced to lower his expectations, abandon those goals, and set different ones.

Soon after the team had completed its work, I converted my notes into a manuscript, entitled "India: A Small Picture," in which I described the team's deliberations and goals and gave my own critical commentary on the team's unrealistic ambitions. After returning to the United States, I showed the manuscript to Ed Hollander, a vice president at Robert R. Nathan

Associates, a Washington, DC, economic consulting firm where I then worked. He was impressed and offered to send the manuscript to a senior editor he knew at Syracuse University Press. The editor shared Hollander's high opinion of my manuscript, and I soon received a commitment from the university press to publish it. But the Maxwell School at Syracuse continued to sponsor programs in India, and, as a precaution, the university press submitted my manuscript for review to the planning team's leader, Bhargava, in India. Not surprisingly, he objected to my observations and conclusions. The press's commitment to publish my manuscript was quietly abandoned.

⬩ ⬩ ⬩ ⬩ ⬩

The most remarkable experiences during our year in India occurred after we left Azamgarh. The program had set aside a generous travel budget allowing us to tour the country for two months. Marcia planned our tour, which was primarily devoted to the study of the art and architecture of ancient India. We spent a night in Agra before viewing the Taj Mahal in the early morning light. We did not think the Taj could possibly be as pristine and uniquely beautiful as it was pictured in art books. But it was.

Later, we boarded a train in New Delhi for Bombay (now Mumbai), where we explored the Hindu and Buddhist Elephanta Caves, built between the fifth and eighth centuries AD. From Bombay, we took an overnight train to the Ajanta Caves, consisting of Buddhist monuments carved over seven centuries, beginning in the second century BC. After exploring the Ajanta Caves, we traveled by bus to the Ellora Caves, one of the largest rock-cut Hindu cave complexes in the world. Inside the caves, we saw spectacular Buddhist and Jain monuments with artwork dating from AD 600 to 1000.

In the state of Kerala on the southwest Malabar Coast, we stayed in a government guesthouse on the beach with a beautiful view of the Arabian Sea. We later went to Cochin, the capital of Kerala, to seek out one of the oldest synagogues in the world, and found it in Jewtown, an ancient district of the capital. The congregation had dwindled to less than fifty members, mostly very elderly congregants. We sat in the empty synagogue, which, sadly, appeared to be more a historic relic than a functioning house of worship.

We then flew south on an Indian Airlines flight to the towering Hindu temples at Madurai, spread over fourteen acres, that had been constructed as early as the first century AD. After visiting Madras, we headed by train up the eastern coast of the country. Our most important stop was at Bhubaneswar, where we viewed the Lingaraja Temple's erotic Hindu sculptures, created in the eleventh century AD and dedicated to the Hindu god Shiva.

In Calcutta, we attended a four-hour concert performed by the master sitarist Ravi Shankar. It was an astonishing musical experience, the beginning of our enjoyment of Shankar's music for many decades. After we returned to the United States, we attended several of his concerts, the last at Carnegie Hall shortly before he died in 2012 at the age of ninety-two.

From Calcutta, we flew to Kathmandu, Nepal, in a twin-engine Indian Airlines plane that navigated precariously between two mountains before arriving at our destination. We could see Mount Everest from our hotel. In a little shop outside of town, Marcia discovered a bronze Buddha caked in mud. We paid a few rupees for it and were certain that we possessed a priceless art treasure. Our high hopes were quickly shattered after we showed our sculpture to a gallery owner in New Delhi. He excused himself for a few moments, returning with an art book that featured a photo of the original bronze sculpture in the Seattle Art Museum.

We were more successful in purchasing four beautiful nineteenth-century Mughal miniature paintings from an art dealer in New Delhi. We later had them appraised at the Freer Gallery in Washington, DC, and were told that, while original, they were neither rare nor especially valuable. The appraisal has not spoiled our enjoyment of the paintings, which we proudly display in our living room.

Before leaving India, we spent ten days on a houseboat in Srinagar, Kashmir. Every day, vendors brought dazzling varieties of flowers to our boat. Floating on the serene waters of Dal Lake, with views of colorful gardens and gentle surrounding hills, it seemed to us like an otherworldly paradise.

Our departure from the airport in New Delhi turned out to be dramatic and stressful. All went well enough until we put our carry-on items on a table for inspection by two customs officials. The officials, who held our passports, refused to return them unless I paid a duty on my typewriter. I was furious, since I had paid duty on the same typewriter when we entered India. It was obvious that they expected a bribe and were in a commanding position to get one, since they held our passports. Fuming, I refused to pay them a single rupee. My friend T. Swayze, who worked for the US Agency for International Development in New Delhi and had accompanied us to the airport, suggested a face-saving solution.

"Jim, you can't take your rupees out of the country," he said. "Give them to me and don't ask any questions."

I did as he instructed in full view of the officials. They immediately returned our passports and, presumably, my friend negotiated a bribe with my rupees. Meanwhile, Marcia and I were hustled onto the tarmac and hurriedly climbed the steps to enter the open door of the plane. Once we were inside, the doors shut, and our plane immediately took off.

• • • • •

Our return trip was almost as fascinating as our tour of India. Since the program required that we return to Oxford to brief the next year's fellows, we could plan an itinerary that took us to countries of our choosing in the Middle East and Europe. Our first stop was Israel, where Marcia's uncle, Sam Schecter, an orthodox rabbi, met us at the Tel Aviv airport at 3 a.m. After the hectic departure from India, the sight of Uncle Sam brought tears to our eyes. He embraced me warmly, though he did not hug Marcia because, under orthodox law, he was prohibited from embracing any woman except his wife.

Uncle Sam drove us to his kibbutz, and we collapsed on the bed in his guest room. Thoroughly exhausted, we slept for most of the next twenty-four hours. Once we awakened, Uncle Sam and his wife, Havah, pampered us with plain but delicious kibbutz food. Several days later, after we sat down to a Sabbath meal, Uncle Sam began to pray for us. We both realized that he was praying that we abide by the laws and practices of Orthodox Judaism. Marcia looked at me and could barely hide her smile. While Uncle Sam was praying for our souls, she knew that I was sending up an anti-orthodox prayer missile to intercept his, so we could be left alone to practice Judaism according to our own beliefs and practices.

After we made a brief trip to my old kibbutz, Kfar Hanassi, we flew to Greece for a wonderful week on the island of Poros, with side trips to the

Acropolis and Delphi. Then we spent a few days in Yugoslavia, still under Communist rule, which seemed gray and depressing. Next, we flew to Budapest, which we enjoyed thoroughly, taking in concerts and art museums, and then to Sweden, where Marcia bought elegant crystal and china. The last stop before Oxford was the Edinburgh Festival and an avant-garde performance of Shakespeare's *Macbeth*, with naked witches stirring the cauldrons.

After we returned to Oxford, I listened with envy to the experiences of many of the other fellows in the Africa-Asia program. They had served in the highest echelons of government in some of the newly independent nations of southern Africa and Southeast Asia (other than India), as lawyers, economists, and public administrators. My experience, by contrast, was profoundly disappointing in terms of what I accomplished. It was, nonetheless, extremely worthwhile.

By any measure, my efforts provided an invaluable learning experience, although one radically different from that of my buoyant days as a Crossroader in Pram Pram, Ghana, five years earlier. After my year in India, I no longer assumed that good intentions necessarily would be welcomed and produce tangible results. I hoped that my idealism would remain intact, but knew that it would be informed by the hard-earned lessons of Azamgarh.

CHAPTER 7

JOURNALIST

Shortly after returning to New York from England in 1965, Marcia and I had dinner with Colin Bradford, a Yale college classmate and close friend, and his wife, Ginny, at a restaurant near Columbia University, where Colin was completing his doctoral studies in international economics. Our conversation immediately turned to our year in India and my misadventures and disappointments in Azamgarh.

Always the optimist, Colin pronounced my experience an important lesson in international development that would serve me well in my first professional job. That job, he suggested, should be with Robert R. Nathan Associates, an international economic consulting firm in Washington, DC. Forget about Mr. Bhargava and his doomed five-year plan for Azamgarh, Colin advised. The Nathan consulting firm was heavily involved in international development at the highest level, having worked with both the Indian and South Korean governments on long-range economic planning.

In mid-September 1965, I met Robert Nathan in his office on the top floor of a stylish townhouse on Sixteenth Street in the nation's capital. Nathan's résumé was intimidating. The son of a Polish immigrant father who had been a fruit peddler in Dayton, Ohio, Nathan had paid for his education at the University of Pennsylvania's Wharton School, earning bachelor's and master's degrees in economics, by selling hosiery, tutoring students, and working in factories. He became a New Deal economist, rising quickly to become President Roosevelt's consultant to the Committee on Economic Security in 1934. During World War II, he was appointed chairman of the War Production Board's planning committee. In 1945, he was named deputy director of the Office of War Mobilization and Reconversion under Fred Vinson, the future chief justice of the United States. A year later, he formed his economic consulting firm.

In our interview, Nathan was especially interested in my experiences in Azamgarh and welcomed my continued commitment to international development. He offered me an entry-level job as a research assistant at his firm, even though I lacked any formal education in economics. He suggested that I enroll in a basic course in economics at night at George Washington University, which I did.

Marcia, meanwhile, was hired as a research assistant to Robert Stewart, chief curator of the National Portrait Gallery. We moved into a charming one-bedroom apartment on tree-lined R Street near the Phillips Art Gallery, where we spent many hours viewing the superb collection as well as listening to chamber music concerts on Sunday afternoons. Weekdays, Marcia took a bus to work while I enjoyed a fifteen-minute walk to the Nathan Associates townhouse.

• • • • •

Marcia received the wonderful news in the winter that she was pregnant with our first child, due in early September 1966. That summer, I bought bleacher seats for a Beatles concert on their third US tour at a large professional baseball stadium on the outskirts of Washington. The concert was scheduled for mid-August, only a few weeks before Marcia was due. What was I thinking? Well, I was young, foolhardy, and, besides, we really wanted to hear the Beatles. On the night of the concert, Marcia and I walked up dozens of steps to our seats in the upper deck of the stadium. The Beatles finally appeared on stage after a seemingly endless procession of musicians we had never heard of. When they began performing a medley of their hard-driving hit songs,

Marcia put her hands on her stomach, then took my hands and placed them where hers had been. We looked at each other. Yes, we agreed, we had felt the thump of our baby keeping time to the music!

On the evening of September 8, the day before Marcia was due, we met my father and one of his clients for dinner at the Knife and Fork, one of Washington's best restaurants. About an hour after we returned to our apartment, Marcia began to have contractions that quickly intensified. By midnight, we were at the hospital. The next morning, shortly after ten o'clock, David Uriah Simon, six pounds, seven ounces, arrived.

After a difficult breech birth, Marcia was exhausted but happy. I was ecstatic. After seeing David for the first time, I drove home to pack more clothes for Marcia. Along the way, I saw one of her closest friends from Pembroke, Helen Klein, pushing a stroller with her baby boy, Abram, next to her friend Cornelia St. John, who was also pushing a stroller with her baby daughter. I stopped abruptly, pulled over to the curb, and shouted the news of David's birth. Had I bought cigars, I would have popped two of them in Helen's and Cornelia's mouths and maybe those of their babies, too. I was almost, but not quite, embarrassed by my predictably zany behavior.

• • • • •

During the final months of her pregnancy, Marcia had been advised to leave her job at the National Portrait Gallery, since pregnant women were not supposed to work in public in those days. Anticipating the arrival of our first child, we had moved into a two-bedroom apartment on Wyoming Avenue. After David's birth, we spent hours in our new apartment simply watching our new baby in his crib or on the sheet spread over our living room rug. Taking care of him, however, was hard work and required almost all of Marcia's time and energy during the week, as well as our combined attention on the weekends. It did not help that we lived in a fifth-floor walk-up apartment.

Meanwhile, I became increasingly frustrated in my research job at Nathan Associates. I found economic research boring. And most of my research was for the domestic clients that made up an increasingly large proportion of the firm's work. By the late fall of 1966, I had begun to write to leading newspapers to inquire about a job as a reporter.

I received an enthusiastic response from the new managing editor of the *St. Louis Post-Dispatch*, Arthur Bertelson, who offered to have me flown to St. Louis on the private plane of Joseph Pulitzer Jr., the newspaper's publisher. That was an offer I did not refuse. In St. Louis, Bertelson told me of his plan to hire a new breed of reporter for the *Post-Dispatch*. He wanted college-educated young men to take their places beside the outstanding veterans on his staff. He offered me a starting salary of $8,000, which was above the minimum wage required under the Newspaper Guild's scale.

I was leaning heavily in favor of accepting Bertelson's offer, but Marcia, understandably, was not excited by the prospect of moving to St. Louis. We both enjoyed living in Washington. Once David advanced beyond the toddler stage, Marcia hoped to return to work at the National Portrait Gallery. Her only trip through the Midwest had occurred when we had driven from New Haven to Fort Worth after my graduation from law school; she changed sunglasses at each state border to break what she considered the monotony of the scenery.

St. Louis was a cosmopolitan city, I assured Marcia. It supported an outstanding art museum and a symphony orchestra, and it had an excellent zoo that would no doubt delight David. The *Post-Dispatch* was one of the leading newspapers in the country with a justly celebrated editorial page and a Washington bureau that had collected more than its share of journalism awards. It was also a beacon of liberalism in the conservative Midwest.

At the age of twenty-eight, I was not confident of receiving a better opportunity to begin my journalism career. With that in mind, I accepted Bertelson's offer. We made plans to move to St. Louis in February 1967.

When I told Robert Nathan that I had accepted a job with the *Post-Dispatch*, he was relieved. We both knew by this time that his firm was not the right place for me. He also was aware of my interest in a journalism career. His senior vice-president, Ed Hollander, had told him of my manuscript describing the Azamgarh five-year plan—the one Hollander had submitted for publication at Syracuse University Press. Nathan later recommended me to a good friend of his, Marshall Loeb, who was a senior editor at *Time* magazine in New York City.

A few hours before the Northwest Moving Company came to our Wyoming Avenue apartment to pack our modest inventory of furniture and clothing, I received a call from Phil Mandelkorn, a friend who was a young reporter in the Washington bureau of *Time* magazine. Phil had told John Steele, *Time*'s Washington bureau chief, about my background and interest in a career in journalism. He told me that Steele wanted me to come in for an interview. Had Steele's invitation come a month earlier, I would have jumped at the opportunity. But Marcia and I were packed and ready to move to St. Louis. And I had made a commitment to Bertelson.

• • • • •

On my first day as a reporter, Bertelson introduced me to my boss, the city editor of the *Post-Dispatch*, or "P-D," as it was widely known. Sam Shelton Jr. was a balding man in his early forties with a fixed, knowing smile who spoke informally but with unmistakable authority. As city editor, he made it immediately clear that, notwithstanding whatever plans Bertelson might have for me and other college-educated recruits, I would be treated exactly like every other cub reporter.

I wrote two-line weather reports, which turned out to be quite challenging. An early effort: "St. Louisans donned their overcoats for the first chilly day of February . . ." But what could I write for the remaining twenty-seven days of February?

On Saturday nights my beat was the city police station. The cops were not natural allies of reporters and certainly not reporters for the liberal P-D. I did not help myself in getting tips from the captain on duty when I refused to personally deliver a free, early edition of the Sunday paper, a common practice among police reporters. I was a journalist, not a lackey, I told my assistant city editor at the desk. For my principled stand, I was rewarded with exactly no tips from the cops.

Since the P-D was an afternoon newspaper, I reported to the city room at 7 a.m. The most difficult early morning assignment was to knock on the doors of the parents of young soldiers who had been killed in Vietnam. I dreaded facing the distraught mothers and fathers, then asking if they could spare a photo of their deceased sons. It was my saddest assignment as a journalist.

Despite the P-D's liberal reputation, it was, in many ways, a shockingly hidebound institution. Women reporters were restricted to the style section of the newspaper and worked at desks separated from the city room's male reporters. The only black face in the city room was a copy boy. And the unwritten rule, enforced by city editor Shelton, was that young reporters were to be seen, not heard.

New reporters were subjected to the P-D's version of boot camp, assigned to the community news section of the newspaper under the hell-for-leather command of its editor, a thick, humorless man who treated every one-paragraph story on a suburban village zoning hearing as if it were the Nazi invasion of Poland. He unleashed blistering tongue-lashings several times a morning, most often directed at Ron Powers, the most talented young writer on the staff, who always seemed to overlook what our editor considered to be a critical detail in a village's deliberations. Powers sought refuge and recognition in the P-D's Sunday feature section, where he wrote one creative article after another.

The tyranny of our masters in the city room inspired the young reporters to forge a professional bond. Bertelson had hired other Ivy Leaguers, including hometown graduates from Harvard and Yale. My favorite companions were Ron Powers, a graduate of the University of Missouri, and Dana Spitzer, a graduate of the University of Idaho, married and the father of three children, and a tenacious reporter. All of the young recruits enjoyed lunches together, played as a team in a softball league, and shared dinners and movies with each other and our families and, in bachelor Ron Powers's case, his dates.

The rigid hierarchy in the city room did not extend to the veteran reporters when all of us, young and old, took long dinner breaks during slow Saturday nights on duty. We always walked to the veterans' favorite Italian restaurant. After a few stiff drinks, the old timers' tales began to flow—about every con artist and crook they had ever covered, embellished with dialects and descriptions that rivaled a Damon Runyon short story. Those dinners provided the best entertainment in the city.

The veterans could also be generous with their time and advice. Bob Collins, the P-D's best investigative reporter, became a mentor and gave me invaluable tips on how to interview corrupt officials who had something to hide. Do your homework, Collins instructed, and make sure you have every piece of relevant information available on your target. When you confront him, look him steadily in the eye with the confident gaze of a reporter who already has the answers but is only checking for confirmation. "Now, do you want to tell me about it?" you ask, and hope he falls for your bluff.

* * * * *

Gradually, I felt as if I belonged in the city room and positively thrilled to the clatter of manual typewriters, especially my own, when I was on deadline. Writing a paragraph and calling out "copy" for the teenage copy boy to snatch the sheet from my hand was pure exhilaration, even if I wasn't sure whether my next paragraph would link up with the one I had just released.

My byline appeared more frequently once I was assigned to the higher education beat. I filed stories on the incipient third-party presidential campaign of liberal US senator Eugene McCarthy (D-MN) percolating on the campus of Washington University. It was an early indication of McCarthy's enthusiastic support among Vietnam War critics across the country, especially on college campuses. McCarthy's challenge influenced President Lyndon Johnson's decision not to seek a second term and later undermined the campaign of the Democratic presidential candidate, Vice President Hubert Humphrey, who narrowly lost the 1968 election to Richard Nixon.

My most exciting story was filed from Southeast Missouri State University in Cape Girardeau, a city in the conservative southeast corner of the state. I was sent there to cover the firing of seven faculty members, all for suspiciously leftist views. It turned out that their most dangerous activities were to be card-carrying members of the NAACP and the American Civil Liberties Union. At a student rally in support of the fired faculty members, the announcement that a reporter from the *St. Louis Post-Dispatch* was covering the story elicited loud, sustained applause. For the first time at the P-D, I felt important, almost heroic. Shortly after my article was published, a P-D editorial citing my story supported the faculty members. Praise from the prestigious editorial board boosted my morale as well as my reputation in the city room.

* * * * *

In the late winter of 1968, Marcia learned that she was pregnant with our second child. Her pregnancy began uncomfortably, and she soon suffered from internal bleeding. Her obstetrician warned that the bleeding meant a probable premature, breech birth. By the early fall, she was often in bed, taking a break whenever possible from our hyperactive two-year-old son.

One morning, when Marcia's condition was at its worst, Sam Shelton called me to his desk to tell me that he was assigning me to a month-long political investigation with a senior reporter. We would divide the 114 counties in the state between us, and each of us would visit half of the county courthouses in search of records that exposed official corruption.

Marcia and I talked about my meeting with Shelton that night and decided that I would ask to be relieved of the assignment. The next morning I met with Shelton and told him of Marcia's condition. I requested that he reassign the investigation to another member of the staff. He refused. He had assigned the investigation to me. No excuse would be accepted.

I was stunned and appalled. But to reject the assignment would almost certainly have jeopardized my job when Marcia was pregnant, and I had no other job prospects. For the first time, I considered returning to Fort Worth to practice law at Simon & Simon. But we needed time to consider such a serious move. Meanwhile, I reluctantly prepared for the month-long investigation. Marcia was miserable, and so was I.

Every Monday morning for the next month, I rented a car and started my weeklong quest driving from one county courthouse in the southern half of the state to the next. The investigation required hard work and attention to detail. Slowly, I began to fill my reporter's notebooks with the minutiae of official records. A pattern began to emerge: there was, indeed, widespread malfeasance on a small but discernible scale.

Every weeknight that month, I called Marcia from the rural motel where I was staying. She was sick and lonely; I felt guilty and was deeply unhappy. I also seethed at Shelton's old-school intransigence. We both looked forward to the weekends when I could return to her and David in our garden apartment in the St. Louis suburb of Creve Coeur.

At the end of October, I completed my investigation and returned to the city room. I spent several days dutifully turning my notes into a meticulously detailed summary of my findings. Shortly after I turned in my copy,

Shelton walked over to my desk to say that I had done an excellent job. His praise did not assuage my smoldering outrage.

On the next Saturday night, I sat at my desk anticipating the publication of the first installment of the investigative series. I knew that it had been written by the veteran reporter of our investigative team, though he had not shown his article to me. When copies of the P-D's first Sunday edition were distributed in the city room in the early evening, I eagerly looked for the story. And there it was, prominently featured on the front page, with the announcement that Sunday's article would be the first in an investigative series.

The byline under the story had only one name—that of the veteran reporter. I immediately rushed to the front desk to confront Dick Jacobs, the assistant city editor on duty.

"Where is my byline?" I asked tensely.

Jacobs, a mild-mannered and decent fellow, replied that the story and byline were printed according to Sam Shelton's instructions.

"It must be a mistake," I insisted. I told Jacobs what he already knew—that I had spent a month on the investigation and expected to receive recognition for my work with a byline.

Jacobs shuffled through his papers to make sure that there had not been a mistake.

"No," he assured me, "there were no additional instructions from Sam."

"There has been a mistake," I repeated. "Please call Sam at home."

"Jim, you don't want me to do that," Jacobs advised.

"Yes, I do," I said.

Against his better judgment, Jacobs called Shelton at home.

"Sam says the story and byline ran as he intended," Jacobs told me.

I listened in disbelief. And then it sunk in. I had spent a month on the road while Marcia suffered at home. And for what? Nothing, absolutely nothing, not even a measly byline as evidence that I had done my professional duty, though reluctantly.

When I arrived in the city room the following Monday morning, Shelton called me to his desk. He was not smiling. He told me that I had been reassigned to the St. Louis County Police Department, commonly understood to be the P-D's Siberia.

• • • • •

On the night of December 13, 1968, after Marcia and I had enjoyed an early dinner with Ron Powers and his date, the four of us settled into our seats for a local repertory theater's performance of Bertolt Brecht's *The Caucasian Chalk Circle*. Halfway through the first act, Marcia's water broke. I helped her out of the theater and across the street to the garage where our car was parked.

Waving my parking ticket wildly, I pleaded with the first attendant I saw. "Can you please get our car immediately," I yelled. "My wife is having a baby!"

The attendant was unimpressed with the urgency of my plea. He was either skeptical or just tired and overworked. In any case, our car did not arrive for another fifteen minutes.

By the time I had eased Marcia into the passenger seat, I was panicked. What if we didn't make it to the hospital? I pushed that scary thought out of my mind and floored the accelerator. I took the most well-traveled boulevard leading to the hospital, hoping to see a police car. None was in sight. I ran one red light after another. Still no police car.

After what seemed to be an eternity, I finally saw the lights of the hospital and quickly pulled up to the emergency room entrance. I helped Marcia out of the car and guided her into the emergency room, where an attendant lowered her into a wheelchair. Much relieved, I parked the car and took a seat in the visitors' waiting room. Minutes later, I saw Marcia's obstetrician walking briskly into the building. Had he come in time to deliver our baby? I didn't know whether to be reassured or frightened.

Forty-five minutes after I had escorted Marcia into the emergency room, a nurse came to the visitors' area to tell me that Marcia had given birth to a baby girl.

"How wonderful," I exclaimed, forgetting my frantic thoughts during that wild ride to the hospital.

I found Marcia lying on a gurney in a hallway. Not the best accommodations, I thought, but I did not complain. She looked tired but happy. "When I held Lauren in my arms," she said, "she opened her eyes and smiled at me." What a marvelous first memory of our baby daughter, Lauren Ruth Simon.

• • • • •

My reporter friends in the city room were accurate in their prediction that I would rarely discover arrests worth reporting from the St. Louis County Police Department. I therefore had many idle hours in the press room to think about my next professional move. Joining my family of lawyers in Fort Worth was an obvious possibility. The problem for me was that, on my best days, I really liked being a journalist. My stories hardly qualified "as the first rough draft of history," as *Washington Post* publisher Philip Graham once said. Still, there was something both exciting and satisfying in shaping a story for publication that could enhance the public's understanding of an important issue.

I decided to go for broke, writing to the most prestigious news organizations in New York City—the *New York Times*, the *Wall Street Journal*, *Newsweek*, and *Time*—to request interviews. I was pleased to receive replies from top editors at the *Times*, the *Journal*, and *Newsweek* inviting me to come in for interviews. The interviews, including one with A. M. "Abe" Rosenthal, managing editor of the *Times,* seemed to go well, but no one offered me a job or even held out the possibility of a future offer. I returned to St. Louis discouraged, nursing a bruised ego and a bad cold.

The day after I returned to St. Louis, I received a telephone call from John Titman, director of personnel at *Time* magazine. He had just returned from vacation and apologized for not having responded to my letter requesting an interview at the magazine. He told me that he was calling at the request of *Time*'s managing editor, Henry Grunwald, to invite me to fly to New York at *Time*'s expense. Grunwald had recently issued a directive to all back-of-the-book sections of the magazine (i.e., after the Nation and World sections) to hire specialists. *Time* would like to interview me for the new position of special correspondent for the magazine's law section.

Marcia and I needed less than a minute to conclude that, yes, we would be very happy to move to New York, if I were offered a job at *Time*. From our first days in St. Louis, Marcia had been worn out by David's seemingly inexhaustible energy, a condition made worse with the arrival of Lauren. It did not help that we lived in a suburban development that offered her no intellectual activity.

I viewed our two years in St. Louis more positively. The P-D, despite its retrograde practices, had offered me a valuable education in reporting for a prominent daily newspaper. I had been assigned my share of interesting stories and was confident that the training would serve me well in the future. I had also enjoyed the company of my fellow young reporters, both in the city room and socially. But it was time to move on. The county police station was a dead-end beat. Even if Shelton eventually relented, after I had learned my lesson not to challenge his judgment, it would be at least six months or a year before I rejoined the staff in the city room.

I prepared carefully for my interviews at *Time*, spending two full days in the Washington University library reading back issues of the magazine with particular attention to stories in the law section. After I arrived in New York City, I could barely contain my excitement as I entered the Time-Life Building in Midtown Manhattan, opposite Radio City Music Hall. Once I reached the fourteenth floor, I was guided through what appeared to be a pre-designed interviewing process, meeting with each of *Time*'s senior editors, beginning with Grunwald. They were friendly and appeared receptive to my answers to their questions about my education at Yale Law School, stories that I had reported during my internship at *Newsweek*, and my two years at the *Post-Dispatch*.

After my interviews on the fourteenth floor, I met with personnel director Titman, who greeted me warmly. Without fanfare, he offered me the job. I would be paid $15,000 a year, almost twice my P-D salary, and would enjoy *Time*'s generous fringe benefits, including comprehensive medical coverage and six weeks of vacation. I accepted and called Marcia with the good news. We were moving to New York!

On my last day at the *Post-Dispatch*, both Bertelson and Shelton asked to see me. The managing editor told me that he had approved my reassignment by Shelton to the county police station and thought it would be a valuable learning experience. I doubted that Bertelson believed that the county police station offered a special educational opportunity for me. I thought it was more likely that the managing editor, who was loathed by Shelton and every veteran reporter, backed Shelton rather than risk a rebellion in the city room.

Shelton said much the same thing as Bertelson, stressing that his decision was not based on any personal animosity toward me, but his professional judgment that it would be another step in my education as a journalist. I was polite but said very little in my brief meetings with them.

After I left St. Louis, I wished I had told both Bertelson and Shelton what I really thought—that I would be the first of many young, ambitious reporters who valued their experience at the P-D but would move on to better opportunities at leading newspapers and magazines that were not so reluctant to abandon old customs and practices. As if to prove my point, a few months after I left St. Louis, two other young P-D reporters chose to pursue their journalism careers elsewhere. Jimmy Singer, a recent graduate of Harvard, was hired by the *Congressional Quarterly* in Washington, DC, and Ron Powers left the P-D for the *Chicago Sun-Times*, where he won a Pulitzer Prize for television commentary.

* * * * *

As I looked out the window of my office on the twelfth floor of the Time-Life Building in early May 1969, I had to remind myself that I was not daydreaming. I was now the special law correspondent for the most powerful newsmagazine in the world, only one month after I had left my lowly job as a beat reporter at the St. Louis County Police Department.

On my first day at *Time*, I was welcomed warmly by Joe Ferrer, a tall, handsome Princeton graduate who was the senior writer for the law section. Joe had been the editor-in-chief of his college daily at Princeton and was hired by *Time* immediately after his graduation.[1] That made him a veteran at the magazine, although he had graduated from Princeton in 1961, the same year that I had graduated from Yale. Joe had an easy, confident manner and was obviously pleased to have a correspondent assigned to his section of the magazine. He promised that I would be covering interesting law stories that would require travel around the country.

Joe introduced me to the other members of the law section team, beginning with the second writer, Howard Muson, a low-key, studious, and

1 Joe's uncle, the actor Mel Ferrer, was married to the famous actress Audrey Hepburn from 1954 to 1968, so Hepburn was Joe's aunt for fourteen years, until the year before I joined him at *Time*. No, unfortunately, I never met her.

pleasant Harvard graduate. The senior researcher for the section was Dorothea Boerne, a large, imposing woman in her early sixties, who spoke with the haughty authority of one who had been working for *Time* when Joe, Howard, and I were in grade school.The junior researcher was Wendy Marcus Raymont, thirty years old, the daughter of the department store magnate Stanley Marcus. I only learned in researching this memoir that Wendy was a summa cum laude graduate of Smith College and one of only a handful of female graduates of the Harvard Law School before clerking for US Supreme Court Justice Abe Fortas. She was married to a prominent *New York Times* foreign correspondent, Henry Raymont, and left *Time* a few months after I arrived. The members of the section met on Monday mornings with Bob Shnayerson, who was the senior editor for the law section as well as several other "back-of-the-book" sections. In his early forties, Shnayerson was pleasant but wielded his editing pencil mercilessly, as I would soon learn.

Within weeks of starting at *Time*, I was immersed in a major national story: On May 23, 1969, President Nixon appointed Judge Warren Burger of the US Court of Appeals for the District of Columbia as chief justice of the United States, replacing the retiring liberal leader of the Court, Chief Justice Earl Warren. After Burger's appointment was announced, I was on the telephone for the next two days interviewing Burger's judicial colleagues and clerks for background and quotes to be used in the *Time* story. I immediately realized that when I identified myself as a correspondent for *Time*, I was treated with respect and often received direct answers to my questions, a far cry from my experience at the St. Louis County Police Department.

Burger's judicial colleagues were circumspect in talking about him. Burger was an outspoken conservative dissenter on the liberal appellate court. In fact, he owed his Supreme Court nomination to his dissents, which often targeted the majority opinions of his liberal colleagues as well as those of the liberal Warren Court, especially decisions that expanded the civil liberties of poor criminal defendants. He also wrote articles and gave speeches criticizing the criminal procedure decisions of the Warren Court. Burger had sent President Nixon copies of those articles and speeches, just in case the president had not read them.

Unlike Burger's judicial colleagues, his law clerks were eager to offer personal observations that I could quote in my reporting for the story. They fondly remembered dinners at his house where Burger, a wine connoisseur, carefully selected and poured excellent wines for his young guests.

In August, I was given my first opportunity to observe Burger in person when he addressed delegates at the American Bar Association's annual meeting in Dallas. I could have booked a hotel room in Dallas but chose to stay in Fort Worth at my parents' house. How sweet it was to return home as the law correspondent for *Time*, the family's secular bible during my teenage years. Predictably, Mother welcomed me home as if I had already won a Pulitzer Prize. Dad was also impressed by my new position but, in his characteristically reserved manner, held his enthusiasm firmly in check. During the week of the ABA meeting, the regular phone calls I received from my *Time* colleagues in New York burnished my emerging reputation among family members and friends as a world-class journalist.

At the ABA meeting, I met the correspondents who regularly covered the Supreme Court for major newspapers and wire services, including the *New York Times* (Fred Graham), the *Washington Post* (Jack MacKenzie), the *Baltimore Sun* (Lyle Denniston), and the Associated Press (Barry Schweid). They were a very smart, sophisticated, and fun-loving group, and they invited me to join them for meals and Court gossip. But I quickly learned that my position as the law correspondent for *Time*, based in New York, did not make me an equal in the eyes of the Supreme Court regulars. Neither Bob Shogan of *Newsweek*, also based in New York, nor I were included in an off-the-record interview that the veteran Court reporters arranged with the new chief justice. It was an early lesson that my *Time* credential did not insulate me from the fierce competition among legal journalists.

The chief justice's speech at the ABA meeting was less newsworthy than the fact that he, unlike his predecessor, Earl Warren, clearly enjoyed meeting and conversing with the ABA delegates. At the ABA annual meeting in London in the summer of 1957, Chief Justice Warren had been so outraged by a special ABA committee's criticism of the Warren Court's so-called pro-Communist opinions that he had resigned from the organization. The ABA committee had singled out for criticism Warren Court decisions that upheld the constitutional rights of suspected subversives to free expression and due process when interrogated by congressional and state committees during the reckless anti-Communist campaign of the 1950s led by US

Senator Joseph McCarthy (R-WI). In contrast, in 1969, Chief Justice Burger courted the ABA members, and a majority of them shared his conservative constitutional philosophy.

In Dallas, Burger's ABA appearance and speech on modern court administration did not make scintillating copy for *Time*'s readers. I nonetheless filled page after page in my notebooks detailing Burger's every move and utterance, including this one-liner: "We have more trained astronauts than trained court administrators." I then sent my files by teletype to Joe Ferrer in New York. My efforts produced a brief story, accompanied by a photo of Burger, for the magazine's law section.

I introduced myself to the new chief justice in Dallas, initiating a polite but arm's-length relationship with him that extended well beyond my five years at *Time*. We met for the last time in the summer of 1985, when, as dean of New York Law School, I was attending the annual meeting of the ABA in London. Marcia and our three children accompanied me on the trip. The five of us were having lunch in a downtown London restaurant when I spotted Burger at a nearby table with his administrative assistant. I led Marcia, David, Lauren, and Sara to his table and reintroduced myself. He was cordial and seemed pleased that I wanted him to meet my family, rather than ask nettlesome questions about his Court opinions.

I was never an admirer of Burger and knew, from my off-the-record interviews with several of his brethren (Justices Harry Blackmun, William Brennan Jr., and Potter Stewart), that he was neither liked nor respected by his colleagues. But on that summer day in 1985, he was still the chief justice of the United States, and I was delighted that I knew him well enough to introduce him to my family.

◆ ◆ ◆ ◆ ◆

Marcia, accompanied by our friend Ginny Bradford, had gone apartment-hunting before the family's move to New York and made what appeared to be an excellent choice for our growing family. It was a bright, spacious second-floor apartment with an additional third-floor bedroom on Rich Avenue in Mount Vernon, New York. A highlight of our time in Mount Vernon occurred on July 20, 1969, when we woke David up in the middle of the night and turned on our black-and-white television to watch Neil Armstrong take man's first steps on the moon. An equally memorable but less uplifting experience occurred when David inadvertently locked Marcia out of the apartment. Marcia called the fire department and a local firefighter climbed a ladder to the second floor to rescue David and Lauren. David thought it was all wonderfully exciting, Marcia less so.

In the fall, I would walk David to preschool, where he was taught by a guitar-playing young woman whom he adored. I then continued my short walk to the Mount Vernon train station for my twenty-minute weekday commute to Grand Central Station, followed by a fifteen-minute walk to the Time-Life Building. Despite my easy commute and David's enjoyment of preschool, the apartment did not turn out to be a good choice for us. We were among the few non-immigrant families on our street, surrounded by the larger, predominantly poor community. Mount Vernon's downtown offered none of the amenities, such as good restaurants and shops, that Marcia and I would have enjoyed. I had begun to make out-of-town trips for *Time*, which gave Marcia, tied down with two small children, a feeling of isolation.

In early December 1969, we began to look for a house to purchase in Westchester County, but quickly realized that we could not afford any house that was attractive to us. Then, one day at work, I received a call from Martin O'Neill, a retiring editor at *Time*, who had heard that we were in the market to buy a house and suggested that we look at his. The following Sunday afternoon, we drove to O'Neill's residence in West Nyack, New York, twenty miles north of the city. Marcia and I immediately fell in love with it. A two-story wood-and-glass structure in the contemporary architectural style of Frank Lloyd Wright, it had a swimming pool and was set back on almost two acres of thickly wooded land.

O'Neill, who was recently divorced and anxious to start a new life on the West Coast, had also invited a senior *Time* correspondent, Karsten Prager, and his wife to look at the house on that same Sunday afternoon. It was obvious to me that the Pragers also loved the house, which meant that I was in competition for the purchase with Karsten, a highly respected *Time* correspondent.

On Monday morning, I learned that an administrator at *Time* had sent Karsten to a nearby Chase Bank branch that did business with *Time* to see if he was eligible for a mortgage to purchase the O'Neill house. I immediately asked for a meeting with the same administrator and made it clear in our meeting that, although I was a relatively new correspondent, I expected to be given the same opportunity to finance the house as Karsten. I was then sent to the same loan officer at Chase. It turned out that Karsten could not afford the terms of the mortgage for the O'Neill house. Thanks to a loan of $8,000 from Dad and $2,000 from Marcia's dad, I was able to arrange for the mortgage. We paid $42,500 for the house and an additional $2,500 for all of O'Neill's furniture as well as his large book and record collections. Quite a bargain.

✦ ✦ ✦ ✦ ✦

My first byline to appear in *Time*, a rarity in the magazine in the late 1960s, occurred in the late fall of 1969, when my exclusive interview with US District Judge Julius Hoffman was published. Hoffman, seventy-four years old, was the federal judge presiding over what later became known as the Chicago Seven conspiracy trial. Originally the Chicago Eight, the defendants included Abbie Hoffman and Jerry Rubin, the leaders of the Youth International Party (known as Yippies), and the Black Panther leader Bobby Seale. They had been arrested during the 1968 Democratic National Convention, held in Chicago that year in August, and later indicted under provisions of the Civil Rights Act of 1968 that made it a crime to conspire to cross state lines to incite a riot. The statutory provisions under which the defendants were charged were widely criticized for conflating dangerous riots with political demonstrations protected by the First Amendment.

The delegates to the Democratic convention had convened in Chicago at the height of anti–Vietnam War protests and after riots in more than one hundred cities following the assassination of Dr. Martin Luther King Jr. in April. Ten thousand demonstrators converged on the city, determined to be heard and seen. Some, like Hoffman and Rubin, had led large protests against US involvement in the Vietnam War previously, but knew that this would be an opportunity to reach their largest audience yet, since the national press corps and the television networks were set up to cover the convention. Others, including Seale, had a different agenda, seeking to bring attention to the federal government's violation of the civil rights and liberties of Black Americans.

Chicago's powerful Democratic mayor, Richard Daley, was determined to host a successful, and therefore orderly, Democratic convention. The city imposed an 11 p.m. curfew and limited demonstrations to a park far from the convention center. The mayor also enlisted twenty-three thousand police officers and National Guardsmen to control the demonstrators. Police were dressed in riot gear and carried tear gas canisters and mace to quickly subdue any rowdy protesters at the convention or in Grant Park, where demonstrators congregated to protest the war.

At an afternoon demonstration to protest the war in Grant Park, police charged the protesters after one lowered an American flag. Protesters hurled food, rocks, and chunks of cement at the cops, who responded by attacking the demonstrators with clubs, tear gas, and mace. Mayor Daley's response was to defend the police and denounce the protesters. But the official Chicago Study Team, led by Chicago lawyer Daniel Walker, that later investigated the clashes between the police and protesters concluded that there was "unrestrained and indiscriminate police violence on many occasions" and that it was "often inflicted upon persons who had broken no law, disobeyed no order, [and] made no threat."

When the trial began in September 1969, it was obvious that the defendants, especially Hoffman and Rubin, who were masterly provocateurs, and their lead lawyer, William Kunstler, had no intention of abiding by the decorum commonly associated with a federal trial. Rather, they treated the trial as live political theater that deserved only ridicule and resistance. And Judge Julius Hoffman, rigid and authoritarian, was their perfect foil.

The defendant Hoffman blew kisses at the jury. And Hoffman, the judge, revealed his utter disgust with Hoffman, the defendant, by commenting in open court that he was "not my son." Hoffman at the defendant's table immediately shouted, "Dad, dad, have you forsaken me?" Another day, defendants Hoffman and Rubin appeared in court dressed in judicial robes. When the judge ordered them to remove the robes, they complied, to reveal that they were wearing Chicago police uniforms underneath. "This court is bullshit," Rubin later yelled.

Judge Hoffman denied defendant Seale's request that the trial be postponed until his attorney, Charles Garry, who was scheduled to undergo gallbladder surgery, could represent him. After the judge then denied Seale's request to represent himself, Seale vehemently denounced the judge for acting unconstitutionally and of being a racist. The judge, in turn, accused Seale of disrupting the trial and had him bound, gagged, and chained to his chair. Defense attorney Kunstler then declared, "This is no longer a court of order, Your Honor, this is a medieval torture chamber."

By the time I arrived in Chicago in November, the vitriolic back-and-forth between the defendants and their attorneys and the judge had become a daily occurrence. During the week I was in the courtroom, Hoffman and Rubin presented Seale with a birthday cake. An incensed Judge Hoffman ordered a marshal to remove the cake. Rubin shouted, "Bobby, they've arrested your birthday cake!" Neither the defendants' antics nor the judge's angry reaction to the unruly courtroom scene was especially newsworthy, at least for publication in *Time*, since both had been reported from the beginning of the trial.

But no reporter had been able to interview Judge Hoffman, which became my primary mission in Chicago. And, surprisingly, the judge was not only willing, but eager to share with me his low opinion of the defendants and their lawyers. When I met with him in his chambers, he practically spit out the name KUNSTLER, as if it were an expletive. In my long interview with the judge, he showed both resentment and prejudice toward the defense lawyers and their clients, a shocking admission by a presiding federal judge.

While the jury deliberated, Judge Hoffman cited all of the defendants and their attorneys for contempt of court and sentenced them to prison for terms ranging from two and a half months to four years. All of the contempt citations were overturned on appeal. All of the defendants were acquitted of the charge of conspiracy, but five, including Hoffman, Rubin, and Seale, were convicted of crossing state lines with the intent to incite a riot. Those convictions were reversed on appeal.

In open court shortly before the trial ended, Judge Hoffman criticized Kunstler for holding press conferences during the trial. Abbie Hoffman immediately responded, "But Judge, you gave an interview to *Time* magazine!" The defendant's rejoinder may have embarrassed the judge, but it was a source of pride to this young *Time* correspondent.

• • • • •

True to Joe Ferrer's word, I was sent on stories across the country. I interviewed the retiring dean of the Stanford Law School in Palo Alto, California; an outspoken liberal federal judge in Madison, Wisconsin; and a brilliant young lawyer who argued, unsuccessfully, before the US Supreme Court that the death penalty was unconstitutional. The most personally satisfying, as well as historically significant, of my profiles for the magazine's law section was that of my Yale constitutional law professor, Alexander M. Bickel. I spent a week in New Haven with Bickel, who had been hired by the *New York Times* in June 1971 to defend the newspaper's constitutional right to publish what would be known in American history and constitutional law books as "the Pentagon Papers."

"The Pentagon Papers" referred to a comprehensive history of the policies of the US government during the war in Vietnam, beginning with the administration of President Harry Truman and ending with the administration of President Lyndon Johnson. The history was written by high-level employees of the Defense Department and was labeled secret and classified. By the late 1960s, Daniel Ellsberg, a former mid-level Defense Department employee who had read the history, had become a fervent critic of US involvement in the war. Having access to the papers, he decided to copy the thousands of pages of the classified documents and give them to the *New York Times* for publication. When the *Times* published the first installment of the Pentagon Papers, it revealed that officials at the highest level of the Johnson administration, including President Johnson himself and Defense Secretary Robert McNamara, had repeatedly lied to the American people about the progress of the massive US military effort in Vietnam.

In June 1971, the Nixon administration was still deeply involved in the Vietnam conflict and sought a temporary restraining order in a federal district court in New York City to prevent the *Times*' further publication of the Pentagon Papers. The administration's lawyer argued before US District Judge Murray Gurfein that their publication would jeopardize national security and that censoring the press was therefore justified. Professor Bickel, representing the *Times*, responded that the administration had failed to show that national security had been imperiled by the publication of the Pentagon Papers, and the *Times* had the constitutional right, under the First Amendment's protection of freedom of the press, to continue publication. In his decision, Judge Gurfein agreed with Bickel, and the Nixon administration appealed.

Daniel Ellsberg, meanwhile, secretly passed a second set of the Pentagon Papers to the *Washington Post*, which began publication. The Nixon administration immediately sought a temporary restraining order in a federal court in the District of Columbia, and when it was granted, the *Post* appealed. The two cases were heard separately, one in the US Court of Appeals in the District of Columbia, and the second before the US Court of Appeals for the Second Circuit in New York. The appeals court in the District of Columbia ruled in favor of the *Post*'s right to publish, but the appellate court in New York sided with the Nixon administration, reversing Judge Gurfein's decision. The conflicting appellate decisions set up a dramatic showdown in the US Supreme Court that would test the limits of a free press under the First Amendment.

Although Professor Bickel was one of the most influential constitutional scholars of the twentieth century, the *Times*' decision to hire him in the Pentagon Papers case was not applauded by every First Amendment scholar. By his own admission, Bickel was not a "First Amendment voluptuary," a term he used for those who believed in the absolute constitutional protection of the free press. Bickel had clerked for Justice Frankfurter, and like his mentor he believed in a careful balancing of individual constitutional rights with the legitimate concerns of the federal government—in this case, the protection of national security. In his successful argument before Judge Gurfein, Bickel argued that the government had not demonstrated that the publication of the Pentagon Papers jeopardized the nation's security and, therefore, that the *Times*' claim of First Amendment protection must prevail.

When Bickel prepared his argument for the *Times* before the US Supreme Court, he knew that he would face two "First Amendment voluptuaries," Justices Hugo Black and William O. Douglas, who believed that the constitutional protection of the press under the First Amendment was absolute.

He could reasonably assume that, in addition to Black and Douglas, two other liberal justices, William Brennan Jr. and Thurgood Marshall, would vote to strike down the Nixon administration's restraining orders as a violation of the press's First Amendment freedom. Finding a fifth vote among the justices in favor of the continued publication of the Pentagon Papers was his crucial challenge.

Bickel concentrated his arguments on the Court's two centrists, Justices Potter Stewart and Byron White. He contended that the Constitution provided broad protection to the press, and that the government could only curb that freedom under the most compelling evidence that publication of the Pentagon Papers posed a danger to the nation's security. In this case, he argued, the Nixon administration had failed to show that the publication would do irreparable harm to the nation's security. His strategy to win a Court majority succeeded. In a landmark constitutional decision, the justices voted 6–3 in favor of the right of the *Times* and the *Post* to publish the papers, with the centrists, Stewart and White, joining the four liberals, Black, Brennan, Douglas, and Marshall. Readers of the *Times* and the *Post* could once again learn of the stunning revelations contained in the Pentagon Papers.

Spending a week in New Haven with Bickel was a fascinating experience for me. I vividly remembered marveling at his mastery of constitutional law in his classroom in 1961. Although I greatly admired him then, I would never have thought to stop by his office for an informal conversation. Ten years later, when we met at his comfortable two-story home a few blocks from the Yale campus, he greeted me cordially. We soon were on a first-name basis. Over the next five days, he laid out his strategies and constitutional arguments, embellishing his narrative with colorful personal anecdotes—perfect for a *Time* profile.

My time with Bickel in New Haven not only led to a *Time* profile that I was particularly proud of, but also to a warm personal friendship that lasted until 1974, when he died of cancer at the age of forty-nine. A year before his death, Bickel recommended my appointment to teach a seminar on the modern Supreme Court at Yale's Ezra Stiles College, while I was still at *Time*. As a result of his recommendation, I commuted to New Haven every Monday afternoon for two years to teach my evening seminar, an extraordinarily rewarding experience that led to my full-time teaching career at New York Law School.

Shortly before Bickel's death, I visited him in his hospital room. He was wan and weak, a shadow of the vigorous man I had so admired in the classroom and, ten years later, at his home when I interviewed him. He refused to talk about his fatal disease or impending death. Instead, he only wanted to talk about the books he was reading. "What are your favorites?" I asked. "Trollope," he replied instantly. On his recommendation, I began reading Anthony Trollope's Barchester series and, later, his Palliser series. Whenever I read one of those superb novels, I thought of my friend Alex Bickel.

CHAPTER 8

AUTHOR

For the first two years that I worked as a law correspondent for *Time*, I found the assignments exciting and intellectually stimulating. Who wouldn't love to meet the extraordinary judges, lawyers, and professors that I interviewed? I also found it satisfying to shape the stories from the mountains of notes I took and sent to Joe Ferrer and Howard Muson in New York.

But there was also a built-in frustration in working as a *Time* correspondent, whether assigned to the law section, as I was, or in the many domestic and foreign bureaus around the world. No matter how penetrating the reporting and eloquent the files, the *Time* correspondent did not have control over the final story that appeared in the magazine, except on the rare occasion of a byline. My filed copy for a single story could run ten to twenty pages. The final story written for the law section in New York typically ran six or seven paragraphs—that is, when it ran at all. Every Friday night, when the magazine was "put to bed," there was furious competition for space among the editors of the back-of-the-book sections (space for the Nation and World sections was inviolate). As a result, the stories scheduled to run in the law section were often severely edited or eliminated altogether.

Friday night complaints and tantrums from correspondents in the field over what they considered to be their mangled files were as predictable as the magazine's appearance the following Monday at newsstands and in homes across the United States and abroad. In 1971, I had the opportunity to see the magazine from the perspective of a writer in New York, as a result of a terrible accident involving Joe Ferrer. Joe was riding his motorcycle to work when he was hit by a truck that ran a red light in Midtown Manhattan. When he was hospitalized with serious injuries to one of his legs requiring several operations, I was pressed into service as a writer for the law section.

As a *Time* writer, I did well enough to earn the new title of contributing editor on the magazine's masthead. But I found writing stories in New York based on correspondents' files in the field as frustrating as my previous work as a correspondent. I also hated the pressure to produce a finished story at the end of the week, which often required waiting for late files from correspondents in the Midwest or on the West Coast. I then had to condense reams of reporters' copy into two or three columns of stories that were routinely returned to me for rewriting with comments or instructions from the law section's top editor, Bob Shnayerson. The process usually meant that I was writing and rewriting the stories well past midnight on Thursdays and Fridays.

Many talented writers in New York thrived under the demands of the *Time* system. I recall meeting two of the magazine's most gifted writers, Gerald Clarke and Stefan Kanfer, roaming the halls late at night in what seemed to me a suspended state of excitement. For them, completing their stories every Friday night seemed to be akin to solving a complicated jigsaw puzzle. Joe Ferrer approached every week's challenge with a similarly ebullient spirit. At the end of an exhausting week, Joe called his wife, Penny, to read his stories to her, even if that meant waking her at 3 a.m. By that hour, I was so tired and emotionally drained that it would not have occurred to me to read my copy to anyone and certainly not to Marcia, who was fast asleep after her own trying day taking care of two active preschoolers.

There were, of course, rewards for me as a *Time* contributing editor, even if I wasn't among the true believers in the system. Within the *Time* organization, my title was prestigious and provided entrée to meetings with those at the top of the magazine's hierarchy, including Managing Editor Henry

Grunwald. More importantly, I gained invaluable experience in writing and editing that would serve me well in my later career as an author. The longest and most ambitious story that I wrote for the law section would lead to my first book contract. The subject of that story was the transition from the liberal Supreme Court under Chief Justice Earl Warren to the more conservative Court under Chief Justice Warren Burger.

"Why don't you expand that story into a book?" asked Carey Winfrey, my good friend and *Time*'s special correspondent for the press section. I had never considered writing a book about the Court's transition or anything else until Carey raised the issue. It seemed to me slightly presumptuous to think that I had that much to say about any subject. But Carey, who had already published one book (a memoir, *Starts and Finishes*, about his relationship with his father, a famous racehorse trainer), suggested that I take his idea seriously. If I wanted to pursue it, he said he would put me in touch with his literary agent, Wendy Weil. I thought about it for a few days, and then asked Carey for Wendy's phone number.

* * * * *

I met Wendy Weil in her office at Julian Bach and Associates to discuss my plan to write a book about the Supreme Court. Although Wendy was my age and the junior partner in the agency, she already represented an impressive list of clients, including the novelist Alice Walker and the feminist writer Susan Brownmiller.

Casually dressed, Wendy greeted me informally, as if we were new neighbors introducing ourselves across a row of bushes. We spoke briefly about our mutual friend Carey, and then she asked me to describe the book I had in mind. I summarized my *Time* story that traced the transition from the liberal decisions of the Warren Court to the conservative rulings under Chief Justice Burger. It was an important subject and topical, I suggested, and she agreed. She instructed me to write a proposal for the book that included a narrative summary and chapter outlines.

It did not take me long to write the proposal because the topic was fresh in my mind. Wendy, now my agent, seemed satisfied with the proposal and said she would send it to a select list of publishers with a particular interest in the Court, and would be in touch with me once she received responses. To my surprise and utter delight, she called a few weeks later with the news that the David McKay Company had offered me a $10,000 advance to write the book. I had not heard of the publisher, but Wendy assured me that it was an excellent small publishing house that would do a fine job with my book.

My initial enthusiasm was quickly tempered by the realization that I had to negotiate a leave of absence with *Time* before I could accept McKay's offer. I was aware that *Time* writers and correspondents frequently asked for leaves to write books, requests that the magazine did not encourage. *Time* grudgingly offered me a ten-month unpaid leave to write my book. Only after my special plea did the magazine agree to continue my benefits during my absence. This meant that I had less than a year to write a major book, a challenge that would have been daunting for most experienced authors, and certainly for a neophyte like me. Even if the writing went well, was it possible for me to support my family on $10,000 (minus 10 percent as Wendy's commission) for ten months? Marcia was understandably skeptical, but I was determined to seize the opportunity. I accepted David McKay's offer.

I met Ken Rawson, the publisher and president of David McKay, who introduced me to my editor, Jim Wade. A recent Harvard graduate, Jim brimmed with enthusiasm for my proposed book, an encouraging sign to me that ours would be a fruitful collaboration. At the beginning of November 1971, a few weeks before my thirty-third birthday, I left *Time* to write my book.

• • • • •

How should I begin? After a few hours at my desk in our bedroom staring out the window, I decided that I needed a professional workspace more conducive to my new life as an aspiring author. I called Elie Abel, the dean of the Columbia School of Journalism and a former correspondent for NBC television news, who was a professional friend and a source for me at *Time*. I asked him if there was a vacant office at Columbia that I might use, and he graciously offered a small office in the university's school of journalism building. I spent the next morning in the journalism school office staring out the window at the Columbia campus. But the result was no different from the previous day. I was paralyzed with fear that I could not write the book.

I thanked Abel profusely for the use of the office but said that my plans had changed; I intended to write the book at home. The next day, again at my desk in our bedroom, I decided that I needed a work plan and strict schedule. I reviewed my proposal with the chapter outlines and devised a plan that allotted one month for each of the ten proposed chapters. For the first two weeks of each month, I would do the research for the chapter. The third week would be devoted to writing a first draft of the chapter. In the final week, I would edit the draft for submission to my publisher. It was a tight and ambitious schedule, but one I vowed to follow.

During the first two weeks of November, I compiled materials for my first chapter, which was devoted to politics and the Court. I focused my research on how politics affected presidential attitudes toward the Court, concentrating on President Richard Nixon's early animus toward Earl Warren as well as his attacks on the liberal decisions of the Warren Court during his successful presidential campaign in 1968. Most of the research was based on my notes and the research files at *Time*, but I also relied on secondary sources, including biographies of Nixon and Warren as well as books on the Warren Court and newspaper articles on Nixon's attacks on the Warren Court. I divided my time between the Spring Valley Library, the largest in Rockland County, and the main branch of the New York Public Library in Midtown Manhattan.

After completing two weeks of research, I looked forward to the next two weeks at home. Having spent a depressing day in a nondescript office at Columbia, I appreciated anew the warmth and surroundings of our house. I arranged a daily schedule for myself that I would adhere to throughout the writing of the book. Never an early riser (except for my two years at the *Post-Dispatch*), I set the alarm for eight o'clock, a crucial time, I was convinced, when I did my best thinking about the manuscript.

After breakfast with Marcia and Lauren, I commuted to my office/bedroom at ten o'clock. Before sitting at my desk, I put on a stack of long-playing Time-Life classical records from Martin O'Neill's collection. My research notes were placed next to my Olivetti manual typewriter. For the next hour, I watched the birds in the woods outside our bedroom window.

I couldn't expect instant inspiration, I told myself. By eleven, I knew I could no longer afford to procrastinate. Slowly, I began to tap out the first paragraphs of the chapter on my typewriter. As the hours passed, I picked up the pace, and my tentative early tapping transformed into the rat-a-tat-tat of a manual machine gun. By noon, I was oblivious to any sound or sight outside of the tightly controlled universe at my desk. With only a brief bathroom break, I worked intensely until midafternoon, when David returned from kindergarten at Birchwood Elementary School.

I remember sitting on the stairs waiting for David on a particularly difficult day of writing. When David opened the front door, I must have had a frown on my face.

"What's wrong, Dad?" he asked.

"I've had a tough day writing," I replied.

"I know what you mean," David said sympathetically. "I'm having trouble with my Bs and Ds."

* * * * *

By midwinter, I had established a rhythm to my workweek and was able to produce a chapter a month, even snatching a few days at the end of each month to start a new chapter. I supplemented my research with interviews in Washington, New York, and New Haven, taking advantage of my *Time* sources, including US Supreme Court Justices Lewis Powell Jr. and Potter Stewart as well as US Senators Birch Bayh (D-IN) and John C. Tower (R-TX). For a chapter on the Pentagon Papers case, I interviewed, in addition to Alex Bickel, A. M. Rosenthal, managing editor of the *New York Times*; Ben Bradlee, who by then had become executive editor of the *Washington Post*; Erwin Griswold, US solicitor general; and Richard Kleindienst, US attorney general. For expertise on the Supreme Court, I interviewed several members of the Yale faculty, including Bickel, Charles Black, and Yale Law School dean Abe Goldstein, as well as Jack Greenberg, director-counsel of the NAACP Legal Defense Fund.

By the summer of 1972, I was confident that I could meet my deadline of completing the manuscript before returning to *Time* after Labor Day. Jim Wade offered very positive feedback on the chapters I had turned in and didn't even complain about the paragraphs I had cut-and-pasted on virtually every page of the manuscript. This was more than two decades before the common use of personal computers.

While my writing was going very well, my advance was not keeping pace with our family's mounting bills. At my request, McKay agreed to send the second and third payments of my advance, and still I could not pay all our bills on time. I remember being both embarrassed and incensed when I received a hostile call from a local dentist's office informing me that my payment was overdue. Didn't the dentist appreciate that I was writing an important book and understand that I could be trusted to pay my bill? The answers were "no" and "no." Even with a $1,000 check from Dad, the result of a windfall royalty payment from one of Poppy's East Texas oil properties, I barely covered our expenses through the summer, the first in which our family had skipped a vacation since Lauren was born.

In my acknowledgments, I thanked Marcia for her editing expertise and compassion and David and Lauren "who at crucial times dragged me away from 'THE BOOK' to play." It was the least I could do. It had been a tough ten months for the family. We had to eliminate virtually every nonessential expense, which meant fewer trips to Dairy Queen. I had no doubt that every member of the family was relieved when, just before returning to *Time*, I posed for a photo holding the last chapters of my manuscript.

* * * * *

The book was scheduled to be published in April 1973. The seven months between my turning in the manuscript and the book's publication required a great deal of work on my part. I had to respond to Jim Wade's editorial suggestions and carefully check the manuscript for accuracy with the assistance of one of *Time*'s researchers, Erika Sanchez, whom I hired for the laborious task. I also was fortunate to receive comments on the manuscript from Alex Bickel, Abe Goldstein, and Albert Rosenthal, a law professor at Columbia. After I received the page proofs from McKay, I did a second line-by-line review.

I was pleased that McKay accepted my title for the book, *In His Own Image: The Supreme Court in Richard Nixon's America*. But I was appalled by McKay's choice of a jacket cover. It showed an image of a blindfolded President Nixon holding the scales of justice but peeking under the blindfold. This was the fall of 1972, almost two years before the Watergate scandal engulfed the Nixon presidency leading to Nixon's resignation in August 1974. I thought the cover was disrespectful of the office of the presidency and immediately called Wade to complain. Wade held his ground, saying that he and Ken Rawson at McKay thought the jacket was appropriately provocative and would sell books. He also told me gently, but firmly, that McKay alone had the contractual authority to choose the jacket design.

In a call to Alex Bickel, I told him of my concerns about the cover and alerted him to the fact that I had no control over the book's jacket. I did not want him to be embarrassed, since I had written about the major role he had played in the Pentagon Papers case in my chapter on that topic and had later asked him to review several chapters of the manuscript. Bickel could not have been more gracious in his response, assuring me that my book would be judged on its content, not its cover. And he was confident, based on the chapters he had read, that it would be reviewed positively. I was grateful and relieved.

The most exciting moment for me as an author was the day in early April when I received the first prepublication copy of my book in the mail. There it was: the title and my name in large letters on the front cover and my photograph on the back jacket. My photo had been taken by Jill Krementz, a *Time* colleague, who later became famous as a photographer of authors, celebrities, and public officials, and who in 1979 would marry the author Kurt Vonnegut. For my jacket photo, I had worn a turtleneck, which I hoped would suggest that I was a hip, up-and-coming young author.

At the beginning of the week of the book's publication, Jim Wade called me with exciting news. He had spoken to the *New York Times'* daily book reviewer, Herbert Mitgang, who had confided in Wade that his laudatory review of my book would be published in the *Times* two days later, which was the official date of the book's publication. Anticipating the review, Wade placed an ad for my book in the *Times* just below the space for Mitgang's review, announcing McKay's second printing before publication. And on Wednesday, April 18, 1973, Mitgang's review was published, describing my book as "a lucid and documented work that is refreshingly objective."

The *Times* daily book review was essential reading for every *Time* editor, writer, and researcher. So it was no surprise that the day the Mitgang review of my book appeared in the *Times* I was greeted with enthusiastic congratulations by my colleagues. I practically floated on air to my desk.

Soon after publication of the Mitgang review, *Time* published its own review, which concluded, "Tomorrow's constitutional historians will certainly have to begin with his [Simon's] text when they record their final judgments on the Burger era." Many excellent reviews from newspapers across the country followed.

McKay arranged for me to promote my book on radio and television talk shows in New York City, Washington, DC, Pittsburgh, and Los Angeles, where my law school classmate Monroe Price, a professor at UCLA Law School, had invited me to speak to his law students. I soon realized that most of my interviewers had not read my book, but asked questions that were hastily written down by their assistants or producers. That was fine with me—just so they repeated the title of my book and told their audiences to buy it.

In Los Angeles, Marcia and I stayed with Monroe Price and his wife, Aimée, who had been a friend of Marcia's since their graduate school days at Yale, where both had studied art history. Monroe, brilliant and slightly quirky, drove us in an old, dilapidated Buick convertible to the high-class Beverly Hills Hilton Hotel, where he picked up US Supreme Court Justice Potter Stewart, for whom he had clerked after law school. Monroe then took Justice Stewart and the four of us on an informal, idiosyncratic tour of Los Angeles, which included a nocturnal stop at Grauman's Chinese Theatre to view the handprints of famous movie celebrities. While we were there, we watched the last scenes of a movie and then crashed a party given by one of Monroe's colleagues. If Justice Stewart was upset by the bizarre evening, he did not show it. He probably expected nothing less from his former law clerk.

• • • • •

While I had won my father's approval with my speech about my summer in Ghana in 1960 at the Fort Worth Rotary Club, our disagreements over the best approach to eliminating racial discrimination continued for more than a decade. In 1972, less than three years before Dad died of a heart attack, we were, thankfully, fully reconciled.

Our reconciliation was obviously complete when I received a warm letter from him shortly before the publication of *In His Own Image*. The letter, dictated in lawyerly fashion, offered ten suggestions for a title, though he admitted some of his entries "might be too flippant" and others "completely inapplicable," since he had not read my manuscript and only had a general idea of the contents of my book. Among his suggestions:

"Who's on Ninth?"—"A rather corny reference to the power that the ninth judge holds in split decisions."

"Dissent, Dissent, Dissent"—"A lead-in to the frustrations of a split court."

"Warren to Burger to Chance"—"Long ago the famous double play combination was Tinker to Evers to Chance. Here Chance would not be the name of the first baseman but the gamble that is inherent in the court decisions."

"Catch Justice"—"I don't know what this means myself."

He promised to keep thinking of titles and predicted that I would soon receive a letter from Mother, "whose first words would be to forget everything above, accompanied by some catchy titles of her own." His letter made me smile, as I'm sure was his intention.

• • • • •

After my book was published, I returned to Fort Worth to sign copies at local bookstores and was greeted as a minor celebrity. My book had jumped to the best-seller list of the *Fort Worth Star-Telegram*, the result, I was sure, of Mother's buying frenzy. Dad was also pleased, especially with the book's dedication to him and Mother, as well as the description on the back jacket flap of the author as a member "of a Texas family with a long, distinguished legal tradition."

Based on my discussions with Dad before his untimely death, I was confident that he agreed with my book's conclusion about *Brown v. Board of Education*: "On May 17, 1954, the country was introduced to a bold new national institution: the Warren Court. That was the day the bickering among the justices over the segregation issue stopped. That was the day that a fifty-eight-year-old legal doctrine was dismissed in a single sentence. . . . 'Separate educational facilities,' Warren wrote in his historic school desegregation opinion, 'are inherently unequal.' . . . The U.S. Supreme Court had spoken for America's best aspirations, had served for the moment not only as the nation's legal counselor, but its conscience."

* * * * *

While in Texas, I was honored as an "outstanding Texas author" at a ceremony in Austin. Luci Baines Johnson, former president Lyndon Johnson's younger daughter, presented my plaque. Later, Jim Wade called to tell me that my book had won the American Bar Association's Silver Gavel Award for outstanding book of the year on a legal subject. The award, he said, would be presented at the ABA's annual summer meeting in Hawaii. Jim hastily added that the award was to be given to the book's publisher, not its author. He assured me that he would proudly accept the honor on behalf of McKay in Honolulu in August.

Although I was miffed that Wade, not I, would make the trip to Hawaii, it was a minor disappointment in an otherwise marvelous experience as a first-time author. A paperback edition of the book was scheduled to be published in April 1974. All my hard work had paid off in a way that I could not have imagined when I sat at my desk that first week in November 1971, wondering if I could possibly write the book. After the success of my first book, I realized that I was no longer committed to a career in journalism. My thoughts, instead, turned to ideas for a second book.

CHAPTER 9

GOODBYE TO JOURNALISM

After the Labor Day holiday in early September 1972, I drove my used Volkswagen bug (decorated with flower decals) from West Nyack to Eighty-Sixth Street, the first leg of my commute to *Time*. I parked my car, took the subway to Fiftieth Street, and waited for the traffic light to change for my short walk to the Time-Life Building. It suddenly hit me: I was not looking forward to my return to *Time*.

A week earlier, I had turned in the final chapters of the manuscript, and I already missed the routine I had established for the ten months that I had worked on my book. Whether doing the research or writing at my desk, I had enjoyed the total freedom to shape my workday. And for the last two weeks of each month, after writing or editing until midafternoon, I had commuted downstairs, where I could play with David and Lauren and spend the evening with the family. Admittedly, the book was never far from my mind. Still, I had savored the whole experience.

After taking the familiar elevator ride to *Time*'s twelfth-floor editorial offices, I was informed by Bob Shnayerson, the law section's senior editor, that my status had changed. The managing editor, Henry Grunwald, had abandoned his idea of assigning special correspondents to the back-of-the-book sections of the magazine. Since Joe Ferrer had returned to write the law section with Howard Muson, I had been reassigned to the New York bureau as a correspondent. I then met with Murray Gart, the chief of correspondents, who welcomed me as a valued new member of the bureau. Gart told me that he was impressed with my reporting at *Time*. His praise helped me cope with the unsettling news of my relocation.

My move to the bureau required that I take the elevator only one floor above my previous office. I was introduced to Marsh Clark, the New York bureau chief, a veteran *Time* correspondent whom I knew by reputation as a savvy reporter with sure instincts for a good news story. You would never guess that Marsh, who was unfailingly courteous and mild-mannered, descended from political royalty: his father, Champ Clark, a prominent Democratic congressman from Missouri, had served as Speaker of the US House of Representatives from 1911 to 1918. Marsh escorted me around the bureau, warmly introducing me to my new colleagues.

Settling into my new office, I was soon fielding regular queries from Joe and Howard in the law section as well as a number of unusually challenging assignments from editors in the Nation and World sections. One of the most memorable came from an editor in the Nation section requesting that I spend a week reporting on two federal prisons in western Pennsylvania and file a story for a new feature in the magazine, "American Scene."

For "American Scene," the idea was to publish a page-long feature demonstrating an unusual aspect of American life. My assignment was to highlight the very different conditions between the two prisons. The first was the maximum-security prison at Lewisburg, where inmates convicted of the most serious felonies, from armed bank robbery to murder, were incarcerated. The second, only a few miles away, was the minimum-security prison at Allenwood, which was perceived, by comparison, as a country club. Well-known white-collar convicted criminals had been sent to Allenwood, including Carmine DeSapio, the former Tammany Hall political boss in New York City, who had recently been released after serving two years for bribing a public official. Author Clifford Irving, who had been convicted of grand larceny for perpetuating one of the biggest literary hoaxes of the twentieth century, was still incarcerated at Allenwood.

My assignment was to concentrate on the country club atmosphere at Allenwood, contrasting it with the brutal conditions at Lewisburg. I went to the Lewisburg prison first, and it lived up to every horrific image of prisons that I had seen in movies or read in novels. The massive concrete walls of the prison hid a menacing community of convicted felons. Although I was carefully escorted through the cellblocks by guards, I was terrified throughout my tour. Palpably relieved when I left Lewisburg, I drove a few miles to Allenwood, where I expected to report the heart of the story on "the country club of prisons."

There were no high walls at Allenwood, but only an ordinary barbed-wire fence that enclosed the prison's spacious grounds. And instead of Lewisburg's sterile, cramped cells, inmates at Allenwood lived in a one-story dormitory, in appearance not very different from housing on a college campus or military base. After entering the dormitory, I spotted Clifford Irving sitting on his bunk and made a beeline to him.

Irving was the author of twenty novels but was best known—and incarcerated—for concocting a supposedly authorized autobiography of the billionaire recluse Howard Hughes, presumably based on his interviews with Hughes. The interviews never took place. Irving had forged letters from Hughes to back up his claim. McGraw-Hill had paid Irving a $750,000 advance to publish the book. *Life* magazine bought the serial rights for $250,000, and Dell paid Irving an additional $400,000 for the paperback rights. Shortly before publication, Irving's claim of an authorized Hughes autobiography unraveled when Hughes publicly denied knowing him. As the incriminating evidence piled up, Irving pled guilty to grand larceny and was sentenced to two and a half years in prison at Allenwood.

Irving greeted me amicably and invited me to interview him. For the next hour and a half he described Allenwood in great detail. He told me that life in the minimum-security prison, for him, was not so bad. Unlike his fellow inmates, he spent most of his idle hours reading stacks of books and writing. But his description of life for his fellow inmates, many of them incarcerated for tax evasion or embezzlement, did not fit the prison's reputation as a country club. Although they were living in a dormitory, not a cell, they felt like caged animals. Constantly monitored by guards, they could never forget they were prisoners. The claustrophobia sapped their energy and sense of self-esteem. Most were deeply depressed, Irving said. I later confirmed the accuracy of his observations in interviews with other inmates.

When I returned to New York, I was eager to begin writing my story that would shatter the myth of Allenwood as a country club. As Irving had told me, it was a living hell for most of his fellow inmates. After I finished transforming my notes into a coherent narrative, I thought I had written a compelling prison article with a surprise ending. But it was not what my editor in the Nation section had in mind. I had described two suffocating prison environments. No story there, he concluded, at least for "American Scene."

• • • • •

A second opportunity to write an unusual feature for the magazine turned out to be more successful. In March 1973, a shocking news story broke over the wire: the governor of Bermuda, the former British colony and island paradise, had been assassinated. It was an international story that, inevitably, would attract reporters from around the world. Marsh Clark came to my office, showed me the wire service story of the assassination, and told me to go home and pack for Bermuda. I immediately called Marcia to see if she could hire a babysitter for David and Lauren, so that she might join me for the week that I expected to be reporting the story from Bermuda. We were both disappointed that she could not arrange for a babysitter on such short notice.

After boarding a plane at New York's JFK airport on a Sunday morning, I noticed that my fellow passengers included reporters from many of the nation's leading newspapers as well as from *Time*'s newsmagazine rival *Newsweek*. We arrived at the Bermuda International Airport in the early afternoon and I took a cab to downtown Hamilton, where I checked into the Hamilton Princess Hotel. *Time* had booked a spacious room for me for the week, but I spent virtually no time there except to sleep.

For the remainder of the day and evening, I walked from block to block in downtown Hamilton interviewing a wide range of Bermudians, from waiters to boutique saleswomen to tourist agents, asking for their reaction to the assassination. I also took copious notes describing the scene, beginning with the policeman, dressed in an immaculate white uniform and pith helmet, deftly directing traffic in the middle of the busiest intersection in the city.

For the next three days, I was in perpetual motion, talking to officials in the governor's office, legislators, and detectives, trying to piece together the details of the assassination and any clues about who might have been responsible. At the same time, I tried to gauge the impact of the assassination on the local economy of this tourist mecca, interviewing scores of officials, educators, and ordinary citizens.

By late Wednesday afternoon, I had filled several notebooks with quotes and observations and begun to outline my story for the magazine. My deadline for filing the story was early Thursday morning. This gave editors in New York from late Thursday morning until Friday afternoon to mark up my copy with their blue pencils. My story would first be sent to an editor in the World section and then forwarded to the "top" editor, one of the executive editors of the magazine. Once my file had gone through those edits, it would be sent back to me by teletype, no later than Friday afternoon. I would then have the opportunity to correct any factual errors or misleading edits before the story went to press late Friday night.

I finished filing my copy by teletype a few minutes before three o'clock Thursday morning, took a cab to my hotel, flopped on my bed, and set my alarm for a few hours later, ten o'clock. Since I would not receive the edited copy until late Friday afternoon, I was free to enjoy Bermuda for the next day and a half. What to do first? The answer was obvious once I opened the curtains of my hotel room. It was a cloudless sunny day. I quickly packed my swimsuit, told the desk clerk where I could be reached, and boarded a shuttle bus outside the lobby for the Princess's sister hotel overlooking the Atlantic Ocean. The shuttle wound its way through the island's narrow streets, lined with palm trees and picturesque, pastel-colored houses, until it climbed the gentle hill to the Southampton Princess Hotel, where I spent the day by the pool.

I devoted the next day to shopping to find gifts for the family. I bought a large silver pin at a fashionable jewelry store in Hamilton for Marcia and an exquisite native Bermudian doll for Lauren. I could not resist buying a novelty toy with moving parts for David from a sidewalk vendor. And before leaving Bermuda, I purchased an aquamarine ring at the hotel's jewelry shop for Marcia for our anniversary.

When the edited copy of my story was returned to me by teletype late Friday afternoon, I was pleased to discover that the editors in New York had kept my narrative essentially intact, including my lead with the description of the white-uniformed policeman directing traffic in midtown Hamilton. And to top it all, they had given me a coveted byline for a full-page feature in the World section.

Early Saturday afternoon I boarded a plane for my return flight to JFK and took a cab from the airport to the Greenwich Village apartment of our friends Ricki and Carl Long. Marcia, David, and Lauren were waiting there to join me for dinner with the Longs. With descriptive flourish, I told them about my difficult week of reporting in Bermuda. David and Lauren kept staring at my deep suntan. I could easily translate those stares into words: "Sure, Dad, it must have been *so* tough for you to spend a week in Bermuda."

✦ ✦ ✦ ✦ ✦

While the Bermuda story was my most exciting assignment, I continued to be given interesting work in the New York bureau. I spent a week with New York City detective David Durk, who had made newspaper headlines for reporting widespread corruption in the city's police department. An Amherst College graduate and Jewish, Durk was not your typical New York City detective. Articulate, well read, and with a wry sense of humor, he was also driven in his determination to cleanse his department of corruption. With his fellow detective Frank Serpico, he made allegations that led to the appointment of a high-level commission to investigate police corruption. The commission later produced a scathing report reinforcing Durk and Serpico's charges.

After my profile of Durk appeared in *Time*, he asked me to meet with him and his literary agent and proposed that I write his "as told to" autobiography. I decided not to do the book, but Durk and I remained friends. He and his wife, Arlene, attended a party at our house where my detective friend packed a pistol in plain view of my mesmerized son.

On the night of October 20, 1973, I was on duty at *Time* when news broke that President Nixon had fired Special Prosecutor Archibald Cox in what became known as the "Saturday Night Massacre." It was the beginning of the end of Nixon's presidency, which had started with the botched burglary of the Democratic National Committee headquarters in the Watergate complex in the nation's capital. The main story, of course, was in Washington, but I reported on the impact of the scandal on Nixon's New York law firm. Later, I was assigned to cover the trial in Lower Manhattan of two of Nixon's cabinet members, Attorney General John Mitchell and Commerce Secretary Maurice Stans, who had also served as chairman of Nixon's reelection campaign in 1972. Mitchell and Stans were charged with criminal conspiracy to stop a Securities and Exchange Commission investigation of financier Robert Vesco in exchange for a $200,000 contribution to President Nixon's reelection campaign.

* * * * *

By the fall of 1973, despite my challenging stories for *Time*, I was convinced that journalism would not be my final career. My mind increasingly wandered to ideas for my next book. At the same time, I began to explore the possibility of a law school teaching career to support my family, supplemented, I hoped, with publishers' advances for future books. At the suggestion of the dean of the Hofstra Law School, Monroe Freedman, I taught a seminar on the modern Supreme Court at Hofstra that fall. To make the 9:00 a.m. seminar at Hofstra every Monday, I set my alarm for 5:30 a.m., to allow time for breakfast and the long commute to Hempstead, Long Island. After teaching the seminar, I drove to the city for work in *Time*'s New York bureau. It was a difficult schedule, to be sure, but one that both Dean Freedman and I hoped would lead to a permanent offer to join his faculty.

Once I began teaching the seminar at Hofstra, I felt an obligation to meet with Murray Gart, *Time*'s chief of correspondents, to inform him that I was seriously considering leaving the magazine to pursue a teaching career, which would allow me to write more books. He was disappointed. If I would make a commitment to *Time*, he promised to find a position in the organization that would satisfy me. A few weeks later, he offered me the opportunity to head a new bureau for the magazine in Houston.

After politely turning down the Houston posting, I told Gart that I could not make the commitment to the magazine that he required. At the time, I had no permanent teaching position or new book contract. In retrospect, it was sheer idiocy for me to tell Gart that I would be leaving *Time* in the near future when I had no tangible plan to support my family. Gart generously said that I could continue to work at *Time* for several months while I made a decision on my next career move.

In late December, Marcia, David, Lauren, and I flew to Fort Worth to be with my family for the holidays, as we had done for many years. David and Lauren looked forward to the Texas trip every year to be with my parents and their cousins. This time I asked my parents to take care of David and Lauren while Marcia and I flew to New Orleans for the Association of American Law Schools (AALS) winter meeting, where the appointment committees of the nation's law schools annually interviewed applicants for faculty positions.

Shortly after arriving in New Orleans, I received the disappointing news from Dean Freedman that a majority of Hofstra's law faculty did not support his proposed offer to me for an entry-level teaching position. Feeling discouraged, I nonetheless forced myself to mingle with other deans and law school faculty members in an effort to arrange for job interviews. Repeatedly I was turned down, primarily, I suspected, for the same reason that had doomed my application at Hofstra: I did not fit the traditional academic profile of a law professor. I had not served on the law review at Yale, and I had not clerked for a federal or state court judge, the requisite credentials for most law school faculty members. My many articles as a legal journalist at *Time* did not count for much. Nor did my critically acclaimed book on the US Supreme Court, which was written for a general readership, not an academic one.

Even Marcia's company and the great food at the famous New Orleans restaurants, Antoine's and Galatoire's, could not lift my spirits. But at the final AALS reception, I caught my one lucky break. Yale Law School dean Abe Goldstein, whom I had told earlier of my desire to leave *Time* for a career in law school teaching, motioned for me to join him in conversation. He introduced me to Professor Daniel Aaron, who held an endowed chair in English Literature and American Studies at Harvard. Aaron was at the AALS meeting to recruit young law professors for Harvard's Law and Humanities Fellowship. Goldstein told him about my work at *Time*, my book on the Supreme Court, and my ambition to teach.

Aaron encouraged me to apply for the Harvard fellowship. He conceded that my résumé did not resemble that of young law professors, who were the typical applicants for the fellowship. But he suggested that my journalism career, especially as a law specialist at *Time*, as well as my book on the Supreme Court, would impress the fellowship committee on which he served. I told him that I would apply for the fellowship. That brief talk with Aaron offered the one snippet of hope in my otherwise depressing series of conversations during the three-day AALS meeting.

Soon after we returned to New York, I began commuting to New Haven by train every Monday afternoon from Grand Central Station to teach my evening seminar on the modern Supreme Court at Yale's Stiles College. I owed the teaching opportunity to Alex Bickel, who had recommended me for the seminar. After my seminar was listed in the college syllabus, approximately one hundred Yale undergraduates signed up for the class, which was limited to fifteen students. The fifteen undergraduates selected by a Stiles College faculty committee were an incredibly bright group. They guaranteed an exhilarating teaching experience for me, which made me more determined than ever to teach full time.

• • • • •

In late January, I received a call from Jim Wade at McKay, who proposed that I write a book patterned on the best seller *The Making of a Surgeon*, in which the author, William A. Nolen, followed a surgeon for a week. Nolen's book provided readers with an inside view of a doctor's dramatic life in the operating room. Jim suggested that I develop a similar narrative for a sitting judge. I liked the idea.

Wade and I agreed that my subject should be a state criminal court trial judge hearing cases in the courthouse at Foley Square in downtown Manhattan. But how should I select a judge to be the subject of the book? I decided to ask reporters from the city's daily newspapers who covered state criminal court cases for their opinions of the best judges in the courthouse. I also polled state trial court judges on the reporters' lists to rate their colleagues. As a result of those conversations, I made a list of state criminal court judges with several indispensable qualities: honesty, high intelligence, competence, and, the most elusive trait, a colorful personality that would project well on the written page.

The judge whose name I heard most frequently was James Leff, a fifty-three-year-old graduate of Harvard Law School. Judge Leff had earned a reputation as a smart, no-nonsense criminal court judge with an outsized personality that was on daily display in his courtroom. I called Leff and asked to meet him in his chambers. In our meeting, I told him of my proposed book. If he agreed to be "the judge" in my book, I said that I would need to sit next to him on the bench for several months. After each session, I would interview him, asking his opinion on each defendant and case that came before him. He was both flattered and intrigued with the idea and agreed to cooperate with me. My next step was to write a proposal that my agent, Wendy Weil, would review and, if satisfied, forward to Jim Wade at McKay.

In early February, Wendy called to tell me that Jim Wade had offered an advance of $17,500 for me to write a book on Judge Leff for McKay. A week later, I received a letter from Harvard's Law and Humanities program informing me that I had been awarded a fellowship for the 1974–1975 academic year. Suddenly, my professional future, at least for the next year and half, had crystallized. I was both relieved and excited.

Marcia was less enthusiastic about my plans, especially about accepting the Harvard fellowship. It meant uprooting our family for a year—renting out our house, finding a house to rent in the Boston area, and enrolling David and Lauren in a new elementary school. Marcia would also need to plan how she might spend her time in the new environment. Making the transition was a daunting task, but she reluctantly agreed to the move.

At *Time*, I had begun to cover the early stages of the criminal conspiracy trial of two of President Nixon's cabinet members, Attorney General Mitchell and Commerce Secretary Stans. The trial took place in the federal courthouse at Foley Square, only a block away from the state courthouse where Judge Leff presided. The Mitchell-Stans trial was a plum assignment, but I knew I would have to relinquish it to start work on the book. I met for the last time with Murray Gart to tell him that I was leaving *Time*, a decision we had discussed in the fall. We shook hands, and he wished me luck in my new career. After saying goodbye to Marsh Clark and my other colleagues in the New York bureau, I left the Time-Life Building for the last time.

CHAPTER 10

HARVARD FELLOWSHIP

For four months, beginning in mid-February 1974, I sat next to Judge Leff on the bench, filling notebook after notebook with details of his criminal cases. We listened to the case of Tillie Martin, who saw Martians and stabbed her "boyfriend," and Martin Johnson, who was arrested and charged with the rapes and robberies of three women within the span of a month. And we heard defendant John Harding, who was charged with robbery and slitting the throat of his boss, reject his attorney's advice to "cop a plea" (plead guilty to a lesser charge to avoid a trial and longer prison sentence, if found guilty).

Most of the cases on the judge's docket were less sensational, often young offenders charged with minor crimes such as shoplifting or purse-snatching. Regardless of the seriousness of the charge, Judge Leff's demeanor never changed. He listened patiently to each prosecutor's and defense lawyer's argument, as well as to the defendant's explanation of the circumstances of his or her arrest, if offered. Speaking gruffly from the bench, he then made it clear to attorneys and defendants alike that he had carefully read the written record and that no amount of posturing was going to sway him. But he interspersed the no-nonsense warning with his irreverent, streetwise sense of humor. Finally, he told them the reasons that he was recommending a plea to a lesser offense or was prepared to set a date for trial, as he did in John Harding's case.

After court adjourned, we retreated to the judge's chambers, where he spoke candidly about each defendant who had appeared before him that morning. He expressed compassion for a few of them, especially first offenders. But he concluded that most were probably guilty of the crimes they were charged with. He did not defend the revolving door of criminal justice in New York City, where most repeat offenders were poor and Black or Hispanic, and represented by public defenders with little time or experience to give them the defense they deserved. But he worked conscientiously, if often futilely, to make the system work. He was critical of many of his judicial colleagues who, he said, did not approach their job with his sense of responsibility. Some were lazy, others incompetent, and, in one instance, dishonest.

Most weekdays we continued our conversations at lunch in the judge's favorite Italian restaurant only a few blocks from the courthouse. While we enjoyed rich pasta dishes, he expanded on his decisions, his colleagues, and the flaws in the criminal justice system. He also spoke personally and frankly about his upbringing in New York City as the only child of a prominent and beloved pediatrician who, according to Leff, was always available to his patients, but rarely to his son. He brushed off the prestige of his Harvard degree with the same abruptness as he did stupid remarks made in his presence.

He adored his wife, Mimi, and soon brought me home to their apartment on the Upper West Side to meet her. I immediately understood his devotion. Mimi, an attractive middle-aged woman with high cheekbones and auburn hair, tinged slightly with a few strands of gray, demonstratively returned his affection. And, just as obviously, she gracefully ignored his gruff manner and feigned commands.

While working on the book, I also met the Leffs' son, John, who was in his final year of law school. Our families became friends. Marcia and I attended the Leffs' annual party at their apartment in early May, in which guests gathered around their television to watch and celebrate the Kentucky Derby, one of the judge's favorite sporting events. In return, we invited the Leffs to meet our family for an informal afternoon at our home in West Nyack.

The reporting for the book was both fascinating and enjoyable, due to the judge's cooperation and rough charm. The greater challenge awaited me at my typewriter. Before we packed for our move to the Boston area, I carefully reviewed my notes, taken over four months with Judge Leff, and organized chapter outlines for the book. But I decided to postpone writing the first draft until we had moved in the late summer.

• • • • •

In choosing a residence in the Boston area, our highest priority was the elementary school for David and Lauren. We quickly focused our search on houses for rent in Lexington, Massachusetts, which had a reputation for operating one of the best school systems in the nation. We rented a sprawling, slightly dilapidated three-story, four-bedroom house on Winthrop Road, within walking distance of David and Lauren's new school.

The transition proved especially smooth for Lauren. At five years old, she possessed a preternatural confidence in the classroom, thanks to her extraordinary preschool teacher, Mrs. McKee, whose sensitive and intelligent nurturing was perfectly suited to Lauren's personality and aptitude. In Lexington, Lauren was placed in an experimental class combining first- and second-graders, where she thrived. Her eager, fun-loving personality and quick high intelligence made her a favorite of her teacher.

Lauren made friends easily both inside and outside the classroom. When she turned six in December, she led a parade of the girls in her class to our house, where Marcia had baked an elaborate three-layer cake. Her best friend, Lara, lived only a few blocks away, and the two girls were inseparable on weekends. Lauren also sometimes confidently walked to the local Woolworth's in downtown Lexington, only two blocks from our house, where she bought trinkets and gum that fit well within her weekly allowance.

David's life in Lexington was more difficult. Although exceptionally intelligent (his high IQ later qualified him for membership in Mensa), he was rarely comfortable in the classroom. His previous teachers had usually liked him, because he was smart, articulate, and energetic. But he often found his assignments difficult to complete. His biggest problems, we later realized, were his undiagnosed dyslexia and his likely attention deficit disorder

(ADD). His third-grade teacher in Lexington was new that year and had no time for or patience with David.

The playground, for David, offered no more relief than the classroom. He had poor eye-hand coordination, which meant that he struggled in ball sports. For a boy, especially a new boy in town, being a valued soccer or baseball player could overcome a multitude of problems in making friends. David loved to ride his bike and, later, would become an excellent downhill skier. But at his Lexington elementary school, he was isolated and unhappy.

At home, he pursued interests that foreshadowed his adult hobbies and professional skills. Music, even at the age of eight, was central to David's life. He listened to his favorite Boston radio station every day and was particularly enthralled with new recordings of the young British singing sensation Elton John. He also demonstrated an exceptional technical understanding of how things worked. Unbeknownst to Marcia and me, he picked up a broken portable television set that had been left on the curb and repaired it. He and Lauren then surreptitiously watched their favorite programs in his room, hiding under the table with his electric trains on it, until Lauren, consumed with guilt, spilled the beans.

And then there were the cars. David was probably in diapers when he first developed his lifelong passion for cars. He played for hours on the floor with his Matchbox cars, and I was often his enthusiastic playmate. For his third birthday, we bought him a large toy gas station to fuel the cars. And when we traveled on vacations or visited family in Texas, he packed them in a customized Matchbox suitcase. On Saturdays in Lexington, the two of us visited the local Buick dealer and then, for the main event, walked a few blocks to the Chevrolet showroom, where we ogled the new red Corvette.

Marcia enrolled in a writing and illustration class taught by Marian Parry, a published children's book author and illustrator, at the Radcliffe Institute in Cambridge. It was the most important class she had taken since she was an undergraduate at Pembroke. Parry, a tall, imposing, but understated instructor, recognized Marcia's creativity as both an artist and writer. Soon enough, Marcia was producing one illustrated story after another, beginning with "Louie, the Louse Mouse." By December, she had begun working on an ambitious children's novel featuring a girl who loved ballet.

When Marcia decided she needed to do more research for her novel, she called Barbara Glazer, who was married to my childhood friend Larry. We had developed a close friendship with the Glazers and knew that Barbara and Larry and their three children had recently moved from Dallas to Short Hills, New Jersey. Marcia was aware that the Glazers' older daughter, Tracy, had begun rehearsals in a minor role for the Paper Mill Playhouse production of *The Nutcracker* in Millburn, New Jersey, not far from Short Hills. Would it be possible, Marcia asked, for her to spend a few days with Tracy at the rehearsals? Barbara enthusiastically supported Marcia's idea and quickly obtained permission for her to sit in on rehearsals and interview the dancers.

Marcia spent several days as the guest of the Glazers in Short Hills, taking copious notes in her interviews of the dancers at the Paper Mill Playhouse. In a long-overdue role reversal, I took care of David and Lauren while Marcia was in New Jersey. She returned more excited than ever about her novel and began to develop a more ambitious manuscript. After we returned to New York, she submitted the completed manuscript to Wendy Weil, who loved it and sold the publishing rights to Harcourt Brace Jovanovich. At the suggestion of her editor at Harcourt Brace, Marcia made the book about Peter, the brother of the girl who was the original focus of her manuscript. Peter loved both ballet and basketball, which created tension with his father and some of his friends. After publication, the book, *A Special Gift*, was made into an episode on *ABC Afterschool Special*, which won a Peabody Award.

* * * * *

The Law and Humanities Fellowship was similar in concept to the Nieman Fellowship for Journalism, also at Harvard. Both fellowships made few formal demands on their fellows, who were otherwise free to take advantage of the many academic opportunities at Harvard. I was one of ten Law and Humanities Fellows who met for the first time in a seminar room on the Harvard campus in early September. There were eight men and two women. At the age of thirty-five, I was one of the oldest fellows and the only one who had not been drawn from the faculties of law schools across the country.

The fellows were required to attend a weekly seminar taught by three young Harvard law professors who offered innovative interpretations of contract, property, and tort law. They were leading members of a new wave of professors who no longer felt tethered to the traditional study of law. I had not liked the traditional study of contract, property, and tort law at Yale Law School and, regrettably, was no more enthusiastic about their new approaches. I preferred our second required seminar, in which we discussed great novels with legal themes, such as Charles Dickens's *Bleak House*. Throughout the year, I enjoyed the company of the other fellows, and I remained friends with several of them after we left Harvard.

I spent most of my time on campus auditing courses taught by renowned professors on subjects of particular interest to me. At the top of my list was a class in constitutional law taught by Professor Paul Freund, who, at the age of seventy, was the preeminent constitutional law authority of his generation. In 1962, Freund had been on President Kennedy's short list for an appointment to the US Supreme Court but was passed over in favor of Deputy Attorney General Byron White. In 1974, when I attended his class, Freund was in his last year of teaching. The lecture hall was packed with law students and auditors who, like me, marveled at the breadth of his knowledge. He liberally quoted Shakespeare as well as Supreme Court Justice Oliver Wendell Holmes Jr. I often stayed after class to discuss with Freund points he had made in his lectures and was pleased when he invited me to lunch several times during the year. He was just as erudite at those lunches as in class, but also charming, exhibiting a finely honed sense of humor.

Second on my must-audit list was a course on American intellectual history taught by one of the university's most popular professors, Bernard Bailyn. There were no empty seats for Bailyn's lectures, and I quickly realized the reason. He covered American intellectual history from the nation's founding with style and in extraordinary depth. Every lecture was an academic tour de force.

I also attended two classes taught by less experienced professors who were already well known for their published works. Anthony Lewis, who in the 1960s had been the first reporter assigned to cover the US Supreme Court full time for the *New York Times*, taught a seminar on major decisions of the Court. He had been awarded a Pulitzer Prize for his book *Gideon's Trumpet*, a fascinating account of the landmark 1963 case of Clarence Earl Gideon, an impoverished drifter and petty criminal who had won his case in the Supreme Court (*Gideon v. Wainwright*) over his right to a defense attorney: the significance of the decision was that it guaranteed the right to counsel for poor criminal defendants. Lewis was teaching his Harvard seminar for the first time in 1974. I quickly discovered that his skill in the classroom did not match his great talent as a reporter and author.

The second professor, Doris Kearns, offered an excellent course on the American presidency. She had recently published a fine biography of President Lyndon Johnson and would later, under her married name, Doris Kearns Goodwin, publish a series of superb best sellers, including *Team of Rivals*, a portrait of President Lincoln's cabinet, and *No Ordinary Time*, a dual biography of Eleanor and Franklin Roosevelt.

• • • • •

My classes were squeezed into two full days at Harvard, leaving the rest of the week for work on my book, which Jim Wade and I had agreed would be titled *The Judge*. The house Marcia and I had rented in Lexington was owned by the Harvard professor John Rawls, who was considered one of the greatest living legal philosophers. I never met Rawls, but, sitting at his desk isolated high on the third floor of his house, I could envision him sublimely deducing philosophical principles.

I wished that I felt similarly inspired. But my overriding emotion was anxiety rather than inspiration. The challenge I faced was unlike any that I had yet experienced. I had spent the past seven years as a journalist, driven by facts and deadlines. The only exception was *In His Own Image*, my first book, which was based on a Supreme Court story that I had written for *Time*. The book on Judge Leff would require a narrative that read like a novel.

At the outset, I faced a critical decision: Should I use Leff's name as well as those of the defendants, lawyers, and judicial colleagues that we had discussed? Leff had given me permission to use his name and had told me not to worry about potential libel suits from those who were on the receiving end of his many scornful opinions. I was especially concerned that I would be sued by one of his judicial colleagues whom he had accused of blatant dishonesty. Before making my decision, I reread my publishing contract, which made it clear that I was financially responsible to defend any lawsuit brought as a result of my book.

I decided to use pseudonyms. My caution protected me from libel suits but risked creating suspicion among my readers that I was taking liberties with the facts. My second decision, to condense four months of trials and plea bargains into a single week, could reinforce the impression that I was an aspiring novelist, not a reporter of a nonfiction courtroom drama in which every salient fact and opinion was backed up by my notes.

While working on the manuscript, I put those concerns aside. I concentrated on constructing a compelling narrative from the stacks of notebooks I had filled during my four months in Judge Leff's courtroom. My monthly work schedule in Lexington was different from the plan I had devised for my first book, when I had spent the first two weeks of every month on research. With *The Judge*, I devoted every day at Professor Rawls's desk to the manuscript.

Over the next four months, I was frequently frustrated and impatient with my efforts. With so many cases to consider, I often felt that I was wasting time with false starts. Once I had winnowed the list down to the most compelling cases, I struggled to make them come alive on the typed page. By early October, however, I had established a rhythm to my daily writing routine. And by December, I was satisfied that I had made the daily churn of criminal cases in the judge's courtroom into a publishable nonfiction drama.

In late December, while making final revisions to the manuscript, I received shocking news from Jim Wade in a phone call from New York. My publisher, David McKay, had been sold to a British publisher. Wade had lost his job, and I had lost my editor. And suddenly, the publication of my manuscript was in jeopardy. I immediately put in a call to Wendy Weil. What was the status of my contract? She was uncertain. I told her that I planned to send my manuscript to McKay within a week and expected her to put pressure on McKay to publish it, even if it was the last book to be published under the McKay imprint. She made no promises but said that she would do her best.

* * * * *

With the future of my manuscript in limbo, I prepared to attend the annual winter meeting of the Association of American Law Schools in Washington, DC, during the first week of January 1975. After I had registered for the meeting by mail, I was sent a list of law schools in the market for new faculty members. I was confident that I was in a stronger position to interview at this meeting than I had been a year earlier at the AALS meeting in New Orleans. I was no longer a full-time journalist with only the Hofstra seminar to show as teaching experience. My updated résumé listed the Yale seminar on the modern Supreme Court that I had taught the previous spring, as well as the fact that I had been invited to teach the seminar again in the spring of 1975, with the title of visiting lecturer in American studies. And I was a Law and Humanities Fellow at Harvard for the academic year, another nice addition to my résumé.

Even with my freshly minted Yale and Harvard credentials, I still faced an uphill battle to secure a law school teaching job. I imposed an additional handicap on myself, limiting my inquiries to law schools in the New York area. Marcia and I agreed that, primarily for David's sake, we would return to our home in West Nyack. We were unwilling to subject him to yet another difficult year of adjustment, away from his friends.

My revised résumé failed to spark widespread interest from New York–area law schools. Only St. John's, among the area's well-known law schools, invited me to interview in Washington, and the invitation did not include the possibility of teaching constitutional law, my preferred subject and area of expertise. The invitation from New York Law School to interview was more encouraging. In the letter I received from Professor Milton Silverman, the chairman of the school's appointments committee, he expressed interest in my résumé and said he looked forward to meeting me in Washington. Before receiving Professor Silverman's letter, I had not heard of New York Law School. I lost no time in learning about the school's history and curriculum.

Soon after I arrived in Washington, I was interviewed by Professor Silverman, the other members of New York Law School's appointments committee, and the school's dean, E. Donald Shapiro. Before asking me a single question, they seemed eager to tell me about their law school. Shapiro, in his early forties, did most of the talking. He did not fit my image of a law school dean. Although he was a graduate of Harvard Law School, his fast-talking pitch for New York Law School reminded me more of an aggressive door-to-door salesman than a buttoned-down Ivy Leaguer. But what he said impressed me.

New York Law School, which was located in Lower Manhattan, was founded in 1891 and soon boasted one of the largest and most distinguished faculties in the city. The future chief justice of the United States Charles Evans Hughes had lectured at the school, and the future associate justice of the US Supreme Court John Marshall Harlan was an NYLS graduate. Shapiro admitted that he was leading a once proud institution that had fallen on hard times in recent decades. He was confident that the school would soon reclaim its past glory under his leadership.

Without further discussion, he urged me to join his newly invigorated young faculty. He was aware of the favorable reviews of my first book and said that I would have the time to write many more books as a member of the NYLS faculty. In my first year, he promised that I would teach constitutional law as well as seminars on the modern Supreme Court and legal journalism. He offered to meet my *Time* salary with comparable benefits. I accepted the offer on the spot. My appointment would begin in the fall of 1975.

Beginning in late January 1975, I commuted by train from Boston to New Haven once a week, as I had done the previous year from New York, to teach my seminar on the modern Supreme Court at Yale. I continued to be amazed by the brilliance and resourcefulness of many of my students. One of them, Vince DiBlasi, was such a powerful advocate on behalf of South Carolina in the seminar's mock argument in *Brown v. Board of Education* that he very nearly convinced the class that segregation in the South's public schools was constitutional. He later finished at the top of his class at both Yale College and Yale Law School and became head of the litigation department at the prestigious New York City law firm of Sullivan and Cromwell.

And there was Jeffrey Leeds, a slender freshman with curly hair and a mischievous smile. Upon hearing that I knew Justice Potter Stewart, Jeffrey proposed that I arrange an introduction for him to the justice, so that he could write his final paper on Stewart's jurisprudence. I called Stewart, who agreed to be interviewed by Jeffrey. On the basis of his interview and original research, Jeffrey wrote a superb paper and received an A+ for the course. He graduated at the top of his Harvard Law School class and clerked for Associate Justice William J. Brennan Jr. After his clerkship, he later told me, he spent a brief, unsatisfactory period of time working as an attorney at one of New York City's most distinguished law firms. Upon hearing that the firm's partners had keys to an exclusive bathroom, he demanded that he be issued a key so that he could urinate with them. His request was denied, and he soon left the firm. He then joined Lazard Frères, the prominent financial investment firm, later started his own private equity firm, and became a multimillionaire.

In early February, I received word from Wendy Weil that McKay would honor my book contract, and *The Judge* was scheduled to be published in the spring of 1976. But with Jim Wade gone, I had no idea if I would receive professional editing of my manuscript. And I had no assurance that the McKay publicity department would provide the enthusiastic support that was so important to the success of my first book. The commitment from McKay was hardly reason to celebrate, but at least I knew that I would have a book to show for the many months I had spent reporting and working on the manuscript.

• • • • •

The telephone call came a few minutes after midnight. "Dad died," my brother said. Our father had suffered a fatal heart attack on February 23, the day after his sixty-eighth birthday. He had not been well since his first heart attack more than a decade earlier. After that first heart attack, he gradually cut back on his workweek at the office and spent more time at home with Mother. He still played golf, including a few rounds with me and Dick, but not with the energy of his pre-heart-attack days.

In 1970, he and Mother had visited our family in New York for the last time. One Sunday afternoon we had driven to West Point, where I watched Dad move very slowly across the campus. In an attempt to lift his spirits, I made reservations at a new Szechwan restaurant in New York City that had received a rave review in the *New York Times*. I thought it would be a special treat for Dad, since I had such fond memories of our many dinners at the Blue Star Inn, his favorite Chinese restaurant in Fort Worth. The owner of the Blue Star Inn was Dad's fellow Rotarian Jimmy Dipp, who always greeted Dad with the warmth of a fraternal brother. Dad invariably ordered either chicken chow mein or chop suey and savored every bite. After we were seated at the New York Szechwan restaurant, Dad looked in vain for chow mein or chop suey on the menu. We were forced to order a variety of spicy Szechwan dishes, none of which, I knew from Dad's pained expression, could match the cooking at Jimmy Dipp's restaurant.

Only two months before Dad's death, we had flown to Fort Worth for the holidays. He seemed especially glad to be with me and expressed an interest in reading my manuscript for *The Judge*. I gave him the copy I had packed in my suitcase. Although I had already turned in the manuscript to my publisher, I sensed that he was eager to serve as my unofficial editor. He spent several days reviewing the manuscript. We then sat down together in the den, where Dad, with the serious demeanor he once reserved for clients, shared his written list of suggested improvements. At first, I was annoyed. "Dad," I silently mused, "I'm the professional writer, not you." But later, reflecting upon our conversation, I was touched that he cared so much.

During the holidays, my brother Dick, my cousin Henry, and I made plans to drive to Irving to attend a Dallas Cowboys football game. Dad asked if he could join us. Given his poor health, I knew it was a terrible idea. I tried to discourage him, but he insisted. Our tickets were in the second tier of the very large stadium. I still have a picture in my mind of Dad climbing up the stairs slowly and with obvious difficulty. I regretted that he joined us that day. But I suspected that he knew he did not have long to live and wanted to spend special time with us. Viewed in that context, the scene still moves me.

After Dick's late-night call to me in February, I made reservations for us to take the first available direct flight from Boston to the Dallas–Fort Worth airport. Dick met us at the airport and drove us to Fort Worth. Mother greeted us at the front door. She was visibly distraught but comforted that we were there. Later, in a private conversation with me, she expressed anger that Dad's longtime cardiologist had not acted more quickly to save his life. After Dad died, his cardiologist had assured Mother that Dad's serious heart condition was beyond repair. She never fully accepted his opinion and returned to the subject in conversations with me again and again, not just during those sad days after his death, but for many years afterward.

Mother told me that she was relieved, nonetheless, that Dad had died first. "He could not have stood it if I had died first," she said. I was surprised. I had always thought Dad was the stronger partner in their enduring relationship. But I later concluded that she was probably right. He would have been lost without her.

In the service at Temple Beth-El, Rabbi Schur extolled Dad's love of family and his many contributions to the temple, to the bar, and to the larger community. I was too sad to pay attention to the details of the service. After we returned home, Uncle Henry told me about his special relationship with his older brother. "Over more than forty years of practicing law together," he told me, "we never had an argument." He choked up when he made that remarkable statement.

Mother gave us Dad's Pontiac to make the drive back East. The three-day return trip served as a welcome time for me to sort out my emotions. The thick sense of loss never left me. But I also was able to recall early, happy memories of Dad and me: Dad playfully twiddling my ears when I was four, while he stood behind me for a family portrait in our living room; Dad reading the comics to me while I sat on his lap; Dad carrying me on his back up our stairs, making the clickety-clack sound of a horse.

After the war, when Dad and I played catch after dinner, he would sometimes tell me, in the authoritative voice of a professional baseball scout, "You really had something on that one." When I was a teenager, we spent less time together. Still, every year we had box seats for the state Golden Gloves finals in Will Rogers Coliseum. And in March 1955, we boarded the Rocket, the Rock Island Railroad's streamlined passenger train, for an overnight trip to Kansas City to attend the NCAA basketball finals. We stayed with Aunt Franny and Uncle Lawrence and their daughters, which was fun. And every night we watched the finals as the phenomenal center Bill Russell led the University of San Francisco basketball team to the first of two consecutive NCAA championships.

On the third day of our return trip East after Dad's funeral, we stopped in New Haven so that I could teach my seminar at Yale. I had missed the previous week's class. After I sat down in the classroom, I noticed an envelope addressed to me. I opened it to find a condolence card signed by every student in the seminar. Fighting back tears, I thanked them. It was the first of many such emotional moments for me that year when I thought about Dad.

CHAPTER 11

LAW PROFESSOR

New York Law School's main building, a nine-story gray stone edifice at the corner of Church and Worth Streets in Lower Manhattan, projects strength and stability. That image was reinforced when I met Dean Shapiro in his mahogany-paneled second-floor corner office during the first week of September 1975. But my tour of the remainder of the building, from the cavernous and poorly lit classrooms to the library that snaked around the top three floors, suggested that the law school was, in every physical and academic aspect, a work in progress.

When I stepped off a freight elevator to find my office on the fifth floor of the adjacent building, I entered an active construction zone with workmen and noise everywhere. My new neighbor, Robert Lancey, a blond, blue-eyed young Australian and recent Yale Law graduate, appeared as mystified by our surroundings as I was. We laughed nervously and wondered aloud whether we had carefully read the small print of our contracts.

At our first faculty meeting later that day, Dean Shapiro attempted to assuage our nerve-wracking introduction to the law school. He explained that the chaos we had witnessed was actually the first step in his grand plan to convert NYLS into a modern facility with newly constructed classrooms and faculty offices. He then introduced the new faculty members. I became

"Professor Simon," a title that sounded odd, but one that I was more than willing to accept.

After the brief faculty meeting, the first hand I shook was that of Professor Milton Silverman, the chairman of the appointments committee who had invited me to interview for a faculty position at NYLS. Milton, an honors graduate of NYU Law School, sported a magnificent handlebar mustache and could have stepped out of one of the mysteries of his literary hero, Sherlock Holmes. In fact, he was a passionate Sherlockian, meeting every month with fellow devotees of Arthur Conan Doyle to untangle one of the author's mysteries.

Milton introduced me to Professor Cyril Means Jr., a Harvard Law graduate and the school's senior constitutional law professor. Cyril possessed a first-rate legal mind. He had published two groundbreaking law review articles supporting a woman's constitutional right to choose an abortion that Associate Justice Harry Blackmun cited in his 1973 opinion for the US Supreme Court in *Roe v. Wade*. Like his best friend, Milton, he was a larger-than-life character. In addition to Cyril and Milton, I met a coterie of young recruits, including Robert Blecker, an intense twenty-six-year-old Harvard Law graduate who had worked as an assistant to the city's special narcotics prosecutor, Maurice Nadjari.

Later that day, I was informed that the four of us—Cyril, Milton, Robert, and I—would become the school's appointments committee. It turned out to be a plum assignment, because Cyril and Milton, both gourmands and wine connoisseurs, scouted out the best restaurants in the cities hosting the AALS winter meetings, from Tucson to St. Louis to Chicago. To add to our enjoyment, Milton and Cyril were world-class raconteurs, guaranteeing that each dinner we shared at the AALS meetings was not only a feast but also a rollicking good time.

Blecker, who became one of my closest friends on the faculty, did not share my enthusiasm for the sumptuous meals. His priorities were of a different order. As his sleepy hotel roommate, I sadly learned that he was a physical fitness fanatic who rose early every morning to complete an elaborate series of strenuous and noisy exercises.

* * * * *

Dean Shapiro kept his promise that I would teach a large class in constitutional law as well as seminars on the modern Supreme Court and legal journalism. The required course in constitutional law was the most challenging. Beginning at eight o'clock every Tuesday and Thursday evening, I attempted to make the dense textbook materials interesting to a class of ninety evening students for an hour and twenty minutes. This was no small task, since the students had already spent eight hours at their day jobs. I decided to lean heavily on my ability, honed over seven years as a journalist, to weave a sustained narrative that would, I hoped, bring the constitutional cases alive in the classroom.

The first case assigned was *Marbury v. Madison*, the decision by the great chief justice John Marshall that established the Supreme Court's authority to declare an act of Congress unconstitutional. Before analyzing Marshall's opinion, I discussed the historical and political forces at work that had brought the case to the Court. I told the story of the so-called "midnight judges" that President John Adams had appointed in the last hours of his presidency, including the commission for Justice of the Peace William Marbury, the plaintiff in the case. Marbury, like the other men who received commissions, was a loyal member of Adams's Federalist Party. The defendant in the case was the new secretary of state, James Madison, appointed by President Thomas Jefferson, the man who had defeated Adams in the 1800 presidential election. Madison refused to deliver Marbury's commission.

Once I had provided the historical context for the case, the intricacies of Marshall's opinion declaring a congressional statute unconstitutional became more understandable to my students. It was a technique I would use throughout the many years that I taught constitutional law. With experience, I learned to calibrate the length and depth of each class discussion depending on the importance and difficulty of the legal issue.

The quality of each class discussion depended on my students, and one of them, John Delmar, was particularly adept at discussing complicated legal issues with sophistication and insight. John had graduated from Harvard College and was then writing book reviews for a Greenwich Village publication. His family pedigree also stuck in my memory. He was the son of Kenny Delmar, a star of the *Fred Allen Show*, one of our family's favorite radio programs in the late 1940s. John's father had been the voice of Senator

Claghorn, a windbag southern senator and one of the unforgettable characters in a feature called "Allen's Alley."

The most agonizing and disagreeable part of my job was grading the three-hour exams at the end of the semester. The blue books were labeled by number to conceal the identity of each student. I felt that I should give students the benefit of the doubt on every question, since their grade for the course depended on what they wrote during those three hours. The only discretion allowed was the bump of a half grade—for example, from C to C+—for class discussion. If a written answer seemed knowledgeable but incomplete, I erred on the generous side.

After grading the first-semester exams, I realized that I could not always identify the top students in the class by who wrote the best exam. While there was a direct correlation between John Delmar's class discussion and his final exam paper, which received an A, that was not the case with a student who was a physicist by day at Bell Laboratories in New Jersey. Even more than Delmar, he consistently made thought-provoking comments in class discussion. But this student, so verbally agile and provocative in class, received a grade of C on the anonymously graded three-hour final exam. When we met to discuss his exam, he was both distraught and embarrassed by his mediocre grade. He subsequently dropped out of law school, and, I presume, enjoyed an outstanding scientific career. The most startling revelation that first semester was the identity of the student who wrote a brilliant exam paper and received the only A+. He had not uttered a word in class.

✦ ✦ ✦ ✦ ✦

The modern Supreme Court and legal journalism seminars were relatively easy to teach. Unlike the required course in constitutional law, both seminars were electives, so students chose to take them because of their interest in the subjects. Both seminars, moreover, followed the format of the seminars I had taken from Fred Rodell at Yale Law School, although I had changed the title of the Rodell writing seminar to "Legal Journalism."

For the modern Supreme Court seminar, which focused primarily on civil rights and liberties decisions, I added many Court decisions of the Warren and Burger Courts that had been handed down after my law school graduation. I had already taught the seminar to undergraduates at Yale and law students at Hofstra, so I entered each class session with more confidence than when I faced the ninety evening students in constitutional law. I also arranged for the class to attend an oral argument at the US Supreme Court and meet with a justice afterward, as Rodell had done for my class at Yale.

For my modern Supreme Court students, spending a day at the Supreme Court was invariably the highlight of the semester and guaranteed a closed-out enrollment every year that I taught the seminar. That unforgettable experience began as soon as we were seated in the magnificent ornate courtroom and stared at the justices whose opinions we had discussed in class. We sometimes were lucky enough to hear an important argument on a First Amendment issue involving free speech or the free exercise of religion. But the justices could electrify the courtroom with their barrage of questions to attorneys even on what appeared to be a dreadfully dull case, such as the interpretation of an obscure provision of a federal statute. Ironically, justices who wrote some of the most important decisions of the modern Supreme Court era, including Harry Blackmun and William Brennan Jr., asked few questions at oral argument. But others, often former law professors, such as Justices Ruth Bader Ginsburg and Antonin Scalia, peppered attorneys with questions.

Over the four decades of our visits to the Court, my classes met with justices who spanned the ideological spectrum, from liberal justices such as Ruth Bader Ginsburg, Elena Kagan, and David Souter to the conservatives, including Samuel Alito and Antonin Scalia. We also met with those considered closer to the center—Justices Stephen Breyer, Anthony Kennedy, Lewis Powell Jr., Sandra Day O'Connor, and Potter Stewart. These discussions lasted for about an hour and we always followed them up with a group photo.

I prepped the students on questions they could ask as well as those that were off-limits, such as issues likely to be argued before the Court. The justices were always cordial and often candid in sharing their views of the law and the Court's role as final arbiter of the Constitution. My favorite answer to a student's question was by Justice Sandra Day O'Connor. When asked to explain her reasoning in an opinion written fifteen years earlier, she replied, laughing, "Well, I can't. I don't remember the details of every opinion I have written, and certainly not one I wrote fifteen years ago." The most erudite member of the Court to meet with us was Justice David Souter, who became a good friend of mine shortly after his appointment to the Court by President George H.W. Bush in 1990. He answered every student's question, whether sophisticated or naive, with such an extraordinary grasp of the relevant constitutional law and history that it seemed as if he were reading from a prepared text.

Over the years, we met with justices appointed by both Republican and Democratic presidents, including Eisenhower (Potter Stewart), Nixon (Lewis Powell Jr.), Reagan (Sandra Day O'Connor, Antonin Scalia, and Anthony Kennedy), George H.W. Bush (David Souter), Clinton (Ruth Bader Ginsburg and Stephen Breyer), George W. Bush (Samuel Alito), and Obama (Elena Kagan).

An added incentive for me in arranging meetings with the justices was that many of them also agreed to be interviewed for my books on the Court. I mailed signed copies of my books to the justices, who unfailingly sent me gracious thank-you notes and, after reading the books, offered generous commentary. My recorded interviews with justices for my books as well as their letters to me are now at the Dolph Briscoe Center for American History at the University of Texas at Austin as part of the Briscoe Center's collection of my professional papers.

I taught the legal journalism seminar as a workshop, assigning the students weekly papers on legal topics, ranging from profiles of judges, lawyers, and law professors to features on Supreme Court decisions and state and local judicial proceedings. For their final papers, the students were required to write a longer paper on a complex legal doctrine. Once a semester, I invited a guest editor to critique the students' papers. My former *Time* colleagues Joe Ferrer and Carey Winfrey served as guest editors, as did William Zinsser, a superb reporter for the *New York Herald Tribune* for many years, whose book *On Writing Well*, which I assigned to my students, became a classic guide on nonfiction writing.

The most popular assignment for my legal journalism students required them to observe the city's arraignment court, where they witnessed the ugly underside of the criminal justice system. They observed a steady stream of bedraggled defendants, mostly Black or Hispanic young men, brought from jail before a judge. The defendants were formally advised by the judge of the charges of minor crimes against them and asked to enter a plea. They were represented by the city's public defenders, always weighed down by overwhelming caseloads, who spent a few minutes with each client. It was our criminal justice system at its worst, but it provoked my students' most inspired papers of the semester.

✦ ✦ ✦ ✦ ✦

My second book, *The Judge*, published in February 1976, was a main selection of the Lawyers' Literary Club, but it received scant public notice. This was disappointing but not surprising. McKay's publicity department had done little to promote the book beyond a press release, modest publicity, and arrangements for a few guest appearances on radio and television shows in New York City.

I was furious, but felt virtually helpless to vent my fury with the publisher. My McKay editor, Jim Wade, as well as the director of publicity, who had both been so supportive of my first book, had left the company after it was purchased by the British firm in December 1974. When I called the publicity department to complain, the young woman who answered the phone told me briefly, but with frosty finality, that the publisher was disappointed in initial sales and had no further plans to promote the book.

The publisher was not entirely to blame for the book's poor sales and nonexistent splash in the media. In retrospect, I wished that I had made clear to the reader that I was covering the four months that I sat in Judge Leff's courtroom, rather than condensing the action into a single week. Moreover, I should have used Judge Leff's name, as he was willing to permit, providing pseudonyms only for defendants and the judge Leff had accused of dishonesty. In that way, I could have shielded myself from lawsuits but avoided any suggestion among readers or reviewers that I had taken liberties with the facts.

I was still proud of the book, which, in my opinion, made an important contribution to the literature on the criminal justice system. It offered a sober, provocative, and accurate view of the state's criminal justice system through the lens of a real judge. And if the book failed to garner public attention, the author's photo alone, taken by my friend Mike Spring, was worth a special place in the family archives. There I am, looking content but extremely young even with my new mustache, stooping down next to the family dog, Touchy. And Touchy is standing at attention in elegant profile, as if he had just been awarded "Best in Show" at the prestigious Westminster Kennel Club's annual canine competition.

CHAPTER 12

THE DOUGLAS BIOGRAPHY

Never a brooder, I began exploring ideas for my next book within a week of *The Judge*'s publication. My attention quickly focused on Supreme Court Justice William O. Douglas, the iconoclastic westerner who seemed to be in the news more frequently than all of his judicial colleagues combined. In 1965, when the justice was sixty-seven, he met twenty-three-year-old Cathleen Heffernan in a Portland, Oregon, restaurant where she worked as a cocktail waitress to pay for her college tuition. His marriage to her, his fourth, made sensational newspaper headlines. Scandal never seemed to bother Douglas, whose divorce from his first wife in 1952 was soon followed by marriages to and divorces from two much younger women.

My interest in doing a book on Douglas went far beyond his unorthodox marital history. By the time he had been appointed to the Court by President Franklin D. Roosevelt in 1939, he had earned a reputation as a brilliant legal thinker, law professor, and New Dealer. Once he was on the Court, Douglas was frequently overshadowed by his liberal colleague Justice Hugo Black. But no one doubted Douglas's considerable contribution to the jurisprudence of the modern Supreme Court, especially in the field of civil rights and liberties. It was Douglas, for example, who developed a theory of the constitutional right to privacy more than a decade before the Court majority recognized it. Douglas wrote the Court's opinion in *Griswold v. Connecticut* in 1965 establishing the right, which was followed eight years later by *Roe v. Wade* extending the right to a pregnant woman's decision to have an abortion in the first two trimesters of her pregnancy.

It seemed remarkable to me that there had not been a full-length biography of Douglas. The only significant published work was the first volume of his autobiography, *Go East, Young Man*, which covered his pre-Court years, from his early life growing up poor in Yakima, Washington, to his rise as an academic star on the faculties at Columbia and Yale Law Schools, and, finally, his appointment by FDR to be chairman of the Securities and Exchange Commission. Although *Go East, Young Man*, became a best seller, reviewers suggested that it suffered the fate of many autobiographies of famous men: the justice had presented a rosier picture of his pre-Court life and achievements than was justified by the factual record.

I was convinced that the time was ripe for a major Douglas biography and quickly began to work on a book proposal. By early March, I had sent a proposal to Wendy Weil, who, in turn, gave it to the senior partner in her agency, Julian Bach. Julian loved my proposal and immediately sent it to Simon Michael Bessie, the senior vice president at Harper and Row. Bessie, sixty, had built a reputation over several decades as an astute editor of nonfiction books. His list of authors included Elie Wiesel, Alexander Solzhenitsyn, and Theodore White, who won a Pulitzer Prize for *The Making of the President, 1960*. Bach called to report that Bessie had offered an advance of $25,000 for me to write the Douglas biography for Harper and Row. I immediately accepted the offer. Within a week, I was invited to Bessie's suite of offices, where he and Brooks Thomas, the president of the publishing house, greeted me enthusiastically and toasted my book's anticipated commercial success and literary honors.

After the meeting with Bessie and Thomas, I was giddy with visions of literary fame. But now I had to write the book. My reporter's instinct told me that I should make contact as soon as possible with Justice Douglas and his wife, Cathy, who was a lawyer in a large, respected Washington firm. I called the justice in his chambers at the Court but was told that he would not see me. I had better luck when I called his wife at her law office. She agreed to see me, and I was soon on a plane to Washington.

Cathy Douglas, a slender, attractive blond, greeted me cordially and spoke with a sophisticated assurance that belied her humble origins growing up in Portland, Oregon. With my notebook out, she provided a long list of the justice's colleagues, clerks, friends, and family members that I should interview. Her list included Douglas's sister, Martha, who lived in Chicago; his friend Kay Kershaw, who ran a dude ranch in the Cascade Mountains next to Douglas's cabin; and, if I could find him, Douglas's son, Bill Jr. She told me that Bill Jr. lived somewhere on the West Coast but had no known address. "He is the world's oldest hippie," she said with obvious affection.

When she completed her list, I asked, "Could I begin my interviews with you?" She politely demurred, saying I should start by interviewing the men and women on the list she had provided. I sought her assistance in interviewing her husband, admitting that he had rejected my initial request. She was noncommittal but advised me to call his office periodically to renew my request for an interview.

Before I left Washington, I arranged to interview former US Supreme Court justice Abe Fortas, who was Douglas's closest friend and confidant. The two men had met at Yale Law School when Fortas was Douglas's best student and served as editor-in-chief of the school's law journal. Fortas later held several high-ranking legal positions in FDR's New Deal administration and was a founding partner in one of Washington's most prestigious law firms. In 1965, President Lyndon Johnson appointed him to the Supreme Court, and three years later he nominated him to succeed Earl Warren as chief justice of the United States. But Fortas's nomination to be chief justice met with a buzz saw of opposition from Senate Republicans. After *Life* magazine reported that Fortas had delivered a series of lucrative outside lectures while on the Court, paid for by a foundation funded by a man then under investigation by the Securities and Exchange Commission, his nomination was doomed. As the pressure mounted, Fortas not only withdrew his nomination to become chief justice but resigned from the Court, a decision that he made against the advice of Justice Douglas.

When I met Fortas in his law office in March 1976, he spoke quietly but with great admiration and affection for Douglas as a law professor, jurist, and devoted friend. I was grateful for his candid recollections. Just as important, I was confident that his willingness to sit down for an interview with me would become known to other close friends of Douglas as well as to Douglas himself and would lead to more valuable interviews.

After I returned to West Nyack, I called Mother to ask if she would do research for my new book on Douglas. I thought she would enjoy the work, but I also expected that it would serve as a welcome intellectual diversion to take her mind off of Dad's absence. She enthusiastically agreed. I suggested that she plan two research trips.

First, I asked her to travel to Independence, Missouri, to work in the Harry S. Truman Library to look for any letters or other references to Douglas while Truman was president. There were widespread rumors in the late 1940s that Douglas was considering leaving the Court to run for vice president on a ticket headed by Truman and, later, to run for president.

The second trip that I proposed for Mother was to the LBJ Presidential Library in Austin, where I wanted her to interview Johnson's widow, Lady Bird Johnson. Douglas and Johnson had been friends since both had come to Washington in the 1930s as enthusiastic supporters of President Franklin Roosevelt's New Deal. I assumed that they and their wives had socialized, so I wanted to know if Lady Bird, who had attended the University of Texas at the same time as Mother, could recall any parties or dinners that the two men and their spouses may have attended. I told Mother that I would make arrangements for the interview. After my book was published, Mother was the subject of a feature story in the *Fort Worth Star-Telegram*, accompanied by an attractive photo of her, in which she described her research at the Truman library and her interview with Lady Bird Johnson.

• • • • •

My month-long odyssey to the upper Midwest and West in the summer of 1976 began where Douglas was born in 1898—the tiny rural hamlet of Maine in northwestern Minnesota near the North Dakota border. I pored over church records at Maine's Presbyterian church where the Reverend William

Douglas, the future justice's father, had preached. Afterward, I stood next to the Reverend Douglas's grave in the church cemetery and tried to imagine life in that desolate, windswept community at the turn of the century.

I then drove my rental car ten miles southwest to the county seat, Fergus Falls, and, to my delight, discovered the Fergus Falls Historical Society. In the society's archives I found an issue of the *Fergus Falls Weekly Journal*, dated October 16, 1898, in which the Reverend and Mrs. Douglas announced the birth of a son, William Orville Douglas. Other articles in the same issue placed Douglas's birth in historical perspective: members of the Chippewa tribe had fired on US troops at nearby Leech Lake, while in Paris, France, a commission was negotiating terms of a peace agreement between the United States and Spain to end the Spanish-American War.

After returning my rental car at the Minneapolis–St. Paul Airport, I boarded a plane for Chicago, where I interviewed Douglas's sister, Martha. She fondly remembered her sickly, high-strung, brilliant younger brother, telling me how they had been cared for by their widowed mother in Yakima, Washington. From Chicago, I flew to Washington state, interviewing Justice Douglas's childhood friends in Yakima and his fraternity brothers at Whitman College in Walla Walla.

My most unpredictable and important interviews occurred later, as a result of my three-day stay at Kay Kershaw's Double K Dude Ranch, next to Douglas's summer cabin high in the Cascade Mountains. It rained for two straight days at the Double K, which meant that I could not ride one of Kershaw's beautiful horses. Even more disappointing, Kay and her partner, Isabelle Lynn, were extremely protective of Douglas's privacy and offered no insights into their longtime neighbor's character or their friendship with him. And despite several requests, Kay refused to tell me where I could find Bill Jr., although Cathy Douglas had told me that she knew.

On my last day at her dude ranch, Kay suggested that I take a hike up an especially steep trail into the Cascades. I spent the entire day on one of those magnificent mountains. When I returned, I enthusiastically recounted to Kay my first day as a mountain climber. She listened with obvious pleasure, satisfied that I had successfully completed her Cascade rite of passage. Before I went to sleep that night, I asked her again if she might tell me where I could find Bill Jr. She scribbled a phone number on a notepad. When I called the number, Bill Jr. answered. He was in Portland, Oregon, and agreed to meet me in a downtown bar the next evening.

Anticipating my interview with Bill Jr., I was concerned that the sight of my tape recorder or notebook would likely inhibit him. The tape recorder, therefore, remained in my hotel room and my notebook stayed in my coat pocket during our extraordinary three-hour interview. Although Bill Jr. was slightly shorter than his father, he bore a striking resemblance to him. He had the same fair complexion, pale blue eyes, and upturned nose. Although we had just met, he was relaxed, trusting, and willing to share his personal memories of growing up in Washington, DC, as the son of a famous Supreme Court justice.

The cameras, it seemed to Bill Jr., were always trained on the "perfect" family of Justice Douglas. The reality was depressingly different. To Bill Jr. and his older sister, Millie, their father was always nervous, in a hurry, and unapproachable. If they had a problem, they sought the counsel of their beloved mother, Mildred. School for the son of a brilliant father was a nightmare. A lackadaisical student, young Bill Jr. had hated school, recalling that he had sat on the curb and cried every morning before boarding the school bus. Even on the rare occasion when his father spent special time with him, the experience was usually disappointing. When the justice, a naturalist and lifelong hiker, took him on a local trail, he was always several strides ahead, with Bill Jr. desperately struggling to keep up.

Toward the end of my interview with Bill Jr., I asked, "Should I try to get in touch with your older sister, Millie?" I assumed that I would have to communicate by letter, since Millie was a schoolteacher who lived in England.

"Oh, you have to talk to Millie," he said emphatically. "Talk to my sister, and you'll know my father. They are exactly alike."

He then gave me an astounding piece of good news. At that moment, Millie was vacationing in the Douglas family's cabin in the Wallowa Mountains in eastern Oregon.

"Do you have a phone number for her?" I asked, attempting not to sound too eager.

"Afraid not," he replied. "There's no phone in the cabin." But he did give me directions on how to find the Douglas cabin.

After I said good night to Bill Jr., I rushed to my rental car, whipped out my notebook, and furiously wrote notes on our extraordinary conversation. When I returned to my hotel, I made plans to check out early the next morning and drive across the state in the hope of finding Millie Douglas at her family's cabin in the Wallowa Mountains.

Driving most of the day, I finally began the ascent on the narrow road that took me up the mountain in search of the Douglas cabin. When I arrived, I immediately recognized Millie from photos. Dressed in jeans, she had curly dark brown hair and piercing brown eyes. I introduced myself and told her that I had spent the previous evening with her brother, who had told me that she was on vacation at the family cabin and urged me to speak to her. Millie did not seem the least bit upset by my intrusion.

Without hesitation, she invited me to sit down on a bench outside her cabin for an interview. She did not mind if I took notes. Her memories of her father reinforced the image that Bill Jr. had painted in such striking detail. Although she resembled her mother in appearance, she admitted that she was the mirror image of her father in spirit. Proud and tough-minded, she confessed to a temper to match her father's and a rebellious streak to boot. Unlike her brother, she challenged her father. "Once he took out a belt and said that he would hit me if I didn't do what he said," she recalled. "I said, 'You wouldn't dare,' and he didn't."

As a teenager, Millie told me, she had engaged in unspoken competition with her father. As an example, she said that she became an expert horseback rider, much better than her father. "He was a terrible rider," she told me. "He had no respect for the horse. He rode like he drove a car, with his foot down on the accelerator until he got where he was going."

She was obviously enjoying herself as our interview progressed, narrating each story about her relationship with her father with gusto. When our long interview came to an end, she mentioned that she had kept a thick packet of family letters, including many her father had written to her and to her mother. "Would you be interested in reading the letters?" she asked. I did my best to reply casually that, yes, I would be interested in reading the letters. I knew intuitively that Douglas's personal letters would provide valuable insights into his character as well as his relationship with his wife and children. Millie wrote down my home address and promised to send me the Douglas family letters after she returned to England.

As I drove down the mountain, I reveled in my unexpected good fortune. Only two days ago, I had had no idea how to contact Bill Douglas Jr., and assumed that his sister, Millie, was in England. Within the past twenty-four hours, I had conducted lengthy interviews with both of Justice Douglas's adult children in two of the most revealing conversations of my professional career. A month later, I received a treasure trove of Douglas family letters in a package that Millie had mailed from England. Wow!

When I boarded a plane at the Portland, Oregon, airport for my return flight to New York at the end of August 1976, my notebooks were filled with insights into Justice Douglas's background and character provided by his children, Bill Jr. and Millie, as well as his sister, Martha. As I had anticipated, the family letters Millie sent to me from England were equally valuable. Many were written by the justice's first wife, Mildred Douglas, Millie and Bill Jr.'s mother, whose letters to them confirmed their descriptions of her as loving, gentle, and sensitive to their feelings. In contrast, Justice Douglas's letters, scrawled in barely legible handwriting, were short, to the point, and devoid of emotion.

After I turned in my NYLS grades in early June 1977, I arranged interviews in Washington with Mercedes Davidson, Justice Douglas's second wife, and Joanie Martin, his third. The justice had met Mercedes in 1950 when he was still married to Mildred. She was the glamorous and high-spirited wife of a prominent member of President Truman's administration at the time. When I interviewed Mercedes, she still expressed fondness for the justice. After they were married in 1954, they seemed to be well matched in temperament and energy, traveling widely and enjoying Washington's busy social life. But eventually the justice's restlessness and roving eye ended their marriage.

While still married to Mercedes, he met Joanie Martin, a twenty-year-old undergraduate at tiny Allegheny College in Pennsylvania, where he delivered a lecture. The next year she interviewed him for her senior thesis on his jurisprudence. She became Mrs. William O. Douglas in 1963. "I was walking around with this enormous name," she told me. "I didn't have any personality anymore." In the spring of 1964, less than a year after they were married, Joanie left. A year later, the justice met Cathleen Heffernan, who soon became his fourth wife.

Over a two-year period, culminating in my interview with the justice in May 1978, a fuller picture of Douglas came into focus. I interviewed Douglas's childhood friends, college fraternity brothers, law school students, New Deal colleagues, law clerks, and brethren on the US Supreme Court. They consistently described him as a man with inexhaustible energy, whether he was climbing mountains, leading long hikes, or writing a series of travel books that might take his reader to the edge of a jagged Himalayan peak in one chapter followed in the next by a lecture on the inequities of the land tenancy system.

Among Douglas's close male friends, he was a practical joker, hard drinker, and fabulous teller of exaggerated tales. Douglas's first three wives loved him but could not keep him home or happy. His law clerks both admired and feared him. Other justices considered him to be one of the most brilliant members of the Court. But they also felt that he often squandered his brilliance in opinions that were written in haste, so that his restless intellect could move on to his next project.

✦ ✦ ✦ ✦ ✦

As I sat in a pew in Washington's National Presbyterian Church on January 23, 1980, to mourn the death of Justice William O. Douglas, my thoughts returned to my conversation with his secretary less than two years earlier. "He controls every situation," she said. And, indeed, he had laid out specific instructions for his memorial service, including a rendition of the old hymn "Shall We Gather at the River?" that he remembered his parents singing when he was a little boy. He would have preferred that "The Lord's Prayer" be sung by a cowboy he knew out West, but the cowboy had died before him, and so the mourners heard the rich baritone voice of Master Sergeant William F. Kugel, a soloist with the US Army Chorus.

Douglas's memorial service had the trappings of a state occasion. President Jimmy Carter and Vice President Walter Mondale sat in the front row. Nearby were the secretary of state, leading members of both houses of Congress, and every member of the US Supreme Court.

Based on the research for my Douglas biography, I could not help thinking of the many ironies suggested by the solemn memorial service. The justice had asked to be remembered as a religious person, a Presbyterian, like his father, the Reverend Douglas. But, unlike his father, Justice Douglas had been married four times, three more than the Reverend Douglas would have approved of. And the justice had little use for dogma, whether religious or political, and never needed a church pulpit from which to deliver his sermons.

William O. Douglas preached his liberal beliefs and hopes for mankind in his many books, on his treks through the wilderness, and, most of all, in his judicial opinions as a member of the US Supreme Court. Throughout his thirty-six years on the Court, Justice Douglas had promoted his causes of human dignity and enrichment, most often pinning his aspirations to the tangible guarantees of the Bill of Rights. His libertarian judicial opinions were calculated, by design, "to take the government off the backs of the people." For Douglas, that meant full constitutional protections for all Americans, including the despised, the defenseless, and the penniless. His controversial ideas, expressed in his books, speeches, and judicial opinions—and his multiple marriages to progressively younger women—enraged his many enemies and inspired four failed attempts by Congress to impeach him.

His idealistic public image was undermined repeatedly by his private conduct. He could be cruel or indifferent to his wives and children, cold to his law clerks, and devious with judicial colleagues. He was easier to admire than to like.

But no one in the National Presbyterian Church on that damp, frigid January day could doubt his profound impact on modern America. "Because of Bill Douglas," declared Clark Clifford, a former secretary of defense, "each of us is freer, safer, and stronger."

◆ ◆ ◆ ◆ ◆

Douglas's death in late January posed problems for my work in progress. Shortly after the memorial service, press reports circulated that the second volume of Douglas's autobiography, covering his years on the Supreme Court, had been finished before his death, and that Random House, his publisher, expected to have books in stores before the end of the year. Harper and Row wanted me to complete my manuscript so that my book could be published at the same time as Douglas's. Even if I could meet my publisher's deadline, my book was likely to come off a distant second best in sales competing with the justice's autobiography. He was a legendary public official whose books, including the first volume of his autobiography, had often been best sellers.

Meanwhile, my relationship with my editor, Simon Michael Bessie, had cooled since our first meeting in the spring of 1976, when we had toasted my book's future success in his suite. Except for receiving a newly published book from his list of distinguished authors every holiday season, I rarely heard from him. And while I rushed to complete my manuscript after Douglas's funeral, he informed me that a young assistant editor would be taking over the responsibility for bringing my book to publication. I never received an explanation from Bessie as to why he had handed my manuscript off to a junior colleague, but it shook my confidence that Harper and Row was fully committed to the success of my book.

I nonetheless forged ahead with final revisions and additions to my manuscript, including reflections on Justice Douglas's memorial service. The publication date was set for late November.

• • • • •

After my biography, *Independent Journey: The Life of William O. Douglas*, was published, I could not have asked for better reviews:

"A superb portrait. Engagingly written and profusely documented . . . corrects, complements, and supplements the self-portrait." *Washington Post Book World*

"Excellent . . . a far more probing yet balanced picture of Justice Douglas than appears in any recent work." *New York Times Book Review*

"Simon brilliantly captures the essential contradictions of his elusive subject [and] provides a sophisticated analysis of the broader contexts of Douglas's life . . . a human, intimate, and stylish account." *Detroit News*

"The best work written on the Supreme Court in recent years . . . a remarkable book about a unique man." *Dallas Morning News*

I was particularly pleased with the reviews in the *Washington Post* and the *New York Times*, because they were written by prolific authors who were also prominent academics. The review appearing on the front page of *Washington Post Book World* was written by a Princeton professor, Alpheus T. Mason, the nation's preeminent political scientist specializing in constitutional law and the authorized biographer of Justice Louis Brandeis. The *Times* review was written by Harvard law professor Alan M. Dershowitz, the author of numerous books on law written for both academic and general readers.

The terrific reviews were not matched by comparably great sales of my book. As I had feared, sales lagged far behind those of the second volume of Justice Douglas's autobiography. This was particularly galling to me since reviewers of both books considered my biography superior to Douglas's autobiography. The reason for the discrepancy in sales was not difficult to understand. Douglas had been a famous Supreme Court justice for more than three decades; I was just a law professor who had written a critically acclaimed biography.

My frustration was compounded by tepid support from the publicity department at Harper and Row. Aside from an ad in the *New York Times* with quotes from the excellent reviews of my book, my publisher was devoting virtually no resources to promoting it. I sought an explanation. By the time of the book's publication, my original editor, Bessie, was no longer involved, and my junior editor had no clout. I therefore called a senior member in the publicity department at Harper and Row and pleaded for more support for my book. He was sympathetic but candidly told me that he had been given a small budget to promote my book. There were no plans for additional advertising, and my scheduled interviews would be confined to New York City and an overnight stay in Washington, DC.

Despite lack of support from Harper and Row, I had many reasons to be satisfied with the Douglas biography, beginning with the stellar reviews. I was also gratified by praise from former Supreme Court justice Abe Fortas, Douglas's closest friend and confidant, who said that my biography perfectly captured Douglas's contradictions as well as his greatness. Fortas had expressed his praise for my book in a private conversation with Mercedes Davidson, Douglas's second wife, who had passed his comment on to me. *Independent Journey* won the annual book award given by the American Society of Legal Writers (Scribes). Paperback rights were bought by Penguin Books.

The most famous admirer of my book was Bob Woodward, the *Washington Post* reporter who, with Carl Bernstein, had exposed the Watergate scandal that had brought down President Richard Nixon. After my Douglas biography was published, Woodward called me to say how much he liked the book. He also said that he appreciated the citations in my source notes to his runaway best seller *The Brethren* (written with coauthor Scott Armstrong), which provided an inside account of the rivalries and infighting on the Supreme Court. *The Brethren* had received many scathing reviews from academics as well as critics in major newspapers, including the *New York Times*. These reviewers were virtually unanimous in questioning the credibility of Woodward's sources, concluding that he only spoke to secondary sources, i.e., law clerks, not to the justices, who they assumed would protect the confidentiality of their deliberations.

The Brethren's critics were wrong. I knew they were wrong, because one of my sources, Justice Potter Stewart, confirmed in our telephone conversation that Woodward's reporting on the justices' deliberations was accurate. In asking Stewart to vouch for the accuracy of Woodward's reporting, I adopted an old journalism technique. I told him that I did not expect him to tell me directly that Woodward's reporting was correct. Instead, I requested that he listen to the passages in my manuscript that were based on Woodward's reporting and to interrupt my reading to say "no" if any passage was inaccurate. Stewart remained silent throughout my reading. I then knew that I could rely on Woodward's reporting. Years later, when Woodward's sources were revealed, I learned the reason that Stewart could speak with authority on Woodward's reporting: he was one of Woodward's sources.

I felt confident in citing Woodward's book in my source notes covering the same Court deliberations after that conversation. In gratitude for my citations to his book, Woodward said that he would be happy to return the favor. We met for drinks the next time I was in Washington, and I reminded him of his offer. He then agreed to contribute a "blurb" (i.e., a quotation) for the paperback edition of *Independent Journey*. Woodward's quote appears on the cover of the Penguin paperback edition: "Clearly the best book on this complex and many-sided Justice . . . far superior to Douglas's own memoirs."

CHAPTER 13

SABBATICAL IN ENGLAND

During the four years that I worked on the Douglas biography, my career at New York Law School thrived. My student evaluations, beginning with my first year of full-time teaching, were among the best of the entire faculty, including those of the most popular tenured professors. My ratings from tenured faculty members who had observed my classes matched the excellent student evaluations. And Dean Shapiro had become a great supporter of mine. He had given me a 10 percent raise in annual salary, praised my teaching, and encouraged my work-in-progress, the biography of Justice Douglas.

With my standing at NYLS secure, Marcia and I decided that it was time to try to have another baby. We were aware of the risks. Marcia was thirty-seven years old, not the ideal age to bear a child. The babies of several of our good friends had been born with either physical or mental disabilities.

By September 1976, after I had returned from my trip to the upper Midwest and West for my Douglas biography, our concerns about having a third child, though not eliminated, had diminished. Marcia had heard about a newly available procedure, amniocentesis, in which the extraction of amniotic fluid from a pregnant woman could determine certain genetic disorders of a fetus. The procedure was available at a clinic in Westchester County and, if a pregnant woman qualified, the procedure was paid for by the March of Dimes Foundation. If Marcia became pregnant, she was likely to qualify for the free procedure because of her age.

And, to our delight, Marcia became pregnant almost immediately. She was told by her obstetrician, Dr. Burt Droga, that she could expect to give birth in mid-June. She then contacted the amniocentesis testing center in Westchester and learned that she qualified for the free procedure. The results of the test revealed no birth defects in the fetus.

For her entire pregnancy, Marcia was virtually pain free. She was not just happy but buoyant in anticipation of our third child. And so was I.

In the late evening of June 2, 1977, we were in bed watching a television production of Thornton Wilder's *Our Town* when Marcia felt the first sharp pains. By eleven o'clock, her contractions had become more frequent. Although the baby was not due for another three weeks, we assumed that Marcia was going to give birth *soon*. Marcia hurriedly packed her suitcase. We woke our kids up and dropped them off at our neighbors, Althea and Ed Reiff.

The streets were deserted when I made the ten-minute drive to Nyack Hospital. Dr. Droga met us there and led us to the obstetrics section, where Marcia prepared to give birth. Dr. Droga checked on her periodically throughout the night while she continued to have severe contractions. Despite my best efforts to comfort and help her cope with them, she was in intense pain. Finally, around 10 a.m., Dr. Droga told me to meet him and Marcia in the delivery room. Shortly after arriving in the delivery room, I watched with awe as Marcia gave birth to our baby girl, Sara Richelle Simon, with her middle name honoring the memory of my father. It was a thrilling sight, unlike any that I had witnessed in my life.

✦ ✦ ✦ ✦ ✦

In my second year at NYLS, I was scheduled to teach an "Introduction to Law" course at the City College of New York in the law school's first joint program with an undergraduate institution. The students in the program were carefully selected for their aptitude and interest in pursuing a legal career. The program proved to be only partially successful, since the top students, upon graduation, were not obligated to attend NYLS. My best student from City College attended Yale Law School. The program did, however, produce a number of very bright and successful NYLS graduates, including Meryl Lieberman, who became a founding partner of an insurance defense law firm that opened offices across the country. She later became a member of the law school's board of trustees.

The greatest disappointment for me in the CCNY program was the failure of one of my most promising students, a young Black man named Michael, who had been admitted to the program despite a history of drug addiction, to complete law school. In my class, he was outstanding, demonstrating a lively and incisive mind. He dropped out of NYLS after his first year and later called to apologize for disappointing me. I encouraged him to continue his legal education, but, as far as I know, he never did.

My student evaluations at CCNY and NYLS were consistently excellent and, after my second year, I was promoted to associate professor. A year later, at Dean Shapiro's initiative, I was put forward for promotion to full professor with tenure. My teaching evaluations, two published books, and my work-in-progress, the Douglas biography, were certainly factors in my favor. But there was also a political consideration. Shapiro's bold reforms to revitalize the institution were opposed by a vocal minority of tenured faculty members who complained that he was moving too fast, ignoring them, and generally favoring young faculty members like me. The dean thought I deserved tenure, but he also looked forward to my support on critical decisions made by the tenured faculty.

While my application for tenure was under consideration, one of Dean Shapiro's most tenacious opponents on the tenure committee came to my office and asked to see a draft of the early chapters of my Douglas manuscript. He had been hired more than twenty years earlier at a low period in the school's history and had not published a book or even a law review article. After a cursory examination of my manuscript, he asked when it would be ready for publication. I told him that publication was probably two years away. He voted to deny me tenure. Fortunately, Shapiro could count on the votes of a majority of committee members without him, so that I was promoted to full professor with tenure after my third year at NYLS.

• • • • •

In early June 1981, at the luncheon preceding New York Law School's commencement exercises at Lincoln Center, Dean Shapiro asked about my plans for my first sabbatical, due in the spring semester of 1982. I told him that I had given little thought to the sabbatical. He suggested that I consider taking a semester in England at the University of Warwick, a modern "red brick" university located on the outskirts of the city of Coventry ninety miles northwest of London. He added that he could arrange the visit because he was good friends with the chairman of the university's law department.

To my surprise, Marcia immediately expressed interest in moving to England for a semester, telling me that she thought it would be a great experience for the family. Marcia's enthusiasm was all the incentive I needed to follow up on the dean's offer. When Shapiro and I next spoke, the dean said he would be happy to speak to his friend Steve Anderman, chairman of Warwick's law department, about a visiting professorship for me the following spring. Shapiro, who loved to do these kinds of favors, assured me that Warwick would be an excellent place for me to spend my sabbatical, because Anderman, a Yale Law School graduate, had modeled Warwick's law curriculum on Yale's.

A few days later, Shapiro invited me to his office while he placed a call to Anderman in England. After he and Anderman were connected and exchanged warm greetings, Shapiro wasted no time in introducing me and telling him of my credentials, including my recently published biography of Justice Douglas. He suggested that my visit would be mutually beneficial to Warwick students and me. Anderman, who spoke in a clipped British accent (although he was a native New Yorker), agreed, suggesting that I could co-teach a comparative constitutional law class with one of Warwick's senior faculty members. He also offered to provide our family with a large university house adjacent to the campus. With my sabbatical salary from NYLS and Anderman's offer of housing, Marcia and I decided that I should accept the offer.

• • • • •

Our plane landed at Gatwick Airport in southern England during the first week in January 1982. I had arranged for a rental car at the airport but had not considered the difficulty of having to adjust to driving on the left-hand side of the road for the four-hour trip to the university. I hit several curbs on the way out of the airport but otherwise navigated well enough. None of us had gotten much sleep on the transatlantic overnight flight. So, while Marcia and the kids slept, my biggest challenge during the drive was staying awake, which I did by stopping periodically at gas station restrooms to douse my face with water.

We arrived at our university-owned house on Gibbet Hill Road on a very cold Saturday afternoon. I drove up a semicircular driveway to the front door of the two-story Tudor-style house. Marcia and the kids were still groggy when I put the key in the front door. We discovered a spacious but frigid set of bedrooms on the second floor and only a hot-water bottle in the master bedroom to welcome us.

When we looked out of our bedroom windows the next morning, we observed a thick blanket of snow on the ground. After breakfast, we took large plastic garbage can lids to use as makeshift sleds and walked to the nearest hill on the Warwick campus for a terrific day of sledding. That night we drove a few miles into the city of Coventry for dinner at what we thought was a British-style McDonald's. We ate awful hamburgers, which, we speculated, were made of horse meat.

My introduction to the University of Warwick was no more promising than our first British hamburgers. After studying the comparative constitutional law materials for my first class at Warwick, I nervously walked to the lecture hall, where I anticipated meeting my co-lecturer, Jeffrey Wilson, a Cambridge University graduate and longtime member of the Warwick faculty. Jeffrey never showed up. He later told me that it was an old "Oxbridge tradition" (i.e., Oxford-Cambridge) to skip the first day of classes. Nobody had told me. I struggled alone at the lectern, wading through the very dense materials, which did not appear to arouse my new students.

My Warwick students, all undergraduates, appeared no more alert or engaged in the seminars than in the lectures Jeffrey and I delivered. My primary intellectual stimulation during the winter term came from my informal discussions with faculty members in Warwick's law department.

I was also able to take advantage of a tradition among faculties at British universities to invite visiting professors to lecture to their faculties on subjects of mutual interest. In my case, my Douglas biography proved to be of great interest to law faculties throughout the United Kingdom. I received no honoraria for the lectures, but my expenses were paid. I spoke to faculties as far away as the University of Kent in southeast England and, hundreds of miles north, at the University of Edinburgh in Scotland. When I lectured at the University of Edinburgh, the distance required a long train ride and overnight accommodations. I then had the added pleasure of staying with the delightfully down-to-earth family of my host, Professor Alan Paterson. My final lecture was at the most prestigious university of all, Oxford.

Life began to pick up for the family after I bought a well-traveled 1973 blue Peugeot sedan with a sunroof and fake zebra-skin seat covers, which enabled us to branch out from the university. On Wednesdays, when I had no classes, Marcia, Sara, and I drove through a series of gently rolling hills to the Cotswolds. On weekends, the five of us toured nearby historic sites, including Warwick Castle, originally built by William the Conqueror in the eleventh century, and Coventry Cathedral, where bombed-out remains were left standing as a memorial to the citizens of Coventry killed by Nazis during World War II. And we attended every new production of the Royal Shakespeare Company at Stratford-upon-Avon, just twenty minutes from our house. We saw *King Lear*, *As You Like It*, and a contemporary version of *Macbeth* in which the men appeared in modern-day leather motorcycle jackets.

• • • • •

London was only a two-hour drive from the university, so we made frequent weekend trips to the requisite tourist stops—Buckingham Palace, London Bridge, the Tower of London, St. Paul's Cathedral, and Westminster Abbey. We also rode on double-decker city buses, looked for bargains for Marcia and Lauren in the city's jewelry district, and took in a matinee performance of Agatha Christie's *The Mousetrap*. Our favorite restaurant offered an "all-you-can-eat" roast beef special, an incredible bargain for David, who threatened to bankrupt the owner with his insatiable appetite.

Before one of our weekend trips, I called Michael Rudman in London, hoping to renew a friendship that dated back to our teenage years in Texas. We had met through our mothers, who were good friends as undergraduates at the University of Texas. I had last seen him when, as undergraduates, we had shared a room in New York City's Biltmore Hotel over a Thanksgiving holiday.

By January 1982, more than twenty years later, Michael was recognized as one of England's most gifted directors in the competitive world of theater. After graduating from Oberlin College, Mike (as he was then called) had received a master's degree from Oxford in English literature and was elected president of the university's dramatic society. He soon earned accolades as a director at regional theaters throughout England. Only a few weeks before I called, he had been appointed deputy director of the National Theater, serving under the distinguished director Sir Peter Hall.

When we met in Michael's London apartment, it was as if we had seen each other a few weeks ago rather than more than two decades earlier. Later, we met his fiancée, Felicity Kendal, then England's most popular actress on television as well as the London stage. Michael gave us tickets to productions that he directed at the National Theater—Tom Stoppard's *On the Razzle* and Arthur Pinero's *The Second Mrs. Tanqueray*. Both starred Felicity, who, with verve and high drama, was superb.

During one of our early conversations, Michael told me that he had read my Douglas biography and proposed that we collaborate on a television miniseries based on my book. I was flattered and eager to work with him on the project. We discussed the broad outlines of the project in telephone conversations, at a "business" lunch in London, and during a round of golf at Michael's country club. After golf, Marcia, Sara, and I met Michael and Felicity for lunch. The celebrated actress was charmed by our four-year-old daughter. "Does she come in boxes?" she asked. "I want one."

Michael discussed our television project with Luis Sanjurjo, his New York agent at ICM Partners, one of the nation's largest literary and entertainment agencies. Luis liked the project and said he would explore sale of the rights to one of the major networks. Michael was excited, viewing the miniseries as an opportunity to demonstrate his directorial talents to a broad television audience. And I began to fantasize about my book being translated into a television series that would reach millions of viewers. But, alas, it was not to be. Shortly before we left England, Luis phoned Michael to say that he had just learned that CBS had committed to a production of a miniseries on Douglas based on the justice's autobiography.

* * * * *

Our family embarked on a month-long trip to western Europe in early March immediately after I had taught my last class of the term. Marcia had charted our itinerary so that we would see great art and architecture throughout France and Italy. We celebrated Marcia's birthday in the early spring in Stresa, a beautiful resort town in northern Italy overlooking Lake Maggiore. Our Peugeot continued to chug along as we drove up the western Italian coast to the French Riviera. Before ending our grand tour in Paris, we arranged to spend several days in southwestern France at the farm of Marybeth Olin, the daughter of our neighbors John and Marian Olin, and Marybeth's French husband, Jean Claude.

No sight on our European tour was more welcome than Marybeth and Jean Claude's farm. We arrived on a bright, sunny spring afternoon and immediately exhaled a collective sigh of relief. We looked forward to three days of rest and relaxation. Marybeth, who had met her husband during her junior year abroad in France, greeted us with her familiar lilting French accent. The next three days on the farm were just what we needed. Lauren and David rode horses with Marybeth's kids and, with Sara, ran around the farm with abandon. My most vivid memory of those days was simply lying down in a field, looking up at the clear blue sky or across to verdant hills and pastures.

We ended our tour of Italy and France with a stay in Paris. After a month abroad, we looked forward to returning to our house in England and sleeping on familiar beds. We were relieved to have a few weeks without any schedule, free to bask in the spring weather with picnics in our spacious backyard. Before our return to the United States, we planned one final excursion—to the Lake District on the northwest coast of England, and to Scotland. In mid-June, we drove to England's largest national park in the Lake District, which included the country's highest mountain and deepest natural lake. We arrived at our hotel very close to the summer solstice. Our kids' greatest pleasure in the Lake District was not observing England's highest mountain or deepest natural lake, however, but running up and down the hill near our hotel at 11 p.m. *in broad daylight.*

We spent our last few days in England frantically packing our belongings and souvenirs as well as a very heavy set of stoneware dishes that Marcia had purchased. The Coventry car dealer who had sold me the used Peugeot with a buy-back guarantee (at a mutually agreed upon price) was not happy when he checked the odometer. We had logged many more miles than he had bargained for, but a deal was a deal. On our return flight, I reflected on our trip abroad. Did it provide the experience we had anticipated? Not exactly. I wished that my classes at Warwick had been more inspiring, and that David and Lauren had attended better schools. But those regrets paled next to our incredibly varied and rich family adventure.

✦ ✦ ✦ ✦ ✦

After returning to West Nyack, I began to draft a proposal for a new book on the rivalry between US Supreme Court Justices Hugo Black and Felix Frankfurter, an idea that I had begun mulling over when we were in England. While I was working on the proposal, I received a phone call from Harvard law professor Vern Countryman, who had clerked for Justice Douglas and was one of the clerks I interviewed for my Douglas biography. He told me that he had recently been interviewed by a man who introduced himself as the producer of a miniseries on the justice to be televised on CBS. Based on the producer's questions, Countryman was concerned that he was following the narrative of my book too closely, raising the possibility of improper use of my work in violation of federal copyright law.

I immediately called Julian Bach, my literary agent, and recounted my conversation with Professor Countryman. Julian quickly arranged for a luncheon at the posh Plaza Hotel in New York City for the television producer, Julian, and me. I was optimistic that the expensive lunch would lead to an offer from the producer to buy the television rights to my book. Such an offer would be justified, I thought, if for no other reason than to eliminate the possibility of a costly lawsuit.

The producer was gracious at the luncheon and assured me that he had read and greatly admired my Douglas biography. But he followed his kind words about my book with his insistence that the script for his television miniseries did not infringe on my copyright. Specifically, he said that the script did not quote directly from my book or follow the narrative of my book in such a way as to raise issues of copyright infringement. His reasons for contending there was no copyright violation left no doubt in my mind that he had consulted with his copyright attorney before our luncheon and had been coached on the position he should take. Even after I told him of the concerns raised by Professor Countryman, he held firmly to his position.

Throughout the lunch, Julian made no effort to persuade or pressure the producer to make an offer. I was so angry at Julian's passivity that I vowed to change agents for my proposed book on Justices Black and Frankfurter. After the disappointing lunch, I still held out a slight hope that I might successfully sue the producer. But the copyright issue became moot a few weeks later when I learned that CBS had canceled plans for the miniseries.

After I completed my proposal for a book on Black and Frankfurter, I did not send it to Julian Bach. Instead, I arranged for a meeting with Michael Rudman's agent at ICM Partners, Luis Sanjurjo. Luis, a slight, handsome Hispanic man in his early forties, was polite but noncommittal. He agreed to read my proposal and represent me if he thought he could sell it. A few days later, he called to say he liked the proposal and was sending it to Alice Mayhew, a senior editor at Simon and Schuster. Alice made an offer of an advance that was substantially higher than the one I had received for my Douglas biography, which I accepted.

Shortly after I had signed the contract and met Alice, Luis died tragically of AIDS. I was then introduced to Esther Newberg, another rising star at ICM, who represented me for the next four decades. Esther became cochair of ICM's New York office and the firm's executive vice president. She was a shrewd, knowledgeable agent, always supportive and protective of my interests, but candid when she did not think one of my book proposals could be sold to a major publisher. She was also a superb negotiator, securing advances for my next five books that totaled approximately half a million dollars (almost double that amount in today's dollars).

CHAPTER 14

LAW SCHOOL DEAN

New York Law School was in crisis when I returned to teach my fall classes in September 1982. Dean Shapiro had been featured on the cover of the September issue of the *American Lawyer* magazine. But the cover art was an unflattering caricature of him, and the title underneath the drawing labeled him "The Entrepreneur–Law School Dean." The story inside the magazine documented Shapiro's moonlighting career as a highly paid member of a dozen corporate boards, including serving as treasurer of a corporation that owned and operated a Las Vegas casino. The article questioned how the dean of a large urban law school could fulfill his academic duties while serving on so many corporate boards. The news department at NBC television followed up on the magazine's story by sending one of its top correspondents, Carl Stern, to the law school as part of an independent investigation of Shapiro's profitable sideline as a corporate trustee and treasurer.

Members of the NYLS faculty were aghast at the public spectacle of Shapiro's wide-ranging corporate activity. The scandal could not have come at a worse time. The law school had begun to earn a reputation as a dynamic institution driven by the talent of a young, ambitious faculty. And Shapiro had been the driving force behind the progress, actively recruiting promising faculty members, renovating and expanding the physical plant, and funding the additional faculty salaries and improved facilities by raising tens of thousands of dollars.

I had long suspected that the dean's enormous energy could not be confined to law school business. My suspicion was heightened when I received a blizzard of memos signed by Shapiro congratulating me on the attached excellent reviews of my Douglas biography. The attached reviews were identical, having appeared in dozens of newspapers that subscribed to the same syndicated service. Neither Shapiro nor his secretary, who sent the dean's signed congratulatory memos to me after he had left town on one of his numerous trips, noticed the redundancy. I smiled at the harmless oversight.

The public exposure of Shapiro's freewheeling corporate life was different, revealing a deeply disturbing neglect of his decanal responsibilities and an existential threat to the law school. My response to the revelations was both anger and sadness. My anger was directed at Shapiro's seeming obliviousness to the potential harm that his outside activities could do to the law school. How could he not have realized that his highly lucrative corporate activities, once exposed, would undermine the law school's growing reputation as a serious institution attracting outstanding faculty and excellent students? But I was also sad, because I considered Don Shapiro a friend and mentor who had been responsible for my satisfying career as a law professor.

Despite my personal affection for and professional debt to Shapiro, I felt that he had to resign. Several tenured faculty members, knowing my close relationship with the dean, asked that I lead a small delegation to deliver the faculty's ultimatum. I agreed to lead the delegation. When our delegation met in the dean's office, I told Don that he needed to resign for the sake of the law school he had done so much to improve. I spoke seriously but with genuine feeling for the man who had hired me.

Shapiro listened impassively. Always the pragmatist, he knew that the board of trustees would support the faculty. His resignation was inevitable. But he insisted that he would negotiate the terms and timing of his departure with the board of trustees, not our delegation.

I left the dean's office relieved but also depressed, having fulfilled what I considered my institutional duty. The news of our delegation's meeting with

Shapiro quickly spread throughout the law school. The dean's intention to resign raised the question on everyone's mind: Who would replace him?

An informal consensus among the senior faculty soon emerged that Professor B. James George should serve as interim dean until the law school could conduct a nationwide search for a successor to Shapiro. Jim George was the obvious choice to take the law school through this transition period. An honors graduate of the University of Michigan Law School with a solid publishing record, George, in his late fifties, appeared to possess the maturity and judgment that were needed at that critical time in the law school's history.

George took over as interim dean within weeks and almost immediately alienated a large swath of the senior staff, associate deans, and members of the faculty. Stories quickly circulated that he treated anyone who disagreed with him with brusque condescension. To those who were subjected to that rough treatment, he acted as if his appointment to the permanent deanship was only a matter of time.

I was stunned by the cascading criticism of George. My relations with him had always been cordial and continued to be so after his appointment as interim dean. He came to my office shortly after his appointment to inform me that he had approved my spring teaching schedule that limited my classes to two days a week, leaving more time for me to work on my new book at home. That accommodation was welcome, although I soon realized that he played favorites, and I was a member of the favored class.

George openly criticized those on the faculty whom he did not favor. He was scornfully dismissive of Robert Blecker's pending application for tenure. Similarly, he treated the associate deans kindly or with contempt depending on his personal relationships with them as well as his strongly held views of their competence. He was a close friend of Associate Dean Arnie Graham, who oversaw the school's finances, and regularly supported his institutional requests. But his benign and cooperative attitude toward Graham did not extend to Margaret Bearn, associate dean for student affairs, whom he did not like or respect.

In a remarkably short time, the school was in an uproar that swirled around George's controversial style and decisions. By January 1983, there was widespread talk in the corridors among faculty, staff, and senior administrators that George should be relieved of his decanal duties. I was not among the faculty members initiating those discussions. I had no problem with George and remained content to teach my classes and work on my new book on Justices Black and Frankfurter. In fact, I may have been the only tenured faculty member who did not have designs on George's job. My attitude, apparently, made me all the more attractive to disgruntled faculty members, staff, and administrators who were seeking a replacement for George.

In late February I received a visit in my office from Associate Professor Blecker and Associate Dean Bearn, two of Jim George's most outspoken critics. They immediately posed a question: Would I consider replacing George as interim dean?

I was surprised and flattered by their question but responded with my reasons to remain on the faculty. I would be leaving a professional life of teaching and writing, which I enjoyed enormously, for an administrative position for which I had no training or experience. And based on the ongoing turmoil at NYLS, I could anticipate many headaches and perils involved in running the law school, even on a temporary basis.

Blecker and Bearn were not deterred by my unenthusiastic response. They reminded me that I had already demonstrated my loyalty to the institution by leading the faculty delegation demanding Shapiro's resignation. My willingness to replace George was just as compelling an institutional obligation. The faculty and top administrators were well aware of my lack of administrative experience, which, they maintained, would encourage their cooperation. It would be in everyone's interest for me to succeed, so that the school would be in good, stable condition to search for a permanent dean.

I did not reject their proposal outright, telling them that I would discuss it with Marcia that evening and speak to them the next day. Marcia responded positively to the idea of my serving as interim dean. What did I have to lose? No one could blame me if I was a failure as an administrator, since it was neither my idea nor my preference. If I was tolerable or even good at it, the faculty, deans, students, and staff would be grateful.

The next morning I told Bearn and Blecker that I was willing to serve as interim dean if I received the support of the faculty and trustees. With lightning speed, my reluctant candidacy was endorsed by votes of both the faculty and trustees.

My brother, Dick (left), with me in 1941. Photo by Stuart Studio, Fort Worth. Simon family photo.

I proudly wore a soldier's uniform during World War II, November 1942. Simon family photo.

My father, Richard U. Simon, in his army uniform, March 20, 1944. Simon family photo.

My family in 1960. From left, my mother, Natalie Levin Simon; my father, Richard; my sister, Mary Elizabeth (Liz); my brother, Richard Jr. (Dick); and me. Simon family photo.

My wedding to Marcia in my parents' living room, 1963. Simon family photo.

My first book, In His Own Image: The Supreme Court in Richard Nixon's America, *was published by David McKay Co. in 1973.*

William O. Douglas on April 17, 1939, the day he was sworn in as a Supreme Court justice. Library of Congress, Prints & Photographs Division, photograph by Harris & Ewing, LC-DIG-hec-26502.

My book Independent Journey: The Life of William O. Douglas *was published by Harper and Row in 1980.*

I was honored to join Associate Justice Harry A. Blackmun along with other trustees and honorary degree recipients at the New York Law School commencement in 1983. Photo by Page One Photography. New York Law School photo.

With my family at Stonehenge in 1985. From left, David, Lauren, Sara, me, and Marcia. Simon family photo.

Former president Jimmy Carter, escorted by Congressman Mario Biaggi and me, walking briskly to his lecture at New York Law School, October 1985. Photo by Steve Friedman. New York Law School photo.

Associate Justice William J. Brennan Jr., second from right, with me and NYLS students Noreen Krasnogar and Sheri Donovan, in Justice Brennan's chambers at the US Supreme Court when he received a plaque honoring his contributions to the protection of civil rights and liberties. New York Law School photo.

As dean, I honored Justices Blackmun and Brennan at a NYLS reception during the annual meeting of the Association of American Law Schools in Washington, DC, in 1985. From left, Justice Blackmun, former US Solicitor General Wade H. McCree Jr., Justice Brennan, and me. Photo by Page One Photography. New York Law School photo.

I introduced Justice Blackmun and his wife, Dottie, behind her husband, at the AALS reception in Washington, DC, in 1985. Photo by Page One Photography. New York Law School photo.

Marcia and I joined Justice Brennan and his wife, Mary, before the NYLS commencement in 1986 when the justice was awarded an honorary degree. New York Law School photo.

I was honored to attend a luncheon at the White House in 1987 with Vice President George H. W. Bush and a group of Jewish donors to the Republican Party. I am on the far left. White House photograph.

Associate Justice Felix Frankfurter, the subject (with Associate Justice Hugo Black) of my book The Antagonists. *Library of Congress, Prints & Photographs Division, photograph by Harris & Ewing, LC-DIG-hec-21699.*

My book The Antagonists: Hugo Black, Felix Frankfurter and Civil Liberties in Modern America *was published by Simon and Schuster in 1989.*

Associate Justice Sandra Day O'Connor and I were awarded honorary degrees at the New York Law School commencement in 1992. New York Law School photo.

Justice O'Connor joined me and my family to celebrate after the commencement ceremony in 1992. Photo by Scott Star. New York Law School photo.

Associate Justice David H. Souter and I with my Modern Supreme Court class in 2000 after we heard oral arguments before the justices.

With my mother, Natalie Simon, September 2002. Simon family photo.

With Justice Souter after I delivered a lecture at the US Supreme Court in 2009. He introduced me before my presentation.

I interviewed Congresswoman Nancy Pelosi for an event at New York Law School in September 2014. Photo by Rick Kopstein.

The Simon family in Bermuda, 2017. Simon family photo.

I signed copies of my book Eisenhower v. Warren *at an event at New York Law School, April 2018. New York Law School photo.*

* * * * *

In early March 1983, my first day as interim dean started quietly enough. I sat down behind the desk in the dean's large, mahogany-paneled office as if I belonged there. I had to smile, because I felt like an actor auditioning for a role. But once the conveyor belt of appointments began—with deans, professors, and senior staff—I realized that this was no play, or joke. Everyone who came into the office wanted something that only I, as dean, could provide. Associate deans required my approval for expenditures for what they described as essential programs. Professors insisted that I fund their new academic projects and summer writing plans. Senior staff warned that unless I authorized additional personnel, their departments would descend into chaos.

Nothing in my professional experience as a journalist, author, or professor had prepared me for this onslaught. The appeals were wrapped in the gauze of extravagant flattery: after each conversation I could be excused for thinking that my decanal appointment was long overdue recognition of my unsurpassed brilliance and, more importantly, my uncanny ability to recognize the merits of the pending request. By the end of this hectic day, I was exhausted. But I was also secretly rather pleased with my nascent ability to deal with the constant pressures of my new job.

When I returned to West Nyack that evening, and virtually every other evening for the next several months, I greeted Marcia with the same head-scratching confession—"You won't believe what happened today!"

The grind of urgent requests quickly became routine, and I realized that I was not required to give an instant answer. If I needed a day or week to think about the implications of my decision, I would do so, without apology. The faculty, staff, and senior administrators, as Professor Blecker and Dean Bearn had predicted, were overwhelmingly supportive and appreciative of my efforts, even if they did not always agree with my decisions. That attitude was underscored at a three-day retreat for faculty, deans, and senior staff at the Thayer Hotel on the campus of the US Military Academy at West Point.

For the remainder of the spring semester, I gained confidence in my ability to competently make tough decisions. At the same time, I realized that there were perks to the job that I had not considered when Marcia and I had discussed whether I should take the job. The first benefit, the prestige of serving as dean, simply fed my ego. Colleagues, acquaintances, and visitors treated me with conspicuous respect for my title, if not for my talent. My status was inextricably linked to my authority to make important decisions for the law school. In starkest terms, I wielded power. As time went on, I became comfortable with the power as well as the title. The interim deanship also offered unique opportunities for me and Marcia to spend time with important and admirable people, beginning with Associate Justice of the US Supreme Court Harry Blackmun, who received an honorary degree at the law school's commencement at Lincoln Center in June 1983.

• • • • •

Blackmun had been recommended to President Richard Nixon for an appointment to the Supreme Court in 1970 by Chief Justice Warren Burger, who had known Blackmun since they had grown up together in St. Paul, Minnesota. Blackmun was Burger's best man at his wedding. When the chief justice recommended Blackmun for a Court appointment, Blackmun was serving as a judge on the US Court of Appeals for the Eighth Circuit, which heard federal cases for the upper Midwest region. A graduate of Harvard Law School and a former trusts and estates attorney in St. Paul, Blackmun had built a reputation on the appeals court as a studious, cautious, and self-effacing jurist. Like Chief Justice Burger, Blackmun was a registered Republican who appeared to be a safe conservative judicial choice for President Nixon.

But in 1973, less than three years after the Senate had unanimously confirmed Blackmun's appointment to the Supreme Court, he had stunned the nation by writing the majority opinion in *Roe v. Wade*, which declared that a woman had the constitutional right to have an abortion in the first two trimesters of her pregnancy. After the decision, one of the most far-reaching and controversial in the history of the modern Supreme Court, Blackmun not only became an outspoken champion for the right to abortion but also a member of the Court's liberal wing, which significantly expanded civil rights and liberties in other areas.

On a Saturday evening in early June 1983, Marcia and I dined with Justice

Blackmun and his wife, Dottie, before the law school's commencement the next day. The four of us hit it off immediately and happily spent the remainder of the weekend together. The justice had a striking physical resemblance to Marcia's father, Ernie Solomon, and spoke with an upper Midwest accent very similar to that of her father, who had grown up in the Canadian Midwest. He also reminded both Marcia and me of Ernie in his warm, mild-mannered personality and understated intelligence. His wife, Dottie, was as unpretentious as her husband and made no secret of her delight in spending a weekend in New York City with her workaholic husband.

After dinner, we attended an exuberant performance of *On Your Toes*, a revival of the 1936 musical by Richard Rodgers and Lorenz Hart. During the performance, Justice Blackmun nudged Dottie in gentle approval with each familiar song. That evening marked the beginning of a friendship for the four of us that resumed when Justice Blackmun and his wife periodically attended law school receptions in Washington, DC. And every time we met, we recalled our pleasure in attending the performance of *On Your Toes*.

The morning after attending the Broadway musical, I was up early and still in my pajamas writing my introduction of Justice Blackmun for our commencement ceremony that afternoon. Old journalism habits are hard to break, and my need to produce a written product on deadline was one of them. I recall that I was satisfied with my introduction, but the highlight of the ceremony came when Justice Blackmun received his honorary degree. He remained in character, modest but also pleased that his considerable accomplishments had been recognized. Marcia and I will always remember that commencement, and especially our weekend with the Blackmuns.

• • • • •

While I dealt with a variety of institutional issues during the 1983 fall semester, the trustee-faculty search committee to recruit a permanent dean was actively seeking someone to replace me. In November, the committee announced that its first choice, Professor Eugene Rostow of Yale Law School, had agreed to become the school's dean, subject to a formal vote of the board of trustees and the faculty.

The appointment of Gene Rostow as dean was considered a coup for the school. Rostow had served as dean of Yale Law School when I was a student there, and later as undersecretary of state for political affairs under President Lyndon Johnson. A superb scholar, he had written two seminal law review articles denouncing the Supreme Court's decisions during World War II that had upheld the constitutionality of the government's exclusion of Japanese Americans from the West Coast. The only drawback to a Rostow deanship was his age—he was seventy years old. But neither the NYLS trustees nor the faculty seemed overly concerned about it and enthusiastically supported the appointment.

Before Rostow could assume the deanship, he suffered a serious heart attack. Although he slowly recovered from the attack, Rostow informed the board and the faculty that, due to his fragile health, he could no longer be considered for the deanship.

In the winter of 1984, the dean's search committee was again at work. By March, the committee had invited half a dozen finalists—deans and associate deans drawn from law schools across the country—to interview on campus. My name was added as a finalist with the support of a large segment of the faculty. They believed that I had done an excellent job under difficult circumstances and deserved the permanent appointment.

I made no effort to argue with my supporters' generous assessment and said that I would accept the decanal appointment if it was offered to me. My experience as interim dean had been intellectually challenging as well as remunerative (I had received a substantial raise from the board when I was appointed interim dean). I was confident that I could do the job well on a permanent basis and wanted the opportunity to prove it. When I saw the list of other finalists, I was encouraged. I thought that my résumé held up well against my competition, and that my experience as interim dean and faculty member at NYLS gave me an edge. After the visiting deans had been interviewed, the faculty overwhelmingly supported my appointment, followed by a formal vote of the board of trustees.

At the age of forty-five, I became the chief executive officer of an institution with an annual multimillion-dollar budget that owned and operated three large buildings in Lower Manhattan, enrolled more than 1,300 law students, employed 60 full-time law professors (and twice that number of adjunct professors), and more than 200 administrative and clerical staff.

* * * * *

Only months after assuming the deanship, I was faced with my first institutional crisis. It came in the fall of 1984 after an inspection team from the Association of American Law Schools filed its report on the school's compliance with its regulations. Every law school in the AALS is subjected to such an inspection every seven years to determine if the school has adhered to the organization's governing regulations covering administration and finance, faculty, curriculum, student-faculty ratio, and classroom and library facilities. On most items, the law school received satisfactory grades. But on two, student-faculty ratio and library facilities, we received failing grades that had to be corrected to preserve our accreditation.

Our student-faculty ratio problem was common among the nation's two-division law schools. NYLS was one of the largest law schools in the country and, like most schools with evening divisions, relied on adjunct professors to teach many of the classes. But adjuncts were discounted in the measurement for the AALS student-faculty requirement. To bring our student-faculty ratio within AALS regulations required the law school to hire more than a dozen full-time faculty members. This put enormous pressure on our faculty appointments committee to find highly qualified candidates, and for me to make offers that they would accept, even if it meant outbidding rival law schools. It also required the law school to substantially increase its annual budget to meet the additional costs of the new salaries. We therefore had to dip into our already small endowment.

Over the next few years of my deanship, we were extraordinarily successful in hiring an outstanding group of new faculty members, including Annette Gordon-Reed, future winner of a Pulitzer Prize for her book *The Hemingses of Monticello*; Ed Purcell Jr., author of several critically acclaimed works of legal history; and Nadine Strossen, an authority on the First Amendment's protection of free speech, who also served for many years as the president of the American Civil Liberties Union.

Improving our library facilities was an even more difficult and expensive challenge. Our library had not changed since I had arrived at the law school nine years earlier. It meandered through narrow corridors and cramped rooms on three floors of our main building. Nothing short of a new facility could meet the AALS regulations. But a new facility would cost several million dollars, money that we would have to borrow at a substantial interest rate.

• • • • •

Bernard Mendik, who would solve our library problem, appeared in my office shortly after I had received the AALS inspection report. An honors graduate of the law school's evening division in 1959, Mendik, fifty-five years old, had recently made a $10,000 gift to the law school. Immediately upon hearing of his gift, I had invited him to my office and to lunch.

When Mendik entered my office, he greeted me with a big grin and warm handshake, as if we had been friends for years. He had made his fortune after his law school graduation by buying old, deteriorating office buildings in New York City, refurbishing and modernizing them, then either renting or selling his properties at considerable profit. He was extremely proud of his success and did not hide its rewards. He wore expensive, perfectly tailored suits; lived during the week with his wife, Susie, in a townhouse on the Upper East Side, where an original Degas pastel hung on the living room wall; and spent weekends at their mansion in Southampton on Long Island.

Despite his extravagant lifestyle, Bernie Mendik never forgot his humble roots. He and his family had immigrated to the United States from Glasgow, Scotland, when he was a child. The family settled in the Bronx, where Bernie's father worked as a handyman. Bernie graduated from the elite Bronx High School of Science and City College of New York before entering New York Law School. He shared fond memories with me of his outstanding law professors at NYLS and took pride in the nuts-and-bolts legal education that he had received.

As I was soon to learn, he had an amazing analytical mind and could quickly calculate the feasibility of a multimillion-dollar building project down to the cost per square foot. He also was a voracious reader, particularly of history and biography. He had read my three books and was eager to talk about them during our first lunch.

At that lunch we began a marvelous friendship that endured throughout my deanship and continued after I returned to the faculty. He was pleased when I told him that I would like to propose that he join our board. After he was made a member at our next meeting, he volunteered to take on the library project. The two of us spoke on the phone many times each week. Bernie's first idea was to sell the parking lot adjacent to the law school (owned by NYLS) to a developer, who would purchase the property at a price that would provide for the law school's library on the lower floors of a high-rise apartment building. But within weeks of floating his proposal to leading developers in the city, Bernie concluded that the project was not feasible.

With typical zeal and confidence, he then focused on his plan B: to buy the five-story building on Church Street, adjacent to the law school's main building, and restore, refurbish, and convert it into the law school's new library. He made inquiries, was told that the selling price of the building was $7 million, and proposed that the board approve the purchase. At the trustee's meeting in which the prospective purchase was discussed, Sam Lefrak, another wealthy real estate developer and longtime member of the board, told Mendik that the law school could have bought the property for half that price just a few years earlier.

"So why didn't you buy it, Sam?" Bernie shot back.

The board authorized the purchase, and employees of the Mendik Company went to work gutting the inside of the building and then restoring and refurbishing it. The result was a stylish new library with large, attractive study spaces, tasteful furniture, bright lighting, and ample shelves and storage for the law school's collection. Bernie made the renovation a gift to his alma mater. We named it the Mendik Library, and it instantly became the jewel of the law school.

In 2006 the law school sold the property for quadruple the school's endowment (prior to the sale, about $50 million) to a developer, who tore down the library to build a high-rise apartment complex. With the proceeds from the sale, the law school built a modern facility on our parking lot with spacious classrooms and lecture halls, an attractive faculty dining room, and a fifth-floor student cafeteria with a glass facade overlooking the lively Tribeca neighborhood below. The new building also included a state-of-the-art library, which retained the Mendik name.

• • • • •

In September 1985, we prepared to welcome former president Jimmy Carter to the law school as the first recipient of the Mario Biaggi Lectureship. Biaggi was a highly decorated New York City policeman who had retired after being injured more than eleven times in the line of duty. He had then studied law in our evening division and, after receiving his law degree, had run successfully as a Democrat for a congressional seat representing the Bronx. He served in Congress for almost twenty years, becoming one of the most influential members of the Democratic caucus and an important ally of President Carter. That former president Carter would agree to be the first recipient of the Biaggi Lectureship was recognition of the mutually beneficial partnership the two men had forged during the Carter presidency.

Plans for the lectureship had begun the previous spring when Biaggi had met with me at the law school. He walked awkwardly into my office with both legs in braces, a result of his injuries as a police officer. He was a handsome man with curly, graying hair, a broad face, and muscular physique above his crippled legs. He was respectful but spoke with the authority of a congressman who had wielded power for many years. We planned a full day for Carter's visit in which the former president would meet with students, have lunch with the faculty and selected guests, and deliver a lecture in the afternoon.

But a week before Carter's visit, weather forecasters predicted that a hurricane would hit the New York area on the day of his scheduled lecture. After hearing the forecast, I consulted with Biaggi on a daily basis. As the hurricane moved toward the city, we decided to postpone the lecture for a month. When Carter arrived at the law school in October, the weather, thankfully, was calm. The former president and his wife, Rosalynn, could not have been warmer or more gracious to the students, faculty, and staff and to our family. We have two prized framed autographed photos: one of Carter posing with our family, holding Sara in his arms; the other of Carter with Congressman Biaggi and me walking briskly on our way to his lecture. As expected, his visit was a publicity bonanza for the law school; we drew both local and national journalists who filed stories, often accompanied by photos, of his meetings with students and faculty and his formal lecture.

We could not have known at the time that former president Carter would be the only Biaggi Lecturer. Shortly afterward, Congressman Biaggi was investigated and later convicted in two separate corruption trials. He resigned from Congress in 1988. His granddaughter Alessandra Biaggi, who was born a year after the Carter visit to the law school, was elected in 2018 to the New York State Senate, where she served as chair of the committee on ethics and internal governance.

For Marcia and me, the high point of that extraordinary day occurred after the formal activities had concluded. The former president and First Lady were our guests at a dinner served by law school staff in my office. Both Jimmy and Rosalynn Carter were tired but seemed relieved to be able to relax. The four of us had a lively, informal conversation that ranged from politics and history to our children. Their daughter, Amy, was then a student at Brown, Marcia's alma mater.

• • • • •

I took considerable pride in the progress that the law school made during my nine-plus years as dean. We built a dynamic young faculty that I considered as good or better than any at the other New York–area law schools with the exception of the top-tier Columbia and NYU.

I was also convinced that our best students could compete with any in the country, although the talent dropped off precipitously in the lower half of our classes. I had raised enough money to finance a new student cafeteria and lounge, a moot court room, and the renovation of several large classrooms. And we opened the Mendik Library to great fanfare in 1989 with New York City mayor Ed Koch and Bernie Mendik cutting the ceremonial ribbon.

Throughout my deanship, I consciously attempted to raise the prestige of the law school by adding leading academics to our board, including Barbara Black, dean of Columbia Law School, and Harry Wellington, the former dean of Yale Law School. I also selected national role models to receive honorary degrees at our commencement ceremonies in Avery Fisher Hall, Lincoln Center. In 1986, I was pleased to be photographed with Associate Justice William J. Brennan Jr., the leader of the liberal wing of the US Supreme Court, before he received an honorary degree. The photo of the two of us was published in the *New York Times* the next day. Justice Brennan later sent me a signed copy of the photo and an accompanying letter with the comment, "I must say that's a couple of handsome dawgs!"

We also awarded honorary degrees to three pathbreaking women: Congresswoman Geraldine Ferraro, Chief Judge Patricia Wald of the US Court of Appeals for the District of Columbia, and Associate Justice Sandra Day O'Connor of the US Supreme Court. In 1984, Ferraro was the first woman nominated by a national political party to serve as vice president of the United States. She ran on the losing Democratic ticket headed by Senator Walter Mondale. Chief Judge Wald was the first woman to be appointed to the federal appellate court and later to lead it. Justice O'Connor was the first woman to be appointed to the US Supreme Court.

Other honorary degree recipients included New Jersey governor Tom Kean, New York governor Mario Cuomo, and Fred Friendly, the former president of CBS News and the creator of the public television series *The Constitution: A Delicate Balance*. At the commencement ceremony in which Friendly was honored, he passed out miniature copies of the Constitution to our graduating students.

* * * * *

A few months before Vice President George H.W. Bush announced his intention to seek the presidency in 1988, he hosted a luncheon in the White House for a small group of major Jewish donors to the Republican Party. There was one additional invitee to that intimate gathering: me. My invitation to the luncheon had been arranged by Professor Marshall Breger, who was on unpaid leave from New York Law School. Breger had been appointed by President Ronald Reagan to serve as his liaison to the academic and Jewish communities. It was an unusual portfolio, but one for which Breger was well suited. An honors graduate of the University of Texas Law School, he was an observant Orthodox Jew as well as a respected law professor. He was also a conservative Republican.

From time to time during my deanship, Breger showed his appreciation for my willingness to preserve his faculty status at NYLS by extending invitations to me, such as the White House luncheon with the vice president. The luncheon discussion focused on the Reagan administration's commitment to the state of Israel. Vice President Bush led the discussion skillfully, assuring his guests that President Reagan stood solidly behind Israel in the volatile Middle East and, implicitly, that a future Bush administration would do the same.

The vice president later sent me an autographed photo of the luncheon showing all the guests seated around him. The photo brought a smile to my face. I relished the idea that I, a lifelong liberal Democrat, had been smuggled into a conclave of deep-pocket conservative Republican donors. One of them had been Ivan Boesky, the Wall Street stock trader who later pled guilty to insider trading and was fined a record $100 million.

Although the White House luncheon was memorable, it could not compare to the official State Department dinner in honor of Shimon Peres, then Israel's foreign minister, that Marcia and I attended, again courtesy of Marshall Breger, in November 1987. Peres had earlier served as prime minister in a unity government that he, a political liberal, had formed with the conservative Yitzhak Shamir that involved a rotation agreement between the two men in the prime minister and foreign minister positions. Marcia and I tried to hide our excitement when we entered the brightly festooned State Department dining room. I was seated next to Marvin Kalb, a prominent television correspondent for CBS. I do not recall our conversation, but I will not forget the US Marine Corps Band's rousing rendition of "Hatikvah," Israel's national anthem.

✦ ✦ ✦ ✦ ✦

The pressures of the deanship had initially prevented me from working on the dual biography of Justices Hugo Black and Felix Frankfurter that I had agreed to write for Simon and Schuster. My editor at S&S, Alice Mayhew, summoned me to her office to demand that I either write the book or return my advance. I then met with NYLS board chairman John Thornton to complain that I did not have the time to write the book. His advice was simple: "Take the time."

Following Thornton's advice, I began to work on my book at home on Fridays, telling my associate deans and senior staff that they could call me at home—but the implicit caveat was that such a call should be so important that it could not wait until the following Monday. I was rarely interrupted. During our summer vacations on Cape Cod, I spent mornings working on the book. I imposed a similar rule on the associate deans and senior staff and was seldom called.

The fruits of my labor appeared in the spring of 1989 when Simon and Schuster published my book *The Antagonists: Hugo Black, Felix Frankfurter and Civil Liberties in Modern America*. The book received many excellent reviews, including one in the *New York Times* by Herbert Mitgang, who had also reviewed my first book, *In His Own Image: The Supreme Court in Richard Nixon's America*, for the newspaper sixteen years earlier. "*The Antagonists* is a palatable lesson in constitutional law," Mitgang wrote, adding that it was "a model of clarity" and "a stronger work historically" than *The Brethren*, Bob Woodward's best-selling book on the inner workings of the Court.

Just as flattering as the *Times* review was the letter I received from US Supreme Court Justice Sandra Day O'Connor after the book's publication. She wrote that she enjoyed the book so much that she had given copies to her close friends as Christmas presents. I later learned that one of the recipients of her holiday gift was the publisher of the *Washington Post*, Katharine Graham.

* * * * *

In 1973 we took our first summer vacation on Cape Cod, where we fell in love with the beautiful bay and ocean beaches. That vacation became the first of many we spent on the Cape in the 1970s and 1980s. In the summer of 1991, which preceded my final year as dean of New York Law School, Marcia and I decided to look for a vacation house to buy on Cape Cod in either Wellfleet or Truro.

To find a house we enlisted the services of an enterprising real estate agent in Wellfleet who seemed to know intuitively the type of house we were looking for. After an offer we made on a beautiful place in Wellfleet fell through, our realtor introduced us to Dick Morrill, a builder who had designed and constructed the house we had hoped to buy. Our realtor told us Morrill could build an identical house at another Outer Cape location. She had found a property for sale in south Truro, in a community of homeowners called Cobb Farm, which was sited on the bay side of the Cape. Residents of

Cobb Farm shared a private beach and tennis court within walking distance of their homes. We made an appointment to meet with Dick the next morning at the Truro property.

We were delighted the moment we saw the tract at Cobb Farm, which was nearly two acres in size. At its highest elevation, we could see the glistening waters of the bay. Less than a mile away stood the Hopper House, where the great American artist Edward Hopper had created many of his famous paintings. And beyond the Hopper House was the skyline of Provincetown, including the historic nineteenth-century tower commemorating the *Mayflower* pilgrims' first landing in the New World. Later, we met Dick and his partner, Jan Potter, at a restaurant in Wellfleet to sign the contract. While at the restaurant, Dick drew on a paper napkin a rough sketch of the floor plan he was proposing. We finally settled into our Cape house in 1992. It soon became the site for our family's summer vacations, as well as for the engagement parties for each one of our three adult children.

* * * * *

In the early fall of 1991, a member of the legislature of the Baltic state of Latvia met with me in my office and made an unusual request. Aware that I had written extensively about the US Constitution, he asked if I would consider traveling to Latvia to advise his legislative committee charged with drafting a new Latvian constitution. He also invited me to give a series of lectures on our constitution. It was a particularly dangerous time for the Latvian government. The citizens of Latvia had overwhelmingly voted to become independent of the Soviet Union in a referendum the previous spring. The Soviet government then attempted a coup d'état, which failed. But the transition from Latvia's status as a Soviet satellite to that of an independent nation was perilous.

I accepted the Latvian legislator's invitation. In late November, Marcia and I flew to Copenhagen and then took a short flight to Riga, the capital of Latvia. As we landed, we could see Soviet tanks and soldiers lining the runways. The scene was no less ominous on our taxi ride into the city, where Soviet soldiers patrolled the streets.

Our hotel had the stolid, nondescript appearance typical of buildings in post–World War II Communist countries. The hotel lobby was almost deserted. Our room was cold but spacious. We suspected that it was bugged. I turned on the television to see the stern face of the Soviet defense minister, a not-too-subtle reminder that Latvia's independence from the Soviet Union was still in jeopardy. It was well below freezing when we took an afternoon stroll through the city. When Marcia pulled out a camera from her purse to take a photo, a Soviet soldier menacingly gestured for her to put it away.

The next day, when I met with the Latvian legislative committee, I could feel the tension among the members. The committee was divided almost equally between those who spoke the Latvian language, including the legislator who had invited me, and Russian-speaking members. Those who spoke Latvian supported a new constitution that guaranteed their citizenship and the nation's independence. The Russian speakers were opposed, determined to protect their rights and ties to the Soviet Union under the existing constitution.

At the request of the committee, I discussed the US Constitution's guarantees of citizenship, both for those born in the United States and naturalized citizens. The Latvian legislators listened attentively; the Russian speakers sat impassively. When a vote was later taken on a motion to draft a new constitution, the members divided almost evenly between those in favor (the Latvian speakers) and opposed (those speaking Russian).

I received a warm reception to my lectures on the US Constitution from a group of Latvian judges and other high-ranking officials. It helped, I'm sure, that I was introduced by the chief justice of the Latvian Supreme Court. He later escorted Marcia and me on a walking tour of the old city, once known as "the Paris of the East." We could visualize the original grandeur of the buildings that, sadly, were in desperate need of restoration.

While I met before the legislative committee and delivered my lectures, Marcia's guide, a Latvian psychiatrist, escorted her to a children's hospital, where she found the low standard of care appalling. The psychiatrist then took her to a local cemetery and pointed to a gravestone with the relief of a father holding his son protectively in his arms. "That little boy was me," he told Marcia. The psychiatrist was Jewish, and the gravestone was a reminder that the Jewish population in Latvia was virtually decimated during World

War II, first by the Nazis and later by the Soviet army. That depressing reality was confirmed when Marcia and I visited a Jewish center in downtown Riga, run by an elderly Jewish lady, that was almost empty.

We celebrated Thanksgiving at the US consulate in Riga, where, without notice, we were asked to explain the festive holiday. We muddled through our presentation before an appreciative audience of guests from the Latvian community and consulate personnel.

On Saturday, a week after our arrival, we were scheduled to board a return flight to Copenhagen. Our week in Riga had been filled with fascinating experiences, but one chilling scene stood out: the intimidating presence of Soviet troops on the city's streets. Eager to leave, we had packed our suitcases well in advance of the time that the shuttle was scheduled to take us to the airport. After taking our seats on the shuttle, we looked nervously out the window as the van moved slowly through a heavy snowstorm. When we finally arrived at the airport, we noticed that the crowd there was restless and unruly. We then learned the reason: all flights that day had been canceled.

Did the cancellation of our flight mean that we would have to wait until the following Saturday for the weekly SAS flight from Riga to Copenhagen? If so, we would also have to reschedule our connecting flight from Copenhagen to New York, delaying our return to the United States for a week. We tried not to sound panicked when we spoke to the SAS attendant at the airline's counter. She told us that, according to her latest information, the canceled flight from Copenhagen had been rescheduled to arrive in Riga the next morning. If the snowstorm persisted into the next morning, however, we faced the grim prospect of being stuck in Riga for another week and an extended separation from our teenage daughter, Sara, who was staying with a friend and her family. While the blizzard raged unabated, we tried to remain calm during the shuttle ride that returned us to our hotel for another night in Riga.

With a feeling of dread, we again boarded an airport shuttle early the next morning. After we entered the airport, we looked at the arrival board and realized that no flights had landed that morning. We waited apprehensively for more than two hours. Shortly after 11 a.m., a small SAS propeller plane landed and taxied to the terminal. It was our flight! After we boarded the plane, we realized that we were the only passengers. A friendly stewardess served us fresh orange juice. We agreed that it was the most delicious orange juice we had ever tasted.

We made our connecting flight to New York with only minutes to spare.

* * * * *

While I served as dean, our family developed in varied and wonderful ways. In the fall of 1984, David enrolled at Clark University in Worcester, Massachusetts. He designed a customized major in music and technology, and his studies anticipated his future career. After graduation in 1988, he got his start in an entry-level job at Russo-Grantham, a music recording company in Lower Manhattan. David married Elyse Wollman, who gave birth to our first grandson, Ethan Jacob Simon, on November 10, 1996. Marcia and I followed the predictable script of all first-time grandparents, overwhelmed with the feeling of disbelief and joy. In 1998 David and Elyse moved to California, where David took a job at Yahoo, the phenomenally successful web portal. He currently serves as senior vice president for marketing at the Los Angeles–based Luminate, a digital company that provides essential data to the music and entertainment industries.

Our daughter Lauren attended Wesleyan University in Middletown, Connecticut, where she found the classes challenging, made lifelong friends, and met her future husband, Tom Irwin. After graduating from Wesleyan in 1991, she began her legal education at the Boston University Law School in the late spring of 1992, where she demonstrated a keen interest and high aptitude for the law. She earned her juris doctor (JD) with honors in 1994. Four years later, her husband, Tom, graduated magna cum laude with a juris doctor degree and a master's degree in environmental law from Vermont Law School. Lauren became a partner in an old, respected Concord, New Hampshire, law firm while Tom served as director of the Conservation Law Foundation's New Hampshire office.

In September 1998, Lauren became pregnant as a result of in vitro fertilization and was told that she could expect to give birth to twins. Her firm granted her a paid three-month leave before the expected births the following June. Shortly before midnight on March 5, 1999, while Marcia and

I were in Fort Lauderdale, Florida, on a fundraising mission for NYLS, we received a telephone call from Cynnie Irwin, Tom's mother. She told us that Lauren, then six months pregnant with the twins, was hemorrhaging and had been driven by ambulance in a heavy snowstorm to Dartmouth-Hitchcock Hospital in Hanover, New Hampshire. Thankfully, Lauren arrived at the hospital safely.

Marcia and I immediately flew to Boston's Logan Airport, where we rented a car and drove to Hanover. We arrived at the hospital around 4 p.m. and rushed to Lauren's room. Much to our relief, she appeared to have suffered no permanent damage because of her hemorrhaging or giving birth to the twins: Natalie and Lindsay. They were being cared for in the hospital's neonatal intensive care unit. Thanks to the extraordinary care that Lindsay and Natalie received at Dartmouth-Hitchcock, their condition began to improve. By the late spring, Natalie was healthy enough for Lauren and Tom to take her home. Lindsay was transferred to Concord Hospital for a few more weeks of supervised care. Marcia and I returned to West Nyack in late April, then made separate trips to Concord in June. The worries that had consumed us at Dartmouth-Hitchcock had abated.

Sara, five years old when I was first appointed dean of NYLS, was completing her freshman year at Clarkstown South High School when I presided at my tenth and final law school commencement as dean in June 1992. During those years, she became an excellent student, a promising ballerina at the Coupé Dance Studio in Nanuet, and a graceful skier at Butternut Mountain in the Berkshires. Sara graduated in 1999 from Trinity College in Hartford, Connecticut, where she studied in an interdisciplinary humanities program. After graduation she earned a master's degree at Columbia Teachers College and became an outstanding English teacher at her old high school, Clarkstown South. In 2007 she married computer analyst Keith More in the idyllic natural setting of a public park in Somers, New York.

In 1985, Marcia discovered her professional calling at Volunteer Counseling Service in Rockland County. She developed a bond with her needy clients, mostly young women, who stayed in touch with her for years afterward. She then enrolled in a master's degree program at Columbia University's School of Social Work. Assuming primary care for Sara while I worked long hours as dean of the law school, Marcia nonetheless made superb grades.

She also demonstrated an unusual ability to empathize with and counsel children in her internships at Rockland Psychiatric Hospital and Upper Nyack Elementary School. In 1991, after graduation from Columbia, she was hired as a school social worker at Felix Festa Middle School, the school that our kids had attended, and later at New City Elementary School. She continued to do exceptional counseling work with students and opened a limited private practice at home for troubled children and their parents.

• • • • •

On June 4, 1992, the board of trustees of New York Law School conferred two honorary degrees. The first was awarded to Associate Justice Sandra Day O'Connor, who served as the pivotal swing justice on many of the US Supreme Court's most contentious constitutional issues. Before her Court appointment, she had earned a reputation as a moderate Republican legislator and judge in her native Arizona. On the Supreme Court, O'Connor took centrist positions that were often supported by members of the liberal wing of the Court. In 1992, shortly after she received her honorary degree from the law school, she joined the Court's liberals in one of the most important decisions of the decade, *Planned Parenthood v. Casey*, which upheld *Roe v. Wade*.

I was awarded the second honorary degree at the commencement. The last paragraph of the citation read: "James F. Simon, for your recognized achievements in scholarship, making the Supreme Court more comprehensible through your perceptive books; for your dedication to the law and to legal education as an outstanding teacher; for your leadership as Dean of New York Law School during a decade of outstanding advancement, the Board of Trustees of New York Law School hereby confers upon you the degree of Doctor of Laws *honoris causa*."

It was an extraordinary day of celebration for me, especially since I could share it with Marcia and our children. After the ceremony, we posed with Justice O'Connor for a photo. She sent us a copy with the inscription: "To the Simons, one and all, with happy memories."

CHAPTER 15

INSIDE THE SUPREME COURT

Soon after the publication of *The Antagonists* in 1989, I began thinking about my next book. My attention immediately turned to the possibility of writing a biography of either Justice Blackmun or Justice Brennan, the two members of the Court whom I knew best. Both justices presented compelling reasons to write their biographies. Blackmun had written the majority opinion in *Roe v. Wade*, the Court's historic 1973 decision that guaranteed a woman the constitutional right to an abortion in the first two trimesters of pregnancy. Brennan was the intellectual leader of the liberal wing of the modern Supreme Court and had either written or influenced scores of decisions expanding civil rights and liberties. If I did not write a biography of either justice, I considered, alternatively, working on an "Inside-the-Court" book, based, I hoped, on interviews with the two justices as well as memoranda and correspondence in their official papers.

I had known Justice Brennan for many years before becoming dean and interviewed him for my biography of Justice Douglas as well as for my dual biography of Justices Black and Frankfurter. I had first met Justice Blackmun in 1983, shortly after becoming interim dean, when the law school had awarded him an honorary degree. Marcia and I had enjoyed the weekend with him and his wife, Dottie, and felt that we had begun a genuine friendship with the couple. Two years later, I had arranged for the law school to honor both Blackmun and Brennan at a reception during the AALS annual meeting in Washington, DC. Dottie Blackmun joined her husband at the reception, which allowed Marcia and me to renew our friendship with the couple. The reception produced one of my favorite anecdotes, reversing NYLS's pecking order with the more prestigious NYU Law School. Among Blackmun and Brennan's colleagues invited to our reception was Chief Justice William Rehnquist. When Rehnquist had first mistakenly gone to the NYU Law School's reception and was greeted graciously by the NYU dean, the chief justice begged his pardon and asked for directions to our reception.

In the winter of 1990, I met with Justice Blackmun in his chambers to discuss the possibility of writing his biography. He welcomed the idea and agreed to be interviewed for the book. But he resisted the idea of granting me access to his papers while he still served on the Court. He did not say, however, that his decision to deny me access to his papers was final. We agreed to meet again to discuss my proposed biography.

Soon afterward, Mother attended a lecture delivered by Justice Blackmun at the Southern Methodist University (SMU) Law School in Dallas. Afterward, she introduced herself to Dottie Blackmun, who told her that her husband was pleased that I might write his biography. But in my next meeting with the justice, he said he had made a final decision not to grant me access to his papers while he served on the Court. That was a restriction I was unwilling to accept.

I then returned to the idea of writing a biography of Justice Brennan or a book on the internal dynamics of the justices' deliberations, based on interviews with Brennan as well as access to his papers. In my previous interviews with him, he had been refreshingly candid in discussing Douglas, Black, and Frankfurter, as well as his other judicial colleagues.

Brennan had remained unusually friendly during my deanship, and he had accepted my invitation to receive an honorary degree from NYLS, one of the first law schools to honor him, in 1986. And he had been his usual charming, outgoing self when we honored him at the law school's reception at the AALS meeting in Washington, DC. I sensed that behind his friendliness may have been an ulterior motive, perhaps to encourage me to write his biography.

But writing a Brennan biography, even more than a biography of Blackmun, would have been an especially daunting task. Brennan had served on the Court since 1956, fifteen years longer than Blackmun, and, as leader of the liberal justices, was destined to be assigned a crucial role in the history of the modern Supreme Court. It was well known that Brennan kept notes on the justices' weekly conferences during his entire tenure on the Court. As a result, I calculated that a Brennan biography would require many years of meticulous research, assuming I could interview him and be granted access to his papers.

While I was contemplating a biography of Brennan or a more focused book on the Court's internal deliberations, I learned that the *Wall Street Journal*'s Supreme Court reporter Steve Wermiel had begun work on a Brennan biography with the justice's cooperation. Wermiel's biography of Brennan, however, did not prevent me from writing a book about the confidential deliberations of the justices, assuming that I could obtain Brennan's cooperation. In the spring of 1990, I arranged a meeting with Brennan to discuss my proposal and was delighted, and slightly surprised, that he agreed to cooperate.

I called my agent, Esther Newberg, with the exciting news. She told me to write a short proposal stressing that my "Inside-the-Court" book would be written with the cooperation of Justice Brennan, though that cooperation would remain confidential. I quickly wrote the proposal. Within a week, I received a call from Esther. Alice Mayhew, my editor at Simon and Schuster, had offered a hefty six-figure advance, by far the largest I had ever received. Alice seemed to be the ideal editor for my book, since she had been Bob Woodward's editor for *The Brethren*, the best-selling book on the Court's private deliberations. I was thrilled and immediately agreed to write the book for Simon and Schuster.

* * * * *

Churning with excitement, I entered Justice Brennan's chambers in June 1990. It was my first research visit to his chambers since signing the lucrative contract for my "Inside-the-Court" book. Based on my conversation with Brennan before signing my contract, I anticipated his full cooperation, assuming he would provide access to his files and his notes on the justices' conferences and that he would make time for interviews with me.

Once inside Brennan's chambers, I sensed that my relationship with him, so cordial for more than a decade, had changed. He greeted me perfunctorily, without his usual wide grin and firm handshake. He seemed tense and gave no hint of our long friendship when he introduced me to one of his law clerks, who, he said, would show me to his Court files.

I spent the day reading internal memoranda between Brennan and his judicial colleagues as well as early drafts of his opinions dating back to his first years on the Court in the 1950s. I carefully set aside the memoranda that reflected Brennan's skills as a negotiator with his judicial colleagues. Those skills were especially impressive when the justices were split on a difficult constitutional issue, and Brennan, with a combination of patience and subtle persuasion, coaxed a wavering colleague to support his position.

By the end of the week, I had accumulated materials that provided insights into the Court's deliberative process. Each day I copied reams of pages from Brennan's files, stuffed them into my attaché case, and lugged them to the elevator, past the Court guards, and out the front door of the building. All the while, I attempted to look as if I were preoccupied with important Court business, giving no hint of the value or weight of the papers that I was carrying. When I returned to my hotel room, I admired my day's catch as if I were a veteran fisherman who had landed a gigantic striped bass or tuna.

Throughout the week, I tried to ignore Brennan's studied indifference to my presence in his chambers. Each day I observed him meeting with Steve Wermiel, his authorized biographer, sometimes over lunch. He never invited me to join them or offered to meet with me privately, as I had expected, based on our earlier conversation. Since I was given no opportunity to interview him, I could not ask to review his notes from the justices' private deliberations, an invaluable source that I assumed he had made available to Wermiel.

I was mystified and profoundly disappointed by Brennan's attitude toward me but soon learned the reason for his strange behavior. Shortly before I began my research in Brennan's chambers, Chief Justice William

Rehnquist and Associate Justice Sandra Day O'Connor had met with Brennan in his chambers and warned him that he was jeopardizing the integrity of the Court by sharing his private notes, papers, and candid opinions in interviews with authors and other researchers writing about the Court. It was presumably too late for Brennan to renege on his commitment to cooperate with his authorized biographer, Wermiel, but he could, and did, call a halt to his cooperation with me beyond allowing me access to his official files. Wermiel, I assumed, would soon be overwhelmed by the enormous volume of Brennan materials, a problem that I had anticipated when I had earlier abandoned the idea of writing the justice's biography. Wermiel's biography of Brennan was published in 2010, more than twenty years after he began the project, and he was assisted by a coauthor, Seth Stern.

Only a month after I began my research, Brennan suffered a stroke and resigned from the Court. After his stroke, I no longer had access to his files. My "Inside-the-Court" research, for all practical purposes, had ended. Even so, I had accumulated internal memoranda and draft opinions that provided invaluable insights into the decision-making process of the justices. I could still write an important book, but my failure to interview Brennan or gain access to his notes on the justices' deliberations meant that my book would lack the detail and human drama that made Bob Woodward's *The Brethren* a best seller.

I also interviewed Chief Justice William Rehnquist and Associate Justices Harry Blackmun, Sandra Day O'Connor, and David Souter, as well as former associate justice Lewis Powell Jr., for the book, but none of them would discuss the Court's internal deliberations in specific cases.

The uneven nature of my research required me to devise a new format for the book. The most valuable materials that I had extracted from Brennan's files dealt with a civil rights case, *Patterson v. McLean Credit Union*, which had been argued before the Court in 1988. The question before the Court was whether the plaintiff, Brenda Patterson, a Black employee of a North Carolina credit union, had been wrongly fired from her job because of her race in violation of a federal civil rights statute. After the argument, the justices had initially voted 5–4 in support of Patterson's claim, with Brennan in the majority. Since Brennan was the senior justice in the majority, he could assign the majority opinion and assigned it to himself.

Justice Anthony Kennedy, an appointee of Republican president Ronald Reagan, had provided the critical fifth vote for Brennan's majority. Brennan knew that his greatest challenge was to write an opinion that Kennedy, the most conservative member of his majority, would join. In draft after laborious draft, Brennan fought to keep a wavering Kennedy with him in the majority. The drafts and exchanges of memoranda between Brennan and Kennedy not only showed Brennan's persuasive skills but also offered a rare glimpse into the justices' internal deliberations. Ultimately, Brennan's skills failed to persuade Kennedy to sign onto his opinion. Kennedy then joined the four original dissenters, the Court's most conservative justices. And Brennan, once the majority opinion writer, was left to write a blistering dissent.

Regrettably, I could not duplicate the compelling narrative of the Patterson case in other Court decisions. Even in the most important cases, the internal exchanges among the justices were usually limited to draft opinions and memoranda with none of the verbal fireworks of the Brennan-Kennedy dialogue in *Patterson*. The result, I felt, still offered readers a unique understanding of the justices' deliberative process, particularly based on the drafts and memoranda in Brennan's files. But no other Court decision revealed the internal friction among the justices so evident in the Patterson case.

After I turned in my manuscript and Alice Mayhew at Simon and Schuster read it in the fall of 1994, she agreed with my conclusion: despite the fact that Chief Justice William Rehnquist was the most conservative leader of the Court in more than fifty years, and that he served with five associate justices appointed by Republican presidents, the Court, remarkably, had not turned decisively to the right. A second surprising observation I had made in the book was that although a sixth justice, Byron White, had been appointed by a Democratic president, John F. Kennedy, he often voted with the conservatives. Alice therefore suggested that we call the book *The Center Holds: The Power Struggle Inside the Rehnquist Court.*

As if I had not dealt with enough problems researching and writing this book, I encountered another one a few months after the book had gone to press in the spring of 1995. At the end of the judicial term in late June, the Court issued a series of civil rights and liberties decisions that appeared to call into question both the title of my book and its conclusion. On July 2,

1995, the *New York Times* headline for the story summarizing the Court's term read, "Farewell to the Old Order in the Court: The Right Goes Activist and the Center Is a Void."

I was badly shaken by the *Times* headline. But upon reading the majority opinions that inspired the headline, I was satisfied that both my book's title and my conclusions were accurate. Each of the Court decisions was supported by only five justices, including Justices Kennedy and O'Connor, who had earned reputations as center-right moderates unwilling to overturn established precedents. Both justices, for example, had earlier voted to preserve *Roe v. Wade*. The majority opinions announced in late June were not sweeping conservative manifestos but rather narrow, fact-based analyses stemming from the relevant statutes and constitutional provisions. I was confident that these decisions, particularly considered in the context of the eight years of the Court's decisions under Chief Justice Rehnquist, supported my book's conclusion.

Despite the jarring end-of-term *Times* headline, I received a thoughtful, favorable review in the Sunday *New York Times Book Review* by Jeffrey Rosen, a professor at George Washington University Law School, who later was appointed president of the National Constitution Center in Philadelphia. On the basis of the Rosen review, the *Times* listed *The Center Holds* as a "Notable *Times* Book of 1995."

Unfortunately, other reviewers of my book were influenced by the spate of 5–4 decisions at the end of the term tilting toward Chief Justice Rehnquist's conservative perspective. A long review in *The New Yorker* by Jeffrey Toobin, the magazine's legal affairs correspondent, focused on those late-term decisions. Toobin's review, accompanied by an artist's sketch of me based on my jacket photo, concluded that the Court's decisions undercut my thesis, despite the fact that my analysis covered almost a decade of rulings. A year later, when the Court decisions for the term fit into the overall pattern I had traced over eight Court terms, Toobin wrote me a note of apology.

At the beginning of the Court's term in October 1995, Stuart Taylor Jr., a columnist for *Legal Times*, reiterated the theme of *The Center Holds*. Taylor wrote, "The Court's current majority comes up about in the center or even, in the case of abortion and religion in the schools, a bit to the left of center." "The bottom line," he concluded, "is that it's hard to think of a single big issue on which the policy judgments implicit in the decisions of the Rehnquist Court are clearly to the right of center, measured by public opinion."

Despite my book's inclusion in the *New York Times* "Notable Books" list, I could not escape the feeling of disappointment. The double whammy—Justice Brennan's lack of full cooperation and the Court's end-of-term decisions that appeared to undercut my thesis at the moment of my book's publication—virtually guaranteed disappointing sales. I worried that the failure of my book's sales to cover my large advance would discourage Alice Mayhew from bidding on a future proposal. But that did not stop me from contemplating my next book project.

CHAPTER 16

PRESIDENTS AND CHIEF JUSTICES

Only a few months after *The Center Holds: The Power Struggle Inside the Rehnquist Court* was published in 1995, I decided my next book project would focus on clashes between chief justices and US presidents throughout American history. I narrowed my research to three confrontations: Chief Justice John Marshall and President Thomas Jefferson; Chief Justice Roger Taney and President Abraham Lincoln; and Chief Justice Charles Evans Hughes and President Franklin D. Roosevelt.

Every constitutional law student is familiar with the clash between Jefferson and Marshall in Marshall's decision for the Court in *Marbury v. Madison*. After Jefferson defeated John Adams in the presidential election of 1800, Jefferson's secretary of state, James Madison, refused to deliver the judicial commission of William Marbury, an appointee of the outgoing Adams administration. Marshall, who had been appointed chief justice by President Adams shortly before Jefferson took the oath of office, had the difficult task of writing an opinion for the Court that upheld the right of Marbury to the commission without inciting an attack by the new president that could undermine the authority of the Supreme Court.

But *Marbury* was only one of the clashes between Jefferson and Marshall that had begun years before they became president and chief justice, respectively. As young men, they had been bitterly at odds over political philosophy. Jefferson believed in states' rights while Marshall was a powerful advocate for a strong federal government. Their disagreements were not just political but also personal. Although they were second cousins, they hated each other.

The Lincoln-Taney clash centered on their contrasting views of slavery. Lincoln believed slavery was immoral and attacked the pro-slavery views of his 1858 Senate opponent, Stephen Douglas, in the famous Lincoln-Douglas debates. In those debates, Lincoln also deplored Chief Justice Taney's majority opinion in *Dred Scott v. Sandford*, the Court's 1857 decision in which Taney declared that the US Constitution did not protect the rights of Black Americans, whether slave or free. After Lincoln was elected president, he and Chief Justice Taney continued to clash over constitutional issues during the Civil War.

The conflict between President Roosevelt and Chief Justice Hughes was over a single issue: whether the popular and frustrated president could "pack the Court" by adding new justices to outvote the conservative Court majority that had struck down major New Deal legislation during the Great Depression.

I considered each of the three clashes between these presidents and chief justices worthy of a book. But I concluded that the Jefferson-Marshall rivalry was the most compelling because of the long-standing, rancorous political disagreements between the two men as well as their personal animosity toward each other. In the winter of 1996, less than a year after my book *The Center Holds* was published, I sent my proposal for a book on Jefferson and Marshall to Esther Newberg, who in turn sent it to my editor at Simon and Schuster, Alice Mayhew. Alice liked the proposal and offered a substantial advance, although considerably less than the amount I had received for *The Center Holds*. I quickly agreed to terms to write my third book for Simon and Schuster with Alice as my editor.

I received a modest grant from the Jefferson Foundation to do research for my book at the University of Virginia's Alderman Library, thanks to a recommendation by my New York Law School colleague Annette Gordon-Reed, whose excellent book on the intimate relationship between Jefferson and his teenage slave Sally Hemings had recently been published by the University of Virginia Press. After taking a flight to Charlottesville and checking into my hotel, I wasted no time in introducing myself to the research staff at the Alderman Library. They led me to a small, windowless inner sanctum, where I was given thin white gloves to handle Jefferson's original letters. I was allowed to examine two letters at a time. After I had read those letters and taken notes, they were taken away, and two more that I had requested were then placed on the table in front of me. Reading Jefferson's letters, many of them written more than two hundred years ago, gave me chills.

After my days of research at the library, I usually had dinner with two Jefferson scholars who were also doing research there, one a professor at the University of Indiana and the other at Washington University in St. Louis. Our dinner conversations were dominated by animated discussions of "TJ," as they referred to Jefferson. Their affectionate reference to him by his initials, as if he were their constant companion, seemed appropriate, as they had spent many years studying the nation's third president.

When I had finished my research at the Alderman Library, I drove to Jefferson's home, Monticello ("Little Mountain"), built on a steep hill a few miles outside of Charlottesville. The home that he had designed and lived in until his death in 1826 reflected his life and accomplishments in remarkable detail.

Upon entering the front door at Monticello, I observed artifacts from Meriwether Lewis and William Clark's historic expedition in 1803, commissioned by President Jefferson, to explore the western portion of the country, which had been newly acquired under the terms of the Louisiana Purchase. To the left of the entrance hall, I walked into Jefferson's study. On his desk was one of his inventions, a device that connected two pens so that Jefferson could write a letter with one and make a copy with the other. Surrounding his desk were shelves of books, many of them on the political philosophy of the Enlightenment. In the elegant dining room, I could envision the dinners that Jefferson hosted surrounded by his neighbors James Madison and James Monroe, both of them successors to the presidency. Near the dining room table was a "dumb waiter," also a Jefferson invention, in which dishes were elevated manually on a lift from the kitchen below.

Outside the mansion, I marveled at the beautifully manicured grounds and gardens. But nearby I also observed dark, dank slave quarters. How, I wondered, could Jefferson, author of the soaring words of the Declaration of Independence, have enslaved more than two hundred human beings?

My final stop at Monticello was Jefferson's grave, located in a small cemetery a short walk from his house. He had requested that only three of his accomplishments be inscribed on his tombstone: his authorship of the Declaration of Independence; his drafting of the Virginia Statute for Religious Freedom; and his founding of the University of Virginia.

From Monticello, I drove to John Marshall's home in downtown Richmond, the capital of Virginia. Unlike Jefferson's Monticello, Marshall's two-story house did not reflect the owner's life and accomplishments. My visit nonetheless allowed me to inspect a few of the chief justice's accoutrements, including his judicial robe and a lock of his wife's hair. More valuable research on Marshall awaited me in Williamsburg, my next stop. I spent several days reading Marshall's original letters at the College of William & Mary, where they were being prepared for publication. Marshall's letters, like Jefferson's, contained frequently candid observations on leading issues of the day as well as a few well-placed swipes at his political enemies, including Jefferson.

Shortly after returning from my research trip to Virginia, I drove to the Massachusetts Historical Society in Boston, where I studied another collection of original Jefferson letters. Those remarkable letters served as the foundation for my book. But I also surveyed the vast literature on Jefferson and Marshall, including biographies, histories of the times in which they had served in public office, and the magisterial opinions of Chief Justice Marshall. I continued to do research on the book in Concord, New Hampshire, on a visit with Lauren and her family. I spent mornings in Concord in the library at Franklin Pierce Law School, only a five-minute drive from their house. To my surprise, I made a valuable discovery in the library. In reading the Supreme Court reporter's summaries of the attorneys' oral argument in *Marbury v. Madison*, the seminal decision written by Chief Justice Marshall declaring the Supreme Court's authority to rule an act of Congress unconstitutional, I gained fresh insights into Marshall's opinion for the Court that I later incorporated into my analysis of the case for the book.

With trepidation, I submitted my manuscript to Alice Mayhew in January

2001. I was slightly intimidated by Alice, although she had been my editor for almost twenty years. She was a tiny woman, barely five feet tall, but spoke in a rasping, commanding voice that exuded authority. As senior vice president at Simon and Schuster, she oversaw the publisher's books on American history, politics, and law. Her authors' list was the envy of every other nonfiction editor in the New York publishing world. It included the historians Stephen Ambrose and Doris Kearns Goodwin, whose books were best sellers and, in Goodwin's case, winner of the Pulitzer Prize, as well as the famous investigative reporter Bob Woodward.

One cold January morning, Alice and I met in her cramped, book-cluttered office. She greeted me in her familiar gruff voice. But she then flashed a rare smile and told me she liked my manuscript very much. Her only suggestion, actually a command, was that I write a new introductory chapter that placed the Jefferson-Marshall clash in the broader context of the politics of the early republic.

Her approval was the elixir I needed to complete the manuscript. Jubilantly, I returned home and wrote a new introductory chapter in less than a month. Alice chose the title—*What Kind of Nation: Thomas Jefferson, John Marshall, and the Epic Struggle to Create a United States*. Roger Labrie, a soft-spoken, highly skilled associate editor at S&S, was assigned the line-by-line editing of my manuscript. When I continued to express reservations about the manuscript as it moved inexorably toward publication, Roger told me that I was too close to it and not to worry.

Alice's and Roger's confidence in the quality of my book was immediately borne out the week of publication in March 2002. *What Kind of Nation* received a lengthy, rave review in the Sunday *New York Times Book Review* by Joseph Ellis, a prominent historian who had won a Pulitzer Prize for one of his books on the early American republic. In his review, he congratulated me on writing the first major dual biography of Jefferson and Marshall and wrote that it was "[a] model of narrative history." The *Times* later made it a "Notable Book of 2002."

In addition to Ellis's laudatory review in the *Times*, I was especially gratified by a letter I received from Justice John Paul Stevens, who said appreciatively that my analysis of Chief Justice Marshall's opinion in *McCulloch v. Maryland* had provided him with new insights into the decision. Marshall's

1819 opinion for a unanimous Court in *McCulloch v. Maryland* established Congress's implied power to create a national bank and rejected Maryland's argument that a state could tax a federally chartered bank.

After the Ellis review appeared in the *Times*, my book briefly made the best-seller lists at Amazon and the *Times*. *What Kind of Nation* sold steadily in hardcover for a year and even better in the paperback edition, which was published in 2003. The paperback edition is still in print and continues to sell a few hundred copies a year to university students assigned the book in American history courses. A Chinese-language paperback was also published; I recently signed a contract for a second Chinese-language printing.

Following the *Times* review, I began to receive invitations to give lectures on the book. I signed up with an agent and, for the first time, made a tidy sum speaking to large groups. One of my most memorable lecture experiences took place in Portland, Oregon, before an audience of about three hundred members of the Oregon Historical Society. I was introduced by former US senator Mark Hatfield, the president of the society. After his generous introduction, I told the audience that I was a lifelong Democrat but nonetheless admired Hatfield, a moderate Republican. At a reception sponsored by the historical society following my lecture, Hatfield asked me to sign his copies of my books. He handed me a stack of books dating back to my first, *In His Own Image*, which I signed with pleasure.

The most unusual gift from my tour was presented after I delivered a lecture to the cadets at West Point—a West Point parade hat with an inscription on the frame underneath that read, "James F. Simon, Guest Lecturer, With Appreciation from Cadets & Faculty." My favorite introduction was given by my daughter, Lauren, before my address to a group of attorneys in the federal court building in Concord, New Hampshire. In Fort Worth, I spoke to more than fifty of my Paschal High School classmates at an event sponsored by two couples—Gene and Nancy Dozier, and Jim and Karen Barlow—who were among my closest hometown friends.

My largest audience was at the New York Public Library, where I spoke to a capacity crowd in the library's auditorium. I was introduced that night by Richard Gilder, a wealthy financier and dedicated student of American history. He had cofounded the Gilder Lehrman Institute of American History, which supports K–12 American history education. Gilder liked my lecture so much that he recommended me to the director of Jefferson studies at Monticello, who invited me to give a lecture on Jefferson's back lawn as part of a summer lecture series. In the summer of 2003, I spoke to an appreciative audience at Monticello, a fitting culmination of my lecture tour.

• • • • •

With the success of *What Kind of Nation*, it was no surprise that I soon wrote a proposal for the second book on my list of clashes between American presidents and chief justices—President Lincoln and Chief Justice Taney. In the fall of 2003, I signed a contract to write the book for Simon and Schuster with Alice Mayhew once again my editor.

My research on Chief Justice Taney began in Frederick, Maryland, where I visited his childhood home, his law office, his home as a young attorney—with slave quarters in the back—and the cemetery where he was buried. From Frederick, I drove to Baltimore to study Taney's original letters at the state historical society. Afterward, I traveled to Springfield, Illinois, Lincoln's home from his days as a young attorney in the state capital until his nomination for the presidency in 1860. I visited his home, his law office, and the state legislative chamber where he delivered his famous "House Divided" speech. I also examined Lincoln's original letters at his presidential library.

My most moving research experience for the Lincoln-Taney book occurred on the outskirts of Gettysburg, Pennsylvania, where the decisive battle of the Civil War was fought. I walked up and down the hills, imagining the horrible toll in human life taken during the bloody three-day battle, and then stood where Lincoln had delivered the Gettysburg Address. I wiped away tears just thinking about the president's speech at that critical moment in American history.

My book *Lincoln and Chief Justice Taney: Slavery, Secession, and the President's War Powers* was published in November 2006. I was especially proud of the endorsement for the book by the famous historian Arthur Schlesinger Jr. that appeared on the back jacket of the book. My favorite letter of appreciation after the book's publication came from Justice Samuel Alito, who wrote that he was eager to read the book but would have to wait until his wife had finished it. The book was later published in a paperback edition and read in an audio recording.

But the Lincoln-Taney book did not enjoy the critical or commercial success of *What Kind of Nation* for a couple of reasons. First, books on Lincoln had become a massive cottage industry; my book was added to a list that numbered more than fifteen thousand publications. It was therefore difficult for any book on Lincoln, including mine, to attract the attention of editors of major book reviews.

The second problem for my book in reaching a wide readership was that Taney, unlike the revered chief justice John Marshall, had the dubious distinction of being the most reviled leader of the Court in American history. In my book, I discussed Taney's admirable career as a private attorney, Maryland's attorney general, and secretary of the treasury under President Andrew Jackson, as well as his many excellent judicial opinions as chief justice. But despite his considerable accomplishments, Taney will be remembered for a single deed: writing the majority opinion for the US Supreme Court in *Dred Scott v. Sandford*, in which he declared that Black Americans, whether slave or free, were not entitled to the protections under the Constitution accorded to white Americans.

• • • • •

Although book sales of *Lincoln and Chief Justice Taney* were not spectacular, they were steady. As a result, I was again invited to give lectures across the country, including to a large book club in Pensacola, Florida; to students and faculty at Skidmore College in Saratoga, New York; and to a Lincoln symposium at Louisiana State University.

Three of my favorite talks were given with family members in attendance. The first was delivered at the Fort Worth Club with Mother on the podium next to me. The occasion was the inaugural lecture of a series to benefit the Fort Worth Public Library. Before discussing my Lincoln-Taney book, I recalled my fond memories of regularly accompanying Mother to the public library in downtown Fort Worth shortly after I had learned to read. I was barely tall enough to reach the check-out counter but had nonetheless proudly presented my books next to Mother's large stack.

The second memorable talk with a family member in the audience was given to my grandson Ethan Simon's fifth-grade class in Lexington, Massachusetts. The invitation from Ethan was inspired by a postcard that I had sent him from Gettysburg with a colorful painting of the historic battle. Ethan seemed pleased with my talk and introduced me to his classmates afterward.

My third lecture on Lincoln and Taney with family members in attendance occurred in April 2009, more than two years after the book's publication, and was the most prestigious. It was delivered in the courtroom of the US Supreme Court. I had been asked to prepare an original lecture on Lincoln and Taney as part of an endowed lectureship series sponsored by the Supreme Court Historical Society. Every lecturer in the series was introduced by a member of the US Supreme Court. I was pleased to learn that Associate Justice David Souter, a friend as well as a justice whom I admired, would introduce me.

The day before my scheduled lecture, I woke up with a terrible cold and called Justice Souter's chambers to report my miserable condition. The justice's executive secretary arranged for me to see the physician in the Court's infirmary. I do not remember what cold remedy he prescribed, but it did the trick. I was robust and ready the next night for my lecture.

The seats in the courtroom were filled for my lecture. I stood at the same podium used that morning by lawyers addressing the justices during their oral arguments. In his introduction, Justice Souter paid me the high compliment of describing my books on the Court as the work of an author who emulated attorneys in the finest common law tradition. He explained that I, like the best common law attorneys, built my books, as they did their cases, from the ground up, analyzing the facts and drawing legal conclusions based on those facts. I could not have been more flattered. My lecture, which focused on the fraught Lincoln-Taney relationship based on their earlier careers in the law, was well received and later published in the Supreme Court Historical Society's journal. A reception followed in one of the elegant rooms adjacent to the courtroom. The evening ended with Justice Souter posing with my family for the Court photographer. That was an evening indelibly etched in my memory.

After delivering my lecture at the Supreme Court, I naturally began to think about my next book project. My Lincoln-Taney book had sold well enough to entice Simon and Schuster to offer me another lucrative contract to write a third book in what had become a series on the clashes between American presidents and chief justices of the United States. I was now prepared to move into the twentieth century to write about the clash between President Franklin Delano Roosevelt and Chief Justice Charles Evans Hughes.

Their disagreement had erupted after an incensed President Roosevelt, fed up with a conservative Supreme Court majority that had struck down key New Deal legislation as unconstitutional, proposed a Court-packing plan. His plan, which he described as a judicial reform measure to bring new energy to an aging Court, would have allowed him to appoint six additional justices to match the six sitting justices over seventy years old. If enacted into law, his proposal would have eliminated the conservative majority that had so frustrated him. But as the president was expressing his concern for the overworked septuagenarians on the Court, Chief Justice Hughes informed the chairman of the Senate Judiciary Committee that the Court was up-to-date on its calendar and needed no help from President Roosevelt or anyone else.

Primary research for my new book required several trips to the Franklin D. Roosevelt Presidential Library and Museum in Hyde Park, New York, as well as visits to the manuscript collection of the Library of Congress to study the revealing letters of Charles Evans Hughes. FDR's library was built on his family's estate in Dutchess County, New York, where Roosevelt had grown up as the only child of wealthy, doting parents. Within walking distance of the presidential library, I toured the Roosevelt mansion, including FDR's study on the first floor, the room in which he not only dealt with matters of state but also spent many hours with his treasured stamp collection. Two miles away, I visited the cottage that FDR had built for his wife, Eleanor, after they ceased living as husband and wife, though she continued to be one of his most valued political advisers.

While working on the Roosevelt-Hughes book, I continued teaching a full schedule of courses at NYLS. During the fall semester of 2010, Marcia raised the issue of our retirement. After many years as a stay-at-home mom raising our three kids, she had made the decision in the mid-1990s to return to graduate school, earning a master's degree at Columbia in social work. The degree had led to a highly successful career as a school social worker in the Clarkstown school district. But as we entered our seventies, Marcia became increasingly concerned about her legal liability in counseling students with suicidal thoughts or physically abusive parents and grandparents. She also worried that our health would fail, depriving us of the pleasure of taking care of our grandchildren and traveling abroad.

Marcia had raised the subject before, but in our early discussions, I was not enthusiastic about retirement, since I still enjoyed teaching and earned a substantial salary. During the 2008 economic recession, my compensation had provided ample income even as our investment portfolio declined in value. By 2010, however, I had several reasons to reconsider Marcia's idea that we should retire. After President Barack Obama's 2009 stimulus bill became law, and the economy slowly began to recover from the recession, our retirement funds appeared secure. Moreover, in the age of the internet, I found my classes less satisfying, as many of my students hid behind their computers, totally disengaged from the class discussion.

An additional reason for me to consider retirement occurred during the 2010 fall semester, when the faculty voted to change the basic constitutional law course. Younger faculty members had petitioned for a one-semester, four-credit course, rather than the two-semester, six-credit course that had been required ever since I had joined the faculty thirty-five years earlier. I opposed the new four-credit course, arguing that the condensed version could not adequately cover essential constitutional materials, but was on the losing side of the vote.

In December 2010, Marcia and I gave notice to our employers of our retirements at the end of the academic year. A few days after I informed the NYLS dean, Rick Matasar (who had succeeded Harry Wellington), of my decision to retire from the full-time faculty, the dean proposed that the law school host a symposium in my honor during the spring semester of 2012. I was delighted with his idea of the symposium as well as his suggestion that the papers presented by the symposium's participants be published in an edition of the *New York Law School Law Review*.

At the end of the 2011 spring semester, Marcia's many years of service as a school social worker at New City Elementary School were celebrated at an evening event. Her principal, Deb Forman, lauded Marcia's many talents and remarkable rapport with students. While I agreed with every word, for me the greatest tributes to Marcia that evening were not delivered from the podium but from her students who attended the ceremony and came by our table. She had counseled some of them individually, while others were members of her "Meet-and-Eat" and "New Americans" lunch groups. "Hi, Mrs. Simon," one after another said, politely but with a grin and look of undisguised gratitude.

• • • • •

Alice Mayhew, my longtime editor at Simon and Schuster, wanted to feature my FDR-Hughes book in the publisher's spring 2012 catalog. This meant that I had to complete the manuscript by the early spring of 2011, which was not a problem. But she insisted that my source notes for the book be delivered to her by mid-June, which was a challenge, since I not only had to compile several hundred source notes but also double-check them for accuracy.

By early June, I still had not completed the source notes but decided to take a weekend off to attend my fiftieth Yale class reunion in New Haven. Marcia and I made plans to stay with our friends Colin and Ginny Bradford in a pleasant bed-and-breakfast near the Yale campus. We enjoyed the weekend with the Bradfords and other classmates and their spouses. But by Sunday afternoon, as we prepared to return to West Nyack, I began to feel pain in my upper back as well as in both shoulders.

After returning to West Nyack, I made an appointment with my internist, who suggested that my pain was the result of stress from working on my source notes. Once I finished the source notes for my book, he expected that my pain would go away. I finished the source notes, but my pain became worse. By early July, after we had driven to our house on Cape Cod, I knew something was seriously wrong and scheduled an MRI. For forty-five minutes, as my body was moved back and forth through the MRI machine, my shoulders were pressed against the machine, causing excruciating pain.

The MRI showed that I was suffering from spinal cord compression but provided no explanation for my shoulder pain. Marcia asked Dr. Paul

Rosman, who was married to Marcia's cousin Syrille, to arrange for me to meet with the chairman of the spinal surgery department at Tufts Medical School. After meetings with spinal specialists at Tufts, we decided that I should have surgery. When I met with the surgeon who would perform the operation, he explained that he would fuse five vertebrae in my upper back, a procedure he had done dozens of times.

Shortly afterward, the pain in my shoulders became progressively worse. The pain was so bad that I called Tufts. The physician on duty prescribed a strong pain medication, OxyContin. Later that night, I woke up feeling faint and asked Marcia to follow me to the upstairs bathroom. Once in the bathroom, I fainted. Luckily, Marcia was able to break my fall. I ended up in the bathtub. She yelled to our son, David, who was downstairs. He rushed to our bathroom and helped me back to our bed.

Marcia called an ambulance, which took us to the emergency room at Cape Cod Hospital in Hyannis. When my pain did not subside and emergency room doctors did not seem to know what to do, Marcia called Paul Rosman in Boston, who arranged for me to be admitted to Tufts Hospital. Marcia ordered an ambulance to take the two of us there, a ride that seemed endless as we crept slowly through heavy traffic for more than two hours.

I spent the next ten days in the hospital while rotating teams of specialists observed and examined me, ordering multiple tests and looking for signs of serious, possibly fatal diseases. Marcia, fearing the worst, insisted on sleeping in my room. No test or specialist appeared to have an explanation for my shoulder pain, which became so intense that I could not get out of bed without assistance.

Finally, more than a week after I had been admitted to the hospital, as my temperature began to rise, it was determined that I was suffering from PMR, or polymyalgia rheumatica, an autoimmune disease that causes stiffness and severe pain in the shoulder muscles, usually in men and women over seventy years old. I was given a high dose of prednisone. It worked almost immediately. Within twenty-four hours my fever disappeared, and my pain began to subside.

The only bad news was delivered by the surgeon who had scheduled the operation on my back: the high level of prednisone I was taking ruled out surgery. After I spent almost two weeks in the hospital, my physicians at

Tufts signed my release and recommended that I be transferred to a rehabilitation center or private residence to recuperate. Our son, David, offered to have us stay with him at his home in Newton, a suburb of Boston, during my recovery, an offer that we quickly accepted. His wife, Lara, and their two children, Audrey and Aaron, were visiting Lara's family in California. David had married Lara after he and his first wife, Elyse, were divorced, and he worked as a marketing executive for an internet firm in the city. David had his hands full taking care of me every morning before his commute downtown. I was still weak, especially in my shoulders. David had to lift me out of bed and waited in the bathroom while I took a shower. After he helped me dress, he took my arm, and we slowly walked downstairs. He then went to work, leaving me to recuperate under Marcia's watchful eye. David returned at dinnertime with takeout from his favorite Newton restaurants.

I did a series of daily exercises prescribed by physical therapists at Tufts to strengthen my arms. Gradually, my physical strength began to improve. My rehabilitation was welcome news to my editor, Alice Mayhew, and Roger Labrie, the associate editor at Simon and Schuster who was responsible for shepherding my manuscript to publication. I had no sooner told them of my improving health than I received by overnight delivery the page proofs for my book: 436 pages of *FDR and Chief Justice Hughes: The President, the Supreme Court, and the Epic Battle over the New Deal.*

When Lara and our grandchildren returned from California, Marcia and I moved to the guest bedroom in the home of Marcia's cousin Syrille and her husband, Paul Rosman, in a different Boston suburb. My days in their home were primarily spent completing my review of the page proofs of my FDR-Hughes book. Paul, who had been responsible for my being admitted to Tufts, continued to pay close attention to my condition. Syrille arranged for a car service to take Marcia and me to Tufts for follow-up appointments. In early September, before Marcia and I returned to West Nyack, David mailed the corrected page proofs to Simon and Schuster for me, meeting the schedule for the book's publication in the spring of 2012.

Once I had reduced my daily prednisone dose to a level permitting an operation, Marcia and I consulted two prominent back surgeons in New York City to determine if I should have the fusion surgery. Both surgeons determined that back surgery was unnecessary. One explained that I ran a greater risk of complications having the surgery than simply going about my normal life. "If your condition worsens," he said, "call me." Braced by their advice, I was happy to get on with my life without back surgery.

* * * * *

In the early fall of 2011, I eagerly returned to the final task required before publication of my FDR-Hughes book—collecting photos for the centerfold display. I asked Adam Rich, my research assistant at the law school, to contact the Roosevelt Presidential Library for photos of FDR throughout his life. Finding photos of Chief Justice Hughes was more challenging since there was no Hughes library. I could use formal portraits of Hughes at the Supreme Court but was more interested in informal shots of him throughout his life.

By a stroke of good luck, I learned that Hughes's grandson, Theodore Hughes Waddell, lived in Dallas and had an extraordinary collection of family photographs, including many of his grandfather. I called him and asked if he would allow my sister, Liz, and her husband, Mike Kennedy, who lived in the Dallas area, to examine his collection and, if he was willing, to allow me to select half a dozen photos to be published in my book. He agreed. Liz and Mike sent me a series of photos of the chief justice, and I chose half a dozen of them for the book's photo display.

I met with Alice Mayhew at Simon and Schuster to make final selections and arrange the order of photos for the book. Alice then collected an impressive array of blurbs for the back jacket cover, as she had done for my previous books. The *Washington Post*'s Bob Woodward offered effusive praise for the FDR-Hughes book, as did the respected FDR biographer Jean Edward Smith. Simon and Schuster forced me into the internet age, setting up an author's web page for me. In addition, the publisher's promotion department arranged a series of talks for me to give after the book's publication in New York City and at the Roosevelt library in Hyde Park.

Following the book's publication, I looked forward with great anticipation to the symposium to be held at New York Law School in my honor. The program featured two panels composed of leading constitutional scholars and journalists who discussed my books on American history, law, and politics, including *FDR and Chief Justice Hughes*. The event was superbly organized by Marcey Grigsby, my former student and editor-in-chief of the *NYLS Law Review*. Marcey had returned to the school as the publisher of the law review after clerking for a federal appeals court judge and then working as an associate in one of New York City's most prestigious midtown law firms.

With characteristic foresight, Marcey had met with me several times in the spring of 2011 to begin planning the symposium. She received acceptances to the symposium from prominent constitutional scholars from the University of Michigan and the University of Texas as well as Yale's Sterling Professor of Law, Akhil Amar. My good friend and colleague Professor Ed Purcell Jr., himself an award-winning constitutional historian, agreed to serve as moderator. The journalism panelists were no less impressive and included the *New York Times* Supreme Court correspondent Adam Liptak and Jonathan Alter, the former managing editor of *Newsweek* and author of a best-selling biography of FDR.

On the day of the symposium in April 2012, I was pleased to see a large crowd seated in the law school's new auditorium. Many of my former students were there, along with research assistants and faculty colleagues. My old friend Sherwin Goldman was there as well, along with Sara, Lauren, and David, and, of course, Marcia. I was bursting with excitement, though I tried with limited success to remain calm. The panelists, who had obviously read my books, took their roles seriously, offering insights and lively repartee. The question-and-answer session that followed was no less entertaining. Afterward, I was escorted into an adjoining room to sign copies of my new book.

Marcey Grigsby then invited participants and guests to dinner in the law school's dining room, followed by an informal conversation between me and Harvard professor Annette Gordon-Reed. I had known Annette for twenty-five years. As dean, I had hired her, the first Black woman to join our faculty, and we had soon become good friends, sharing an avid interest in constitutional history and biography. In 1997, the University of Virginia had published Annette's groundbreaking book *Thomas Jefferson and Sally Hemings: An American Controversy*. Based on her original research, Annette had concluded that contrary to Jefferson's most respected biographers, the nation's third president had an enduring, intimate relationship with his teenage slave Sally Hemings. With publication of her book on Jefferson and Hemings, Annette became an academic superstar. After she had won the Pulitzer Prize in 2009 for her superb history *The Hemingses of Monticello: An American Family*, Harvard had lured her away from NYLS, appointing her to an endowed university professorship in both the law school and history department.

In our conversation following dinner, I noted that both Annette and I were recipients of prestigious awards for our books—Annette's Pulitzer Prize and my Silver Gavel Award from the American Bar Association. I archly offered to exchange my Silver Gavel Award for her Pulitzer, an offer she graciously declined. Our conversation, which primarily focused on the research for our books, was always easygoing and fun and seemed to please everyone in attendance.

CHAPTER 17

EISENHOWER VS. WARREN

In January 2013, I began research for a dual biography of President Dwight D. Eisenhower and Chief Justice Earl Warren that would focus on their disagreements over issues of civil rights and liberties. By late February, I had drafted a proposal for the Eisenhower-Warren book. It would be my ninth book and the fourth on the clashes between American presidents and chief justices of the United States.

Eisenhower, the victorious World War II commander of Allied forces in Europe, was elected president in 1952 with the important endorsement of Earl Warren, the popular three-term Republican governor of California. Shortly after his election, Eisenhower nominated Warren to be chief justice, praising his leadership qualities and moderate Republican policies. Less than a year after he took office, Chief Justice Warren wrote the landmark opinion for a unanimous Supreme Court in *Brown v. Board of Education*, mandating the desegregation of public schools in the South. In his press conference after the *Brown* decision was announced, President Eisenhower was asked to comment on the Court's historic decision. He responded in a single sentence, saying only that *Brown* was the law of the land and should be obeyed. He then quickly moved on to the next question from the press corps.

Chief Justice Warren was infuriated by Eisenhower's brief public comment on *Brown* and silence on *Brown II*, the Court's implementation decision, having expected the president to emphatically put the moral authority of his office behind the Court's decisions. Eisenhower's tepid support for *Brown* was interpreted by segregationist governors in the South as a signal that they could resist the Court's mandate with impunity, and they did so successfully for many years. Warren never forgave Eisenhower for what he considered the dereliction of his presidential duty. The two men's relationship immediately deteriorated and ultimately ended in private, mutual recriminations.

In my written proposal for the Eisenhower-Warren book, I contrasted the earlier career of Eisenhower, the World War II military hero, with that of Warren, the consummate politician. I then discussed their initial political alliance, and, as president and chief justice, their bitter disagreements over important civil rights and liberties issues, beginning with the *Brown* decisions. It seemed to me to be a compelling proposal. And with original research, particularly at the Dwight D. Eisenhower Presidential Library in Abilene, Kansas, I was convinced that I could produce a fine dual biography. I was therefore stunned when Alice Mayhew, my longtime editor at Simon and Schuster, did not make a bid to publish the book.

Alice's decision surprised and annoyed my agent, Esther Newberg. But Esther, always the pragmatist, explained to me that the publishing industry was increasingly pressed financially, primarily as the result of competition from social media on the internet. This meant that the financial bottom line, always important, dictated publishers' decisions more than ever. The sales of my FDR-Hughes book were modest, too much so for Alice to offer me another contract, Esther concluded.

Soon after Esther gave me the bad news from Simon and Schuster, she called to say that a young assistant editor at Liveright, a division of W. W. Norton, was enthusiastic about my proposal and had sold it to his senior editors. I followed Esther's recommendation to accept Liveright's offer, although the advance was far less than those I was accustomed to receiving from Simon and Schuster.

After I signed the contract, Will Menaker, the young editor at Liveright who had championed my proposal, called to invite me to lunch at a Turkish restaurant near the Morgan Library in Midtown Manhattan. When we met at the restaurant, Will was nervous and deferential toward his new author, in stark contrast to Alice Mayhew, who was gruff and always in command at our meetings. Slightly built and blond, Will was in his early thirties, roughly forty years my junior. But Esther had assured me that editorial talent ran in the family. His father, Daniel Menaker, had served as senior fiction editor at *The New Yorker* for many years and later as executive editor-in-chief of Random House; his mother was an editor at the *New York Times*. During our lunch, Will appeared to relax, spoke glowingly of my Eisenhower-Warren proposal, and expressed his high hopes for the book's publishing success. In response, I told him I was eager to start my research with a trip to the Eisenhower library in the summer.

✦ ✦ ✦ ✦ ✦

Before making my first research trip to the Eisenhower Presidential Library, Marcia and I considered how we should celebrate our fiftieth wedding anniversary in the spring. We decided to take the entire family—adult children, spouses, and grandchildren—to Bermuda for the occasion. We stayed at the Fairmont Southampton, the resort hotel where, forty years earlier, I had spent a day at the swimming pool. In 1973, having filed my story as the *Time* magazine correspondent assigned to cover the assassination of the Bermuda governor, I had enjoyed a sunny afternoon at what was then known as the Southampton Princess Hotel.

Accompanied by Sara, her husband, Keith, and their four-year-old twins, Justin and Ryan, our anniversary trip began with the ninety-minute flight from New York to Bermuda. As our jet circled the small island in late morning, we gaped at the turquoise water of the Atlantic Ocean lapping against the renowned pink beaches. It seemed as if we had entered a different universe. After the plane landed and we had gathered our luggage, taxis took us through the winding streets of Hamilton, the island's capital, past the blue, yellow, and pink pastel cottages that dotted the landscape. Finally, we arrived at our destination, the imposing six-story resort hotel, painted pastel pink, that overlooked the Atlantic Ocean. Lauren, David and their families arrived later that day.

For the next four days, the family, all fifteen of us, dined on great food in the hotel's four restaurants. The only serious decision we made each day was which lounge chairs to sit in at the hotel's beautiful beach, nestled in a cove just a short shuttle ride from the hotel. The sun was bright, the temperature in the low seventies, and the water refreshingly cool. It was the best anniversary celebration ever.

* * * * *

The Bermuda vacation was the first of three splendid trips in 2013. The second was to Paris with our grandson, Ethan, where we stayed at the Hotel du Louvre, named for the world's most famous art museum, which we could see from our hotel room window. We went sightseeing to all the usual places in the beautiful city, including the Arc de Triomphe, Notre-Dame, and the Eiffel Tower. But the musical highlight of the trip was a concert in an eighteenth-century cathedral. Our hotel concierge had arranged for us to be seated in one of the front rows of the cathedral, where we heard an incredible tenor sing arias of Bach, Vivaldi, and other Baroque composers. For our third trip abroad, Marcia and I flew to Athens, Greece, where we enjoyed a three-week tour of the art, architecture, and archaeological treasures of Greece and Turkey. In Athens, we toured the Parthenon. Marcia and I had seen the temple years earlier, before we met, but this time we agreed that it was especially remarkable.

After a tour of the Temple of Apollo at Delphi, we went by bus to the port city of Piraeus, where we boarded *Le Boreal*, a small French cruise ship that sailed the Aegean Sea to the Greek and Turkish islands on our itinerary. Sailing into Turkish waters, we docked at Troy, the ancient city made famous in Homer's *Iliad*, but were disappointed by the lack of extensive archaeological remains. The modern reconstructed horse made me think of Disney World more than the giant wooden horse the Greek soldiers used to defeat the Trojans. On the next island, Ephesus, we spent an afternoon touring one of the largest and most complete Roman archaeological sites, dating to the first century AD, which more than made up for our letdown at Troy.

Our final destination was Istanbul, home to one of the world's great architectural wonders, Hagia Sophia, built in AD 537. We also visited the seventeenth-century Blue Mosque and the city's vast central market. But for us, every attraction was an anticlimax after Hagia Sophia. We were exhausted at the end of our three-week trip but also exhilarated. For the incredible art and architectural treasures alone, we rated it the best since we had toured India for two months in our mid-twenties.

* * * * *

In late June 2013, shortly after Marcia and I had returned from our trip to Paris with Ethan, I traveled to Abilene, Kansas, to conduct research for the Eisenhower and Warren book at the Eisenhower Presidential Library. It only took a few minutes for me to drive down the main street of Abilene (pop. 6,802) before turning into the parking lot for the library. The library was just one of the buildings dedicated to the nation's thirty-fourth president spread over several acres of carefully manicured lawns. The complex also included the Eisenhower museum and the two-story white clapboard house where Eisenhower and his five brothers had been raised by their parents in the late nineteenth and early twentieth centuries.

The library is a researcher's dream: two floors of stacks housing Eisenhower's letters, diaries, notes, memoranda, and drafts of speeches, all neatly cataloged and overseen by research assistants paid to help those, like me, working on books, articles, and doctoral theses on Eisenhower. In my first visit to the library, I concentrated on Eisenhower's childhood and early military career, from his West Point graduation to his work under Army Chief of Staff Douglas MacArthur in the 1930s. Reading through reams of documents, I searched for revealing diary entries, letters, notes, and memoranda that would help me to better understand Eisenhower the man as well as Eisenhower the future Allied commander and US president.

In my early research I quickly learned that the prevailing public image of "Ike" (as he was known throughout his life) as the affable, not especially bright, consensus-building leader was woefully inaccurate. Contrary to that public image, Eisenhower's private papers revealed him to be exceptionally intelligent, calculating, and ambitious, even as a young military attaché in the 1930s. As MacArthur's assistant in Washington, and later in the Philippines, Eisenhower wrote lucid, insightful reports on every aspect of the army under his boss's command. Later, in his diaries, Eisenhower was anything but affable, complaining bitterly about MacArthur's vanity and venting his own frustrations in not being given command of a combat unit.

I did my research at the library from the time it opened at 8:30 a.m. until it closed at 5:00 p.m., so I always arrived at the entrance a few minutes before 8:30 and never returned to the motel until the stacks had closed. I was disappointed that the library shut down for an hour at noon, but tried to make the most of the lunch hour by visiting the Eisenhower museum or grabbing a sandwich at a nearby café and reviewing my notes from the morning.

When I left Abilene, my briefcase was packed with notebooks and copies of original documents, and I was more enthusiastic than ever about my new book project.

✦ ✦ ✦ ✦ ✦

Sybil Shainwald, a wealthy New York Law School trustee, called me in July 2014. Sybil, who had established an annual lectureship at the law school in honor of her late husband, told me that she had invited Congresswoman Nancy Pelosi, the first woman to serve as Speaker of the House of Representatives, to be the Shainwald Lecturer in September. Would I be willing to interview Pelosi? she asked. Sybil explained that Pelosi had agreed to come to the law school but did not want to deliver a formal lecture. Instead, she would sit for an extensive interview, and Sybil wanted me to conduct it.

I was enormously flattered that Sybil chose me to interview Pelosi, who would follow an impressive list of Shainwald Lecturers, including US Senators Ted Kennedy and John Kerry and US Supreme Court Justice Stephen Breyer. But I hesitated to accept Sybil's invitation. Even in retirement, it was difficult for me to slow down when I was working on a new book. And that summer I was deeply immersed in writing a draft of an early chapter of my Eisenhower-Warren book. I politely declined to interview Pelosi.

In retrospect, I was appalled at my initial response to Sybil's invitation. Was I really too busy with my Eisenhower-Warren book to prepare for an interview with a woman widely considered to be one of the greatest majority leaders in congressional history? After I hung up the receiver, I told Marcia of my decision. She understood how important the Eisenhower-Warren book was to me, but gently suggested that I might later regret passing up the opportunity to interview Pelosi. I went to bed thinking about my decision. Early the next morning, I realized I had made a mistake. I called Sybil and told her that if the invitation was still open, I would happily accept. She said that it was, and we were both pleased.

I then dropped all work on my book and asked Bill Mills, my research liaison at the NYLS library, to send me major newspaper and magazine articles on Pelosi as well as a copy of her book *Know Your Power: A Message to America's Daughters*. Over the next month, I read both the book and every significant story about Pelosi that I could find. By the end of August, I felt confident that I had a firm grasp of Pelosi's life and career, from her rise as the youngest of seven children (and the only daughter) in a devout Italian-American Catholic family in Baltimore to the liberal, tough-as-nails leader of the Democratic congressional delegation. As Speaker, she was credited with shrewdly corralling the votes in the House to pass President Barack Obama's Affordable Care Act, which provided health care to more than twenty million Americans. Pelosi's rise to power was a remarkable, quintessentially American success story that I could not wait to explore when I was scheduled to interview her at New York Law School on September 16, 2014.

When we met at the luncheon preceding our interview, Pelosi was wearing a stylish tailored light gray pants suit. At the age of seventy-four, she was an extremely attractive woman who greeted me with graceful assurance, putting me at ease. I instinctively anticipated a lively, extended conversation in front of our large audience.

As a journalist, and, later, as an author interviewing prominent public officials, I always began with what I regarded as "softball" questions to ease into conversations that I expected would later touch on more sensitive topics. After we took our seats next to each other on the dais, I first asked Pelosi about her Catholic upbringing. She replied that she had considered entering a Catholic convent as a young novitiate. As a nun, she said, "you could pray all the time and do good deeds. But I just thought I might check out the world."

Her last sentence gave me the opening to ask about her ardently liberal political views, surprising for a devout Catholic. Those views included support for a woman's right to choose an abortion and a gay couple's right to marry. She replied, "I was taught to honor the dignity of every person. Part of that dignity is the free will to be responsible for your own life. Whatever my thoughts are, what business is it of mine to insist on that for someone else?"

I asked her about the determined opposition to President Obama's proposed legislation by the House Republican majority led by Speaker John Boehner. She replied with cheerful disdain. The Republican House majority was "anti-government, anti-science, and anti–Barack Obama," she said. "What they've said to the president is, 'Anything you want, we're not interested, nothing is the agenda, never is the timetable.'" She added, with a laugh, "Pardon me for that partisan word."

Our interview lasted for more than an hour, but I thought those exchanges succinctly illustrated Pelosi's core convictions and ferociously combative political style.

✦ ✦ ✦ ✦ ✦

My mother breezed through her seventies and eighties with the energy and spirit of someone twenty years younger. Neighbors became accustomed to seeing her in her jogging suits and well-worn sneakers, setting a brisk pace for her daily walk of two or three miles through Tanglewood. When Marcia and I made trips to Fort Worth every six weeks or so, we kept to a busy schedule, which often included walks in Tanglewood or the city's botanical gardens with Mother, lunch at a crowded cafeteria on University Drive, a quick browse through the women's clothing racks at Talbots, and a visit to the Kimbell or Amon Carter museums (where Mother had worked for years as a volunteer docent). Afternoons concluded with a glass of wine along with cheese and crackers before dinner at a great barbecue restaurant.

She seemed unstoppable as she approached her ninetieth birthday. But one day in February 2002, returning from her daily walk, she slipped on a curb and hit her head. She picked herself up, even though her head was bleeding, and kept going until she reached her house. When she called my brother, Dick, he noticed that her words were slurred. He drove to her house and took her to Harris Hospital, where she was diagnosed with a subdural hematoma. I flew to Fort Worth and found her in her hospital room after surgery, impatient to be released. Two months later, the family gathered for brunch at Colonial Country Club to celebrate her ninetieth birthday.

In her nineties, Mother began to slow down. For her one hundredth birthday, on April 6, 2012, our family and her close friends celebrated the event with a wonderful party. No one enjoyed the party more than Mother, who stood up throughout the celebration to greet and talk to every one of her guests. In January 2014, when Marcia and I visited her in Fort Worth, she seemed more fragile than ever. I promised that we would return for her 102nd birthday in April. But upon returning to New York, I speculated that she might not live through the year and suggested to our children that they should visit her as soon as possible. David and Lauren flew down separately for visits in February, and Sara accompanied us in early April for Mother's birthday. During our visit, Mother and I took walks in the city's botanical gardens, as we had for many years. I especially cherish the memory of the two of us sharing a bench among the roses.

Mother died on June 4. At her memorial service, Sara, Lauren, David, and Dick's daughter, Nancy, each reminisced about "Grandma," their stories filled with humor and told with deep affection.

They loved her dearly, as did I.

◆ ◆ ◆ ◆ ◆

In early June 2016, Marcia and I took a trip to France to celebrate the seventy-second anniversary of the successful Allied landings on the beaches of Normandy on June 6, 1944. Sponsored by Brown University, the group tour featured lectures by David Eisenhower (accompanied by his wife, Julie Nixon Eisenhower) on his famous grandfather, Dwight D. Eisenhower, who commanded the Allied forces that landed in France on what is now known as D-Day. David Eisenhower gave an introductory talk on D-Day on the bus that transported our tour group from the coastal port of Calais to the beaches in Normandy where the Allies landed. Both David and Julie Eisenhower were gracious and spoke knowledgeably about the Allied landings on D-Day as well as the French resistance to the Nazis. Once we left the bus, David took over, describing the Allied landing in dramatic detail, the highlight of the entire trip for me. Later, he presided at a somber ceremony adjacent to the cemetery where the fallen Allied soldiers were buried.

Later, our group crossed the English Channel on board the French cruise ship *Le Boreal* for a tour of the British Isles. *Le Boreal* was the same vessel on which Marcia and I had toured the Greek and Turkish islands. On board *Le Boreal*, David Eisenhower delivered two outstanding lectures on General Eisenhower as the Allied commander in Europe during World War II. Following his first lecture, I introduced myself and told him about the book I was writing about his grandfather and Chief Justice Warren. I asked if I could interview him after we returned to the United States, and he immediately agreed to meet with me. When he gave me his card with his email address at the University of Pennsylvania's Annenberg School for Communication, where he was on the faculty, I put on my best reporter's poker face, but I could hardly hide my pleasure in anticipating our interview.

✦ ✦ ✦ ✦ ✦

Soon after completing our trip abroad, I made another visit to the Eisenhower Presidential Library in Abilene, Kansas, for an intensive week of research. When I returned to West Nyack, I emailed David Eisenhower to suggest that we meet for our interview in his office at a time convenient for him. I received no response, so I sent a second email at the end of the summer proposing the interview during the fall. Still, I did not hear from him. In the late fall I nervously called his office at the Annenberg School, leaving a message for him to call or email me. He did not return my call or email. By this time, I was very close to finishing the Eisenhower-Warren manuscript and realized that if I did not interview him soon, it would be too late to include any information or direct quotes from the interview in my book.

How could I reach Eisenhower, I wondered, short of knocking on his office door in Philadelphia? I recalled telling him in our conversation on board *Le Boreal* that I was a graduate of Yale Law School. He had smiled and said that Monroe Price, a fellow graduate of the law school, also taught at the Annenberg School and occupied the office next to his. Monroe, I replied, was my law school classmate and good friend.

Eureka! Why had I not thought of enlisting Monroe in my now frustrating attempt to set a date for an interview with Eisenhower? I immediately called Monroe, recounting my conversation with Eisenhower on the cruise ship, his agreement to let me interview him, and my subsequent difficulty in arranging the interview, or, indeed, even making contact with him. Monroe said that he would get in touch with Eisenhower on my behalf, which he did. Almost immediately afterward, I received an email from David saying that he would be happy to see me. He suggested a date and time in early March 2017, and I agreed.

Marcia and I drove to Philadelphia the morning of the scheduled interview, and once we had checked in at our hotel, I emailed Eisenhower and left him a message on his answering machine. I told him that I had arrived in Philadelphia and looked forward to our interview, reminding him that it was scheduled for four o'clock that afternoon. When I received no reply, I sent a second email and made another call to his office. Again, no response.

"We're taking a taxi to his office for my scheduled interview," I told Marcia. "If I have to break down his goddamn door, I'm going to get that interview!"

After we arrived by taxi at the Annenberg School, Marcia went to the school library to wait for me, and I knocked on the door of Eisenhower's office.

"Jim," exclaimed David Eisenhower after opening the door. "So glad to see you!"

I pretended that his gracious welcome was expected; my frustration in the months it took to set up the interview was quickly forgotten. For the next hour and a half, we engaged in a wide-ranging conversation. He then invited Marcia and me to be his guests for dinner at a nearby restaurant and apologized that his wife, Julie, could not join us, because she was attending the ballet recital of one of their grandchildren.

I had prepared for our interview in much the way I had approached my interview in 2014 with Nancy Pelosi. I had read everything I could on David Eisenhower as well as his memoir recalling his close relationship and many conversations with his grandfather after his second presidential term. I began with general questions about his background and slowly worked my way toward crucial questions about his grandfather's relationship with Chief

Justice Warren. Our conversation about his grandfather continued at dinner, but I did not take out my notebook at the restaurant. Once we had said goodbye, I hurriedly scribbled notes on our dinner conversation.

In both my afternoon interview and our dinner conversation, I carefully probed for firsthand corroboration for my conclusion that Eisenhower, after appointing Warren to be chief justice, had bitterly regretted his decision. Getting David Eisenhower, on the record, to reinforce my conclusion was important, especially since there was not a trace of criticism of Warren in President Eisenhower's memoirs. But according to Eisenhower biographer Stephen Ambrose, the president had told friends that his biggest mistake during his two terms as the nation's chief executive was appointing "that dumb son of a bitch Earl Warren." Ambrose did not provide documentation for the quote, which was disputed by high-ranking members of the Eisenhower administration as well as later biographers of the former president.

I asked David if the Ambrose quote was true. He paused to consider my question. "Maybe," he replied ambiguously. But then he lent credence to the Ambrose quote by suggesting that his grandfather most likely made the remark to his southern friends to deflect criticism of Warren's opinion for the Court in *Brown v. Board of Education* that struck down segregation in public schools in the South. Later in our interview and dinner conversation, David elaborated on President Eisenhower's antipathy toward the chief justice, recalling his own conversations with his grandfather in which he said the basis of Warren's opinion in *Brown* was more political than judicial. He further recalled that his grandfather, who was not a lawyer, complained that the Warren Court had discovered new "inherent rights" not enumerated in the Constitution. "Eisenhower," David said, referring to his grandfather, "was concerned about judicial activism as inappropriate, not just in the desegregation decision but later with school prayer, reapportionment, and criminal procedure decisions." The Warren Court struck down New York's Regents Prayer as an unconstitutional violation of the First Amendment's prohibition against the establishment of religion. It also ruled that malapportioned state legislatures were prohibited by the Fourteenth Amendment's Equal Protection Clause and that criminal suspects were entitled to additional constitutional protections after their arrests. David said his grandfather thought "these were good ideas gone amuck."

David Eisenhower provided me with the most direct evidence of the fraught relationship between the president and Chief Justice Warren. When Marcia and I returned to West Nyack, I inserted direct quotes and summaries of our conversations from my notebooks into the manuscript's epilogue. A few weeks later, I turned in the final chapters and epilogue to my publisher.

In the spring of 2017, my publisher, Liveright, announced that the publication date of James F. Simon's *Eisenhower vs. Warren: The Battle for Civil Rights and Liberties* would be March 2018. My book was already listed on Amazon for prepublication sales! I was, of course, gratified to read Liveright's announcement. It offered tangible evidence that my four years of work on the Eisenhower-Warren manuscript would soon be transformed into a hardcover book.

But that giddy feeling soon evaporated when I realized that I still faced the time-consuming, onerous tasks that had to be completed before my manuscript could be published. My immediate challenge was to respond to each query from my Liveright editor, Katie Adams, in the margins of my manuscript. Katie had replaced my original Liveright editor, Will Manaker. My agent, Esther Newberg, assured me that Katie, whom she had known for years, would be an excellent editor of my manuscript. Katie sent me several books, both fiction and nonfiction, that she had edited. I was impressed. Once I was done answering queries, I needed to compile source notes for all four hundred pages of the manuscript. To meet the March 2018 publication date, those two critical assignments had to be finished by the end of June. The old journalist in me kicked in. I rose before seven o'clock every morning and I made the deadlines with a few hours to spare.

* * * * *

In February 2018, Marcia and I attended a performance of the New York City Ballet in the State Theater at Lincoln Center. During an intermission I was approached by an old friend, Leon Friedman, whom I had first met in the early 1970s when working at *Time* magazine. He had been an attorney with the New York Civil Liberties Union at the time. Leon congratulated me on the excellent review of my Eisenhower-Warren book in the leading prepublication journal, *Publisher's Weekly*, which I had not seen, but quickly read on the internet.

A few weeks later, I received an email from a former student at New York Law School telling me that a glowing review of my book had appeared in the March issue of *The Atlantic*. The reviewer had written that *Eisenhower vs. Warren* presented "the most thorough and balanced assessment of the two men's fraught relationship yet written." Comparably positive reviews soon followed in the *Washington Post*, the *New York Times* (online), and the *Wall Street Journal.*

Shortly after the reviews appeared, the New York Law School dean, now Anthony Crowell, hosted a celebration of the publication of my book in the school's large auditorium, which was televised on C-SPAN. Dean Crowell asked my former research assistants, including some who had worked on my books in the 1970s and 1980s, to stand for a round of applause. I was introduced by my former student Meryl Lieberman, a member of the NYLS Board of Trustees and founding member of a prominent insurance defense law firm. NYLS professor Ed Purcell Jr. and I then took the stage for an extended conversation about my book, followed by a question-and-answer session. It was a grand evening.

During the summer following the book's publication, I was interviewed by two correspondents from the BBC, who were making a documentary on the US Supreme Court. Not long after the BBC interview, the managing editor of the *National Law Journal* called from Washington, DC, and conducted an interview for a profile of me that appeared in the publication in the early fall. At the end of the summer I received an email from my Yale College classmate Ed Cantor inviting me to give a talk about my book at a class reunion in New Haven the following spring. As it turned out, my talk was sandwiched between those of some of the Yale faculty's most renowned lecturers. When it was my time to speak, I told my classmates that my predicament reminded me of a quote from then newly appointed Supreme Court justice William J. Brennan Jr. "I feel like the donkey entered in the Kentucky Derby," he had said. "I don't expect to distinguish myself, but I do expect to benefit from the association." That Brennan quote elicited chuckles throughout the room, and my classmates applauded heartily after my talk.

One of my classmates, Mike Samuels, approached me after my New Haven talk to invite me to speak in Washington, DC, at the historic Metropolitan Club (est. 1863). Its past members included Presidents Theodore and Franklin Roosevelt as well as prominent cabinet members and US senators. Marcia and I stayed overnight at the club before my luncheon talk, which was attended by former US senator Christopher Dodd (D-CT) and his brother, a professor of international affairs at Georgetown University. Both of them joined us and other guests for lunch afterward and were delightful conversationalists.

I thoroughly enjoyed my book talks as well as the reviews for *Eisenhower vs. Warren*, among the best I had received since *What Kind of Nation*, which had been published almost twenty years earlier. But, regrettably, the sales did not compare to those of the Jefferson-Marshall book, a result I attributed, at least in part, to the high price ($35) Liveright had placed on the hardcover. Despite the moderate sales, I was extremely proud of the book. In terms of original research and the quality of the narrative, I considered it among the best of the nine books I had written.

After I completed the final chapters for *Eisenhower vs. Warren* and turned eighty, Marcia and I continued our travels. We joined our entire family in Bermuda for a second glorious vacation on that beautiful island. A year later, we once again boarded the small French cruise ship *Le Boreal*, and sailed to Tallinn, Estonia; St. Petersburg, Russia; Helsinki, Finland; and Copenhagen, Denmark. We completed our tour with an extended railroad and boat trip through Norway. In late May 2019, we visited the Badlands National Park and Mount Rushmore. That trip included an expedition to Yellowstone and Grand Teton National Parks. Later that year, we flew to Sicily and boarded a small sailing ship for a tour of the island's great art and architectural treasures. We visited Palermo's early Christian churches and, on the last day of the tour, watched from the deck of our sailing ship as a volcano erupted spectacularly on the island of Stromboli.

• • • • •

Only a few months after we returned from Sicily, the COVID-19 virus, which had originated in China in December 2019, spread to the United

States. At last count (mid-2024), more than a million Americans have now died from the virus and its variants, the deadliest pandemic since the Spanish flu epidemic that began in 1918. The pandemic was frightening and caused us, and everyone we knew who was lucky enough to stay healthy, to alter our daily lives in ways that we would never have imagined before the outbreak.

It meant that we stayed in or close to our West Nyack house for almost three years. But there were advantages to being in our eighties during the most devastating period of the pandemic. We did not have to worry about jobs or taking care of small children. In fact, Marcia and I sheltered in place quite easily. While our everyday activities, like everyone else's, were severely limited, we appreciated our time together, perhaps more than ever.

In the afternoons, I spent several hours writing this memoir, while Marcia read or took Zoom classes online. In the spring of 2021, I took a break from writing to prepare for a Zoom talk on "American Presidents and the U.S. Supreme Court from Washington to Biden," which I delivered to my Yale College classmates as part of our sixtieth reunion.

In February 2021, we were given the first of two Pfizer vaccinations, allowing us to gather with our family that summer. We later received booster shots, which freed us to cautiously resume a normal life, such as having dinner with friends and family and returning to one of our favorite New York City cultural treasures, the Metropolitan Museum of Art.

CONCLUSION

Prior to the onset of the COVID-19 pandemic, in late November 2018, Marcia and I attended a 130th birthday celebration (Lauren's 50th, my 80th), which took place in a private dining room at one of Manchester, New Hampshire's excellent restaurants. Best of all, our family was there to celebrate with us—Lauren and Tom and their children; David and his children; Sara and Keith and their children.

Turning eighty naturally focused my attention on aging, but it also prompted memories of a life that spanned tumultuous times in world and American history. I was born only a few weeks after the Nazis' destruction of synagogues and Jewish businesses throughout Germany, the ominous prelude to World War II. After the war, I grew up in a blissfully innocent time in American history, at least for a privileged white kid in Fort Worth, Texas. The US Supreme Court's decision in *Brown v. Board of Education* in 1954 outlawing racial segregation in public schools became the catalyst for the nation's civil rights movement that led to the Civil Rights Act of 1964 and the Voting Rights Act the following year.

That eightieth birthday also stirred memories of my own awakening, after *Brown*, to racism in the city where I had grown up. Slowly, I had become aware of the scourge of racial discrimination in Fort Worth as I witnessed prejudice against Black men in two of my summer jobs. After my junior year at Yale, I had joined a small interracial group that traveled to Ghana to work with Ghanaian students to build a schoolhouse for children growing up in a fishing village on the southern coast of the former British colony. The larger purpose of our Operation Crossroads Africa project was to create understanding between young Americans and West Africans. Crossroads was the precursor to President John F. Kennedy's Peace Corps, which sent young (and not-so-young) Americans to towns and villages across Africa, Asia, and Latin America to work and enhance international understanding.

The Crossroads experience made an indelible impression on me. Although I was not a direct witness to history three years later, when Dr. Martin Luther King Jr. delivered his "I Have a Dream" speech in front of the Lincoln Memorial, I was only a few blocks away. As a *Newsweek* intern, I watched the televised speech in the office of the newsmagazine's Washington bureau chief, Ben Bradlee, with Bradlee and the other *Newsweek* reporters who were not outside covering the speech. I was so excited by King's speech that I called Marcia, then in our apartment in Arlington, Virginia, to ask her to join me in Washington, so we could walk down the streets together, along with thousands of other Americans, Black and white, to celebrate the occasion.

◆ ◆ ◆ ◆ ◆

My summer internship at *Newsweek* convinced me that I should pursue a career in journalism, not law, although I returned to New Haven to complete my final year at Yale Law School. At the time, I could not have known that my legal education would be crucial to my future career as journalist, professor, dean, and author.

At *Time* magazine, where I worked as law correspondent and contributing editor, I had written a long article on the transition from the liberal US Supreme Court under Chief Justice Earl Warren, which expanded civil rights and liberties, to the Court under Warren's successor, the conservative chief justice Warren Burger. It had led to the first of my books on the US Supreme Court and its justices, primarily focused on civil rights and liberties.

In doing research for those books over the course of five decades, I was fortunate to count among my most valued sources many members of the Court, whether they were appointed by Democratic or Republican presidents. In the present state of our polarized national politics, which has also infected the Supreme Court, the kind of access to the justices that I enjoyed would be impossible. The irony does not escape me, as a lifelong registered Democrat, that most of my sources on the Court had been appointed by Republicans—Brennan and Stewart by Eisenhower; Blackmun and Powell by Nixon; O'Connor and Rehnquist by Reagan; and Souter by George H.W. Bush. Only Chief Justice Rehnquist would count as a dependable vote with today's conservative majority. My other Court sources nominated by Republican presidents were either nonideological centrists (O'Connor, Powell, and Stewart) or members of the liberal wing of the Court willing to expand civil rights and liberties (Blackmun, Brennan, and Souter).

Today, none of these liberal or centrist justices would pass muster with the Federalist Society, the conservative organization that exercises a virtual veto over the nominees of Republican presidents. Consider, for example, how these justices would have voted in the 2022 decision *Dobbs v. Jackson Women's Health Organization*, the case that overturned *Roe v. Wade*. Blackmun wrote the majority opinion in *Roe*, supported by Brennan, Powell, and Stewart. The 1996 joint opinion in *Planned Parenthood v. Casey*, upholding *Roe*, was written by Justices Kennedy, O'Connor, and Souter and supported by Justices Blackmun and Stevens, all appointees of Republican presidents.

• • • • •

Reflecting on my long life, I am grateful for so much fun and adventure, my many enduring friendships, my loving family, the decades I have spent in a rewarding career, and especially the opportunity to write books on the Supreme Court and its justices.

I recently completed a major project—sorting, labeling, and packing fifteen boxes of my professional papers, dating back to my years as a journalist for the *St. Louis Post-Dispatch* and *Time* magazine, and including my notes, recorded interviews, and drafts for my nine published books, as well as letters I have received from Supreme Court justices. The boxes have been shipped to the Dolph Briscoe Center for American History at the University of Texas in Austin. In addition, my digital files for my last four books, as well as my lectures on my books over the past twenty years, have been sent to the Briscoe Center.

It has been a pleasure to work with the Briscoe Center's executive director, Don Carleton. The center's outstanding archival collection is the reason I wanted my papers to be housed there. But the center also has special meaning to me. My mother and father met at the University of Texas during the Great Depression when Dad was a law student and Mother an undergraduate. And, of course, my formative years were spent in Texas, growing up in Fort Worth.

Now in my mid-eighties, I have one more ambitious writing project in mind: a dual biography of President Lyndon B. Johnson and Associate Justice Abe Fortas. The two men could not have been more different in backgrounds and personalities. Johnson was a tall, rough-hewn Texan from the Hill Country, while Fortas was a short, soft-spoken child of Eastern European Jewish immigrants who graduated with top honors from Yale Law School. They met in Washington, DC, in the 1930s as committed New Dealers during President Franklin D. Roosevelt's first term. The ambitious LBJ was serving his first term in Congress, while Fortas held a series of high-level administrative positions in the Roosevelt administration. They developed a deep friendship and mutually beneficial professional relationship over more than thirty-five years.

Fortas successfully defended Johnson's narrow, disputed Senate victory in court in 1948 after it was challenged by Johnson's opponent, former Texas governor Coke Stevenson. When Johnson became Senate majority leader and later vice president, Fortas remained his close friend and confidant. After President John F. Kennedy was assassinated in 1963, President Johnson asked Fortas to serve as US attorney general. Fortas turned him down, preferring to remain in his lucrative private law practice. LBJ later named a reluctant Fortas to serve as an associate justice on the Supreme Court.

Both LBJ's and Fortas's public careers ended tragically. In 1968, President Johnson, unpopular and distraught by the failure of US troops to win the war in Vietnam, announced that he would not seek reelection. Before his presidential term ended, he nominated Fortas to succeed Earl Warren as chief justice. The nomination ended in disaster, successfully opposed by Senate Republicans (and secretly by President Richard Nixon), who were aided by press revelations that Fortas had accepted lecture fees from the foundation of a potential defendant before the Court. Fortas ultimately resigned from the Court.

I have a working title for the book: *Lyndon and Abe: The Meteoric Rise and Tragic Fall of President Lyndon Johnson and Supreme Court Justice Abe Fortas*. Just two small tasks remain: to research and write the book. At this stage in my life, it would be foolish to assume that I will complete the manuscript. But I can't wait to get started! As the great historian and biographer David McCullough once wrote, "Real success is finding your lifework in the work that you love."

ACKNOWLEDGMENTS

I wrote the first draft of this memoir during the COVID pandemic, intending to make copies for members of my family. Later, at the suggestion and with the guidance of Don Carleton, executive director of the Briscoe Center, I revised the manuscript to focus more on my career as a Supreme Court historian, while retaining a significant portion of my personal history. Don then placed the revised memoir in the capable hands of Holly Taylor, head of publications at the Briscoe Center, who expertly guided it toward publication. Kathy Streckfus did an outstanding job as copy editor. I am also grateful for the excellent work of Derek George, the book's designer, as well as Amanda Wilson, who compiled the index. Aryn Glazier and Marisa Jefferson at the Briscoe Center scanned many of the photos, and Camille Broussard and Michael Roffer from the New York Law School Library helped track down other photos from my time as dean.

Finally, I thank my family for their love and joyful diversions during the writing of this memoir—children and spouses, spirited grandchildren, and foremost and always, my wife Marcia.

INDEX